High Performing Healthcare Systems

DELIVERING QUALITY BY DESIGN

High Performing Healthcare Systems

DELIVERING QUALITY BY DESIGN

G. Ross Baker, Anu MacIntosh-Murray, Christina Porcellato,
Lynn Dionne, Kim Stelmacovich and Karen Born

Longwoods Publishing Corporation
Toronto

Toronto
Printed in Canada

www.longwoods.com

ISBN: 978-0-9810089-0-5

Library and Archives Canada Cataloguing in Publication

High performing healthcare systems : delivering quality by design / G. Ross Baker .. [et al.].

Includes bibliographical references and index.
ISBN 978-0-9810089-0-5

1. Medical care--Quality control--Case studies. 2. Health services administration--Case studies. 3. Health facilities--Administration--Case studies. I. Baker, G. Ross, 1950- II. Title.

RA425.H54 2008 362.1068 C2008-905902-6

This publication made possible through the financial assistance of the Ontario Ministry of Health and Long-Term Care and the Change Foundation.

To Paul B. Batalden
whose insights have guided many
in their efforts to improve healthcare.

Contents

Canadian Case Studies

Foreword

Quality remains one of the great trade-offs in Canada's healthcare system. Every person working in the system agrees with the importance of quality, and many make it an explicit part of their personal and professional missions. Today, for example, when confronted by clear evidence of poor quality in their own practices and organizations, clinicians and administrators rarely question the validity of the information and they respond quickly to solve the problems identified. At the same time, however, most clinicians and administrators believe that large-scale improvement is unaffordable.

Although quality continues to rise in importance, and nearly every study published identifies room for improvement, something stops us from achieving the high quality we desire. The work of G. Ross Baker – who led the Quality by Design initiative and, with Peter Norton, the landmark study on patient safety in Canada – lays out the challenge clearly. Every day in Canada's healthcare system preventable errors arise in hospitals, long-term care facilities and physicians' offices. These errors lead to extra costs, poor health and, in many cases, avoidable deaths. Yet the pursuit of safety and quality remains the something extra that many of the people working in our system can follow up on only at the end of a busy day.

There are a number of potent examples to the contrary in the case studies that follow. These are portraits of healthcare systems that have made the pursuit of quality and safety a core element of their strategies, a part of everyone's work and the way they differentiate themselves from their competitors. Constant improvements in quality and safety are integral to their workplace cultures and central to what is expected from everyone employed in those systems. In a presentation based on one of the following case studies, Sven-Olof Karlsson, the chief executive officer of Jönköping County Council, put it most succinctly: "Everyone has two jobs: to do their job and to do that job better." In the systems profiled in this book, quality and cost are not opposing goals; rather, quality is one of the ways to improve cost control. Moreover, these systems are not rich healthcare systems or systems that serve only the rich. The examples collected here include Canadian systems, as well as systems from the United Kingdom, Sweden and the United States that offer care to incredibly diverse populations.

The Ontario Ministry of Health and Long-Term Care (MOHLTC) provided a grant for the Quality by Design project because we believed it was important to try to identify the common elements of high-performing healthcare systems from around the world. Our sincere thanks go to the research team and to the leaders of the systems who graciously participated. The MOHLTC's Health Quality Council has defined characteristics of a high-performing healthcare system, attributes that range from equity to efficiency. Each of the systems profiled in this book strives to meet those characteristics. And each provides an example to leaders at all levels of Canada's healthcare system of how to design our structures and processes to achieve the outcomes desired by the people we all hope to serve.

None of the systems discussed in this collection presents the ideal recipe for better quality. Rather, each case illustrates that high quality results only from a mix of good incentives, helpful information technology, clear goals, accountability systems and the constant application of quality improvement techniques made possible through widespread improvement training. Moreover, each system proves that high quality is more the result of a culture that pursues quality than of any single investment or policy. The systems the Quality by Design team profiles in this book pose a provocative challenge for the rest of us because they overcame familiar obstacles in order to deliver high-quality and sustainable care every day. We must do the same.

Adalsteinn Brown
Assistant Deputy Minister, Strategy
Ministry of Health and Long-Term Care

1

Introduction
Learning from High-Performing Systems: Quality by Design

Improvements in science, technology and care have offered the promise of better healthcare and improved health. But many healthcare systems have been unable to cope with the acceleration of knowledge growth, thus creating a gap between the care that is possible and the care that is delivered. Many commentators bemoan the inconsistent quality and increasing costs of current healthcare and fear the future burdens posed by aging populations and the costs of adopting emerging therapeutic and diagnostic innovations. Providing consistent, high-quality care is a challenge even in the countries that spend the most on healthcare (Institute of Medicine 2001). The increasing complexity of healthcare systems in industrialized countries has further exacerbated the quality chasm, thereby leading to a healthcare delivery system that is complicated, inefficient and uncoordinated.

Improving the safety and quality of care is an increasingly important objective in all health systems. Advances in measurement have helped to highlight variations between organizations, and across regional and national health systems. For example, the Commonwealth Fund, a health foundation based in the United States (US), has sponsored multi-country surveys of patients and physicians for 10 years, releasing the results of these surveys annually.[1] The results demonstrate that the US system, which is the most expensive of the seven systems studied, performs poorly in most dimensions compared with other countries (see Table 1). The Canadian system is the most expensive of the non-US systems; however, its performance is the lowest on several dimensions of quality, including the provision of appropriate, coordinated and patient-centred care, and next-to-lowest in most other dimensions (Commonwealth Fund 2007). The Organisation for Economic Co-operation and Development (OECD) recently released a report based on administrative data. It revealed wide variations in performance between Canada and the other OECD countries. For example, in 2005 the 30-day mortality rate from acute myocardial infarction was lower in Canada than the average for OECD countries, while the 30-day stroke case fatality rate was higher (Organisation for Economic Co-operation and Development 2007).

Table 1. Commonwealth Fund rankings

	Australia	Canada	Germany	New Zealand	United Kingdom	United States
Overall Ranking (2007)	**3.5**	**5**	**2**	**3.5**	**1**	**6**
Quality Care	4	6	2.5	2.5	1	5
Right Care	5	6	3	4	2	1
Safe Care	4	5	1	3	2	6
Coordinated Care	3	6	4	2	1	5
Patient-Centred Care	3	6	2	1	4	5
Access	3	5	1	2	4	6
Efficiency	4	5	3	2	1	6
Equity	2	5	4	3	1	6
Long, Healthy, and Productive Lives	1	3	2	4.5	4.5	6
Health Expenditure per Capita, 2004	$2,876*	$3,165	$3,005*	$2,083	$2,546	$6,102

* 2003 data.
Source: Calculated by the Commonwealth Fund based on the Commonwealth Fund 2004 International Health Policy Survey, the Commonwealth Fund 2005, International Health Policy Survey of Sicker Adults, the 2006 Commonwealth Fund International Health Policy Survey of Primary Care Physicians, and the Commonwealth Fund Commission on a High Performance Health System National Scorecard. Commonwealth Fund (2007).

[1] The Commonwealth Fund surveys began with comparisons of the US, Canada, the United Kingdom, Australia and New Zealand. Results from Germany and the Netherlands have been added more recently.

As these results suggest, no country has succeeded in demonstrating a consistently high level of performance. Moreover, the national variations incorporate a range of performance within each country for different geographic regions and/or health systems. On individual measures, for instance, some regions in countries that rank low may perform better than regions in countries that rank high. Country rankings provide useful indicators of the effectiveness of national policies and structures; however, they are clearly insufficient as guides to the elements of success. Moreover, examining the variations on their own does not explain why some regional systems or hospitals are able to achieve better outcomes than their peers. Indeed, despite agreement on the goal of improving quality in all healthcare systems, there remains considerable disagreement on effective and affordable means to improve performance. Few studies have attempted to examine whether any regional or local systems are capable of achieving consistently better outcomes across different disease programs, levels of care and local delivery organizations.

Identifying such high-performing health systems and understanding the strategies and investments they have made is more than an academic issue. The practices these healthcare systems employ can inform strategy development and guide the allocation of resources in systems seeking to improve their performance. Identifying improvements to current care delivery structures and translating approaches from high-performing systems to local delivery organizations will help to spread more reliable and cost-effective care. While there are many examples of local successes, too often these are "islands of excellence in a sea of mediocrity" (Rogers and Bevan 2002) rather than reflections of consistent approaches to good practice. High-performing healthcare systems are those that have created effective frameworks and systems for improving care that are applicable in different settings and sustainable over time – but is this an achievable goal in systems that are not high-performing?

The search for sustainable and affordable quality is not a problem unique to healthcare. Indeed, in many industries there has been a search for strategies and investments that yield consistently better results. Among notable success stories are the achievements of Toyota Motor Corporation based on the development of the Toyota Production System, an approach to manufacturing that has revolutionized the auto industry (Womack et al. 1990). The critical first step for achieving such high performance levels is to recognize that quality must be defined as a system property and not as a characteristic of individuals who work in a system. Healthcare has traditionally defined excellence in terms of individual physicians or other caregivers. In this view high quality results from the practice of highly trained expert clinicians. Yet patient safety experts such as James Reason (1995) and Lucian Leape (1994) have long argued that safety cannot be improved by urging individual clinicians to be more careful. Instead, we must design systems that reduce the likelihood of errors, make errors more visible and provide the means to remediate before harm occurs.

The same reasoning applies to improving quality. In their seminal report *Crossing the Quality Chasm*, the Institute of Medicine's Committee on Quality of Health Care in America noted,

> Health care has safety and quality problems because it relies on outmoded systems of work. Poor designs set the workforce up to fail, regardless of how hard they try. If we want safer, higher-quality care, we will need to have redesigned systems of care, including the use of information technology to support clinical and administrative processes. (Institute of Medicine 2001: 4)

The recognition that quality is a property of systems and not just individuals or operating units begs several questions:

- What aspects of healthcare systems are key to facilitating high performance?
- What do we know about the relationships among these elements and among various important outcomes?
- What is the best way to study these issues?

What is a system capable of improvement?

Calling a group of healthcare organizations a "system" has become common practice. As Ackoff (1974, 1994) and others have noted, however, true systems involve a functionally related group of interacting, interrelated or interdependent elements forming a complex whole with a common aim. In simpler terms, system elements must be capable of working together to achieve shared goals; otherwise, they are merely individual parts with separate missions. Batalden and Mohr (1997) devised an exercise to show how improvement activities relate to an organization's daily work. They emphasize the need to understand three sets of interdependent components of any given system (see Figure 1):

- *Why an organization produces its services* – Who are the customers and what are the broader social needs the organization fulfills?
- *How those services are produced* – What are the processes of daily work or, in other words, the means of production?
- *How the organization improves its services* – What are the improvement activities or means of improvement?

Efforts to improve healthcare services are often termed "quality improvement." Quality improvement is an umbrella term that includes many overlapping concepts, such as continuous improvement, organization-wide commitment and worker participation, knowledge of customer needs, systems thinking, systematic analysis of processes, use of scientific data-driven analytic methods and involvement of interdisciplinary and cross-functional teams (Blumenthal and Kilo 1998; Lucas et al. 2005; McLaughlin and Kaluzny 1994; O'Brien et al. 1995; Øvretveit and Gustafson 2002). The knowledge and skills necessary for this improvement work draw from a variety of disciplines. Different improvement methods emphasize different tools, but most quality improvement approaches include methods to analyze and improve (or design) work processes, techniques to collect and integrate information about the needs of patients and other key customers to inform the design of work, and methods for testing and implementing improvements.

Figure 1. A system capable of continual improvement

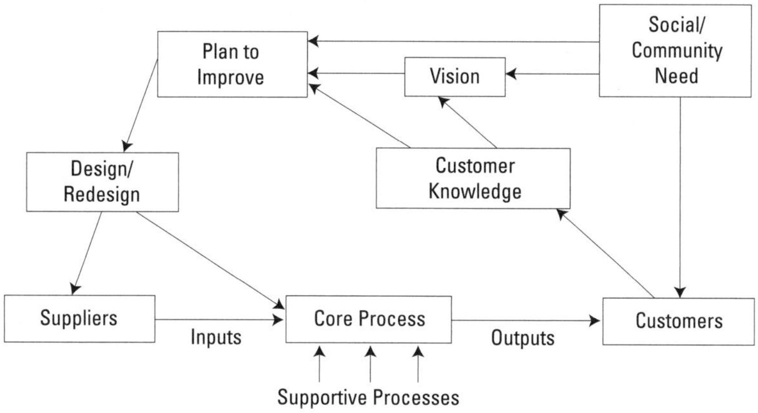

Source: Batalden and Stoltz (1993), based on Deming (1986).

Much of the improvement literature describes work at the front lines – or "clinical microsystems of care" – involving caregivers, patients, support staff, the information and materials they need and the activities and outcomes they generate. High-quality care results from the effective practices and interactions of caregivers in such microsystems. A successful microsystem is able to make multiple and sustained improvements in care based on factors such as the following:

- Members' understanding of their clinical unit as an interdependent group with the capacity to make changes
- The development of a common purpose and collaboration to improve outcomes

based on an understanding of current system performance and of the methods and tools necessary to improve performance (Batalden and Splaine 2002; Mohr and Batalden 2002; Nelson et al. 2007)

Efforts to improve performance at the front line depend on a range of supports both within organizations and from the broader environments in which they operate. Because improvements at the local level depend on leadership and action at higher levels, successful leaders of the large systems in which clinical microsystems are embedded need to support local leadership and provide resources to clinical microsystems. While clinical improvement is rooted in high-performing clinical units, the development of fertile cultures and effective unit leadership depend on support from above. This point is made by Ferlie and Shortell (2001: 282), who argue for "a more comprehensive, multi-level approach" to improve the quality and outcomes of care. Changes at any one level must take into consideration the other levels within an organization's strata in order to anticipate and deal with barriers. For example, team-level interventions take place in the context of an organization, which must have the necessary systems and resources in place to support its teams undergoing change. In this context, Berwick (2002) argues that there are four levels of analysis nested within each other:

- The experience of the patient
- The functioning of the microsystem
- The functioning of the organization
- The aspects of the broader environment, including policy, payment, regulation and other critical factors that shape the organization's behaviour

Similarly, Walshe and Freeman (2002: 85) note that a receptive organizational context is "a crucial determinant" of the effectiveness of quality improvement initiatives.

What are the key elements that facilitate improvement work?

The relationship between a system's levels and the dependence of microsystems on supportive environments suggests a need to understand what organizational and inter-organizational resources are necessary to promote improvements in care. Although many healthcare systems articulate strategic improvement goals, as Berwick et al. (2003: I35) note, "the ability to change should not be taken for granted. It implies a set of specific organizational processes (the processes that facilitate and manage systemic change), which constitute the organizational infrastructure for improvement." These commentators specify the elements of this organizational infrastructure necessary for improvement, including the following:

- The reliable flow of useful information
- Education and training for staff in improvement theory, methods and techniques
- Understanding of time and change management necessary to change core processes
- Alignment of strategic organizational incentives and improvement goals
- Leadership to guide and inspire improvement

A number of other authors also discuss the various organizational processes and the ways they interact with one another. For example, Adler et al. (2003) describe five components of capability, including the following:

- Skills: Technical, business and social skills
- Systems: Organizational systems and information systems
- Structures: Performance improvement staff groups and performance improvement project structures
- Strategies: Priorities and strategy processes
- Culture: Norms, values and identities

Ferlie and Shortell (2001) identify four essential core properties of successful quality improvement work:

- Leadership at all levels
- A pervasive culture that supports learning through the core process
- Emphasis on the development of effective teams
- Greater use of information technologies for both continuous improvement work and external accountability

Øvretveit and Gustafson (2002) identify eight important factors that motivate and sustain quality improvement programs. Like Ferlie and Shortell, they include leadership commitment and a supportive culture. They also add a number of structural factors (physician involvement, sufficient resources, careful program management and training) and a strategic focus on customer needs. Other analyses of critical factors supporting improvement have been made based on various data sources (see Barron et al. 2005; Franco et al. 2002; O'Brien et al. 1995). While the names for these critical factors and supportive processes vary, the main elements they contain are largely consistent. Table 2 provides an overview of the nine key attributes and component elements derived from a synthesis of these and other studies.

If scholars in several countries with differing approaches have developed similar lists of key elements, then some might wonder why more healthcare systems have not achieved

Table 2. Attributes of successful improvement

Attribute	Elements
Culture	* Organization/leaders support and expect learning and innovation. * Organization/leaders value staff and empower all members to participate. * Organization/leaders focus on customers/patients. * Organization/leaders value collaboration and teamwork. * Organization/leaders are flexible.
Leadership	* Strong administrative leadership that provides role models for organizational values. * Leadership celebrates and even participates in improvement initiatives. * Emphasis on developing, fostering and inclusion in decision-making for clinical leadership and champions. * Board support: Board sets expectations by asking for reports on improvement initiatives and results. * Board provides continuity of expectations if administrative leadership changes.
Strategy and policy	* Leaders set clear priorities for improvement. * Improvement plans are integrated in the overall strategic plan as the means to achieve key strategic goals. * Leaders demonstrate both constancy of purpose and flexibility. * Operational policies and procedures, including human resources policies, provide incentives, rewards and recognition. * Incentives, rewards and recognition are aligned to support improvement work.
Structure	* Roles and responsibilities for improvement are clearly articulated. * Steering/oversight committees provide direction. * Teams and teamwork are part of structure.
Resources	* Organization provides time for staff members to learn skills and participate in improvement work. * Financial and material resources and human resources are available for improvement. * Quality improvement support/expertise: A core group of improvement experts is available to help teams and individuals. * Quality improvement department coordinates and supports initiatives.
Information	* Needed clinical and administrative data are readily available. * Information is available to support improvement.
Communication channels	* Organization has vehicles to communicate with stakeholders regarding priorities, initiatives, results and learning. * Ample forms of communication, including newsletters, forums, meetings and intranet sites.
Skills training	* Includes training in improvement methods, team and group work, project and meeting management, and epidemiology.
Physician involvement	* Physicians are involved in planning improvement initiatives and participate as team members. * Opportunities for physician and clinical leadership of improvement. * Clinicians "own" improvement.

Source: MacIntosh-Murray et al. (2006).

high levels of performance and reliability. The reasons for this are complex, but they likely stem from several factors. First, many of the elements identified as supporting high performance are difficult to achieve. For example, healthcare organizations must provide relevant and timely data on clinical processes in a format that guides improvement. This requires overcoming substantial technical and logistical challenges. Many organizations have found it difficult to develop skills for improving care and to create environments in which physicians "own" improvement. These components of high-performing healthcare systems are not widely shared, and there are many broader policy and resource barriers to developing them.

Second, in many cases these elements are interdependent. High-performing healthcare organizations are *systems* of interacting, interrelated and interdependent clinical microsystems. There are also supportive elements and structures that are aligned with (and sometimes pushing against) broader health system policy and structures. Fulfilling only some of the characteristics of successful systems is insufficient for achieving high performance. Instead, high-performing systems need to develop many, if not all, of the characteristics noted above.

Third, the path forward to achieve these attributes is rarely clear. Typically, we assess a system on a set of measures and judge it to be better or worse than others. But such an assessment is inevitably static; it does not tell us which strategies, structures and processes were critical for creating the system's high level of performance. Nor does it detail the leadership processes and strategic investments required over time.

Fourth, when offered a list of attributes associated with high-performing systems, the temptation is to create a checklist to assess other systems that wish to emulate such performance. But reality is more complex than a checklist. Developing a high-performing system is a journey that cannot be judged solely by examining current performance. Instead, we must assess the environment and challenges the organization faced; understand the strategies and investments its leaders made; and assess the learning, mid-course corrections and current efforts made to maintain and spread high performance. Nor can we assume that the decisions one organization made will be appropriate for others that face different challenges and possess different resources.

Exploring systems capable of improvement

The goal of the Quality by Design project was to investigate a small number of high-performing healthcare systems to examine the leadership strategies, organizational processes and investments made to create and sustain improvements in care. Although most comparative health policy literature focuses on differences in national systems (e.g., Anderson and Hussey 2001; Arah et al. 2003; Saltman and Figueras 1998), the variation in performance *within* national systems suggests that important learning can be gained from assessing strategies used by regional systems or other subnational units that have achieved high performance. And although it is clear that successful improvement must take place at the microsystem level where patients, clinical professionals and other staff members interact, these microsystems depend greatly on the leadership, resources and strategies of leaders in their broader organizations.

Nelson et al. (2007) have recently published a study of high-performing microsystems. Although they discuss the elements of the broader macrosystems that support the work of successful microsystems, their primary focus is on the tools and unit-level strategies for creating improvement at the front lines. By contrast, the emphasis in this study is understanding the strategies and investments of high-performing health systems. This fills a gap in the literature between studies of national healthcare policies, on the one hand, and the analysis of clinical microsystems and the methods and tools used to secure front-line improvements, on the other hand.

This focus is not unique. Several frameworks have been developed in recent years to assess performance excellence in organizations. In the US, the Malcolm Baldrige National Quality Program was created to recognize companies that have been successful in improving the quality of their goods and services and to stimulate improvement in other US firms. The Baldrige awards were first given in 1988 and the first award to a healthcare organization was made in 2002 (National Institute of Standards and Technology 2007). The criteria on which organizations are judged are based on a framework that assesses performance in seven areas: leadership; strategic planning; customer and market focus; measurement, analysis and knowledge management; human resources; process management; and, results. As of 2007 eight healthcare organizations had won the Baldrige Award. Senior leaders from several of these organizations have written detailed accounts of their organization's efforts to improve quality (e.g., Ryan 2007; Stubblefield 2005). Similar awards in Canada (e.g., the National Quality Institute's Canada Awards for Excellence) and Europe (the European Foundation for Quality Management's Excellence Awards) have established similar criteria and processes for judging excellence (European Foundation for Quality Management 2003; National Quality Institute nd). Healthcare organizations have used these awards programs as guides to assessing and improving their performance.

Mary Jean Ryan (2007) and other winners of the Baldrige Award identify the Baldrige framework and criteria as a useful guide to assessing their organizations and helping to direct the leadership of improvement. Many thousands of copies of the Baldrige criteria have been downloaded or purchased, and both Baldrige and other award criteria have been used to inform or evaluate leadership strategies (e.g., Goldstein and Schweikhart 2002; Nabitz et al. 2000). However, by themselves the long lists of criteria and questions in these assessment frameworks are daunting and require considerable effort to complete. Moreover, the frameworks are similar, but not identical (MacIntosh-Murray et al. 2006), and possible gaps in them have been identified (Counte and Meurer 2001). Lastly, many descriptions of award-winning organizations emphasize their current performance rather than the strategies that led to it.

The accounts by Baldrige winners do, however, describe their journeys and are useful sources of ideas. Yet these accounts emphasize different issues and focus only on US organizations. There are, therefore, few studies that have employed consistent methods for assessing high-performing healthcare organizations in different policy environments. Two notable exceptions are the recent book by Bate et al. (2008), who examine quality improvement efforts in seven hospitals in the US and Europe, and McCarthy and Blumenthal's (2006) study of the work of six US organizations that have been leaders in patient safety strategies.

Approach and methods: Selecting and profiling systems capable of improvement

There are no international performance data that rank regional healthcare systems. Therefore, in order to select the systems studied in this project we devised a nomination and selection process that relied on experts to identify health systems that have successfully invested in improvement resources and demonstrated measurable performance improvements over time. We asked 21 international experts in quality improvement and health systems monitoring to nominate health systems (defined as regional authorities, trusts and/or networks/systems of organizations, as opposed to single hospitals) they believed had made significant investments in quality improvement and had achieved demonstrable, measurable improvements as a result of those investments. These experts were chosen according to their reputations in the fields of practice and academia as being knowledgeable about systems that were successful in improvement. Among our experts were individuals from the European Society for Quality in Healthcare, Institute for Healthcare Improvement and the Joint Commission for the Accreditation of Healthcare Organizations International, as well as health system providers, researchers and decision-makers.

Fourteen experts submitted 40 nominations of 22 health systems. Of the 22 systems, 13 were in the US, 5 were in Europe and 3 were located elsewhere. Seven systems were nominated more than once. We examined the accomplishments of these seven systems and selected five based on their capabilities in sustaining quality improvement efforts and results. Our team collected information on the chosen systems through a review of publications and data available on the Internet and from other sources. From May

2006 through September 2007, between two and four team members paid one visit to each of the five sites. In advance of each visit, the researchers reviewed a range of background documents provided by system informants, including, for example, strategic plans, annual reports, terms of reference, improvement reports and Baldrige Award or other detailed applications for public recognition. Site visits included meetings and interviews with system leaders, clinicians, administrators and educators as well as local and national health system leaders and policy-makers.

The case studies were crafted based on thematic analysis of extensive notes recorded during the interviews, integrating details from the strategic and operational documents from each site. Key interview participants at each of the five sites reviewed the draft reports to ensure factual accuracy. A study advisory committee comprised of leaders from health organizations in Ontario and elsewhere in Canada met twice to discuss the study framework as well as case report drafts. Members of this committee provided helpful insights and guidance, and validated the relevance of the major themes in the Canadian context.

In addition to the five international cases, we investigated two Canadian systems. These cases were selected with guidance from members of the study advisory committee as representative of better-performing Canadian healthcare systems that exemplified elements present in the international cases. While none of the systems originally nominated by our experts were Canadian, we included Canadian cases in response to interest from several advisory committee members about whether characteristics of high-performing systems could be identified in Canadian organizations. The two cases provide evidence that Canadian health policies, financial environments and regulatory frameworks do not prevent the emergence of high-performing systems. These two cases were approached in a somewhat different fashion than the five international ones. Two members of the team spent several months on site – one team member at each – as part of practicum experiences for their master's degrees in health administration. During this time they collected information and conducted interviews. Other members of the team collected additional interviews and information, and drafts of the cases were reviewed and revised by several team members.

Drafts of the international and Canadian cases were given to leaders in the respective organizations so they could identify factual errors in our descriptions. In addition, we sought input from external experts who knew the organizations, and we reviewed other case analyses of and literature on the healthcare systems we studied. In a few instances system leaders disagreed with some of the interpretations we made of their organizational strategies. We have duly noted where these disagreements occurred.

As with any study, there are limitations inherent in the Quality by Design approach. For example, the nomination method for systems to study was influenced by expert opinion, health system visibility and case visit feasibility. The choice of other experts might have led us to different systems. However, we do not claim that our study comprises an exhaustive list of high-performing health systems internationally, nor was that our intent.

In each of the cases we discuss a number of areas in which the organizations have been successful, describing the strategies, methods and tools used at a senior leadership level, detailing the organizational infrastructure and approach, and examining the methods and tools used at the front lines of care. Still, none of these systems' representatives would claim their performance is exemplary in all domains, and each one noted areas they are targeting for improvement. One of the characteristics of highly successful healthcare systems is a paradoxical stance toward success. All the organizations we studied were proud of their achievements and often sought recognition of their successes to support further efforts and reward staff members. Yet all were striving to spread their successes throughout their organizations to improve more areas of care. Indeed, an impatience – rather than satisfaction – with current performance appears to be a hallmark of high-performing healthcare systems.

Variations in performance also mean that in some areas these high-performing systems may be merely "average." There is no Toyota in healthcare: no one system clearly outdistances its competitors in virtually all its products and services. In selecting the systems we chose for our case studies, and in collecting and analyzing information on those cases, we sought evidence that the seven organizations had developed robust strategies and approaches. Nevertheless, some performance measures in each organization are not at the level to which system leaders might aspire.

Canadian healthcare policy expert Steven Lewis has observed, "[We need to] become more adept at learning which features of international systems we can and cannot easily import, and recognize that what ails our system originates in design rather than the laws of nature" (Lewis 2007: 19). The focused case study approach allowed us to describe in more detail the developmental stories of five international and two Canadian organizations as they worked to become – and remain – high-performing systems. None of the cases is a precise road map for other systems in Canada or elsewhere. But all provide useful insights into the strategies, investments and lessons learned on the journey to excellence.

A key strength of our approach is that the case narratives highlight details of the *how:*

- The often difficult processes these varied organizations have gone through
- What they have done and why
- What they believe has worked (or not)

By reading the stories from each system, comparing them with our own organizations and considering the policy environment and resources that provide a context for performance, we can begin to identify ideas to import. Learning from these case studies requires that we acknowledge the differences between policy contexts and timing. Moreover, in addition to recognizing the strategies and ideas that may be transferrable we need to determine the "obstacles that have to be addressed in translating practices from one system to another" (Ham 2005: 192). From country to country – and even within the same country – healthcare systems are widely divergent in terms of histories, contexts, policies, structures and other determining factors. Our study focused on high-performing systems that have very different structures, exist in policy environments that range from highly directive to facilitative and embody very different histories. Despite these differences we believe that careful study of international and local successes better enables us to evaluate the assumptions and decisions in our own environment, aspects of health system planning and operation that sometimes go unquestioned. In other words, the case studies can help us to learn about what we might try to do differently in our own systems' pursuit of quality – not by chance, but *by design*.

References

Ackoff, R. 1974. *Redesigning the Future.* New York: John Wiley & Sons.

Ackoff, R. 1994. *The Democratic Corporation.* New York: Oxford University Press.

Adler, P.S., P. Riley, S. Kwon, J. Signer, B. Lee and R. Satrasala. 2003. "Performance Improvement Capability: Keys to Accelerating Performance Improvement in Hospitals." *California Management Review* 45(2): 12–33.

Anderson, G. and P.S. Hussey. 2001. "Comparing Health System Performance in OECD Countries." *Health Affairs* 20(3): 219–232.

Arah, O.A., N.S. Klazinga, D.M.J. Delnoij, A.H.A. Ten Asbroek and T. Custers. 2003. "Conceptual Frameworks for Health Systems Performance: A Quest for Effectiveness, Quality, and Improvement." *International Journal of Quality in Health Care* 15(5): 377–398.

Barron, W.M., C. Krsek, D. Weber and J. Cerese. 2005. "Critical Success Factors for Performance Improvement Programs." *Joint Commission Journal on Quality and Patient Safety* 31(4): 220–226.

Batalden, P.B. and J. Mohr. 1997. "Building Knowledge of Health Care as a System." *Quality Management in Health Care* 5(3): 1–12.

Batalden, P.B. and M. Splaine. 2002. "What Will It Take to Lead the Continual Improvement and Innovation of Health Care in the Twenty-First Century?" *Quality Management in Health Care* 11(1): 45–54.

Batalden, P.B. and P.K. Stoltz. 1993. "A Framework for the Continual Improvement of Health Care: Building and Applying Professional and Improvement Knowledge to Test Changes in Daily Work." *The Joint Commission Journal on Quality Improvement* 19(10): 424–447.

Bate, P., P. Mendel and G. Robert. 2008. *Organizing for Quality: The Improvement Journey of Leading Hospitals in Europe and the United States.* Abingdon, UK: Radcliffe Publishing.

Berwick, D.M. 2002. "A User's Manual for the IOM's 'Quality Chasm' Report." *Health Affairs* 21(3): 80–90.

Berwick, D.M., B. James and M.J. Coye. 2003. "Connections between Quality Measurement and Improvement." *Medical Care* 41(1): I30–I38.

Blumenthal, D. and C.M. Kilo. 1998. "A Report Card on Continuous Quality Improvement." *The Milbank Quarterly* 76(4): 625–648.

Commonwealth Fund. 2007. *International Survey: U.S. Adults Most Likely to Report Medical Errors and Skip Needed Care Due to Costs*. New York: Author. Retrieved February 28, 2008. <http://www.commonwealthfund.org/newsroom/newsroom_show.htm?doc_id=567035>

Counte, M.A. and S. Meurer 2001. "Issues in the Assessment of Continuous Quality Improvement Implementation in Health Care Organizations." *International Journal for Quality in Health Care* 13(3): 197–207.

Deming, W.E. 1986. *Out of the Crisis.* Cambridge, MA: MIT Center for Advanced Engineering Study.

European Foundation for Quality Management. 2003. *The Fundamental Concepts of Excellence.* Brussels: Author. Retrieved August 15, 2006. <http://www.efqm.org/Portals/0/FuCo-en.pdf>

Ferlie, E. and S.M. Shortell. 2001. "Improving the Quality of Care in the United Kingdom and the United States: A Framework for Change. *The Milbank Quarterly* 79(2): 281–315.

Franco, L.M., D.R. Silimperi, T. Veldhuyzen van Zanten, C. MacAulay, B. Askov, B. Bouchet and L. Marquez. 2002. *Sustaining Quality of Healthcare: Institutionalization of Quality Assurance.* Bethesda, MD: Quality Assurance Project. Retrieved August 15, 2006. <http://www.qaproject.org/pubs/pubsmonographs.html>

Goldstein, S.M. and S.B. Schweikhart. 2002. "Empirical Support for the Baldrige Award Framework in U.S. Hospitals." *Healthcare Management Review* 27(1): 62–75.

Ham, C. 2005. "Lost in Translation? Health Systems in the US and the UK." *Social Policy & Administration* 39(2): 192–209.

Institute of Medicine. 2001. *Crossing the Quality Chasm.* Washington, DC: National Academy of Sciences.

Leape, L.L. 1994. "Error in Medicine." *Journal of the American Medical Association* 272(23): 1851–1857.

Lewis, S. 2007. "Can a Learning-Disabled Nation Learn Healthcare Lessons from Abroad?" *Healthcare Policy* 3(2): 19–28.

Lucas, J.A., T. Avi-Itzhak, J.P. Robinson, C.G. Morris, M.J. Koren and S.C. Reinhard. 2005. "Continuous Quality Improvement as an Innovation: Which Nursing Facilities Adopt It?" *The Gerontologist* 45(1): 68–77.

MacIntosh-Murray, A., C. Porcellato and K. Born. 2006. *Quality by Design Literature Review* (v. 1.2). Unpublished.

McCarthy, D. and D. Blumenthal. 2006. "Stories from the Sharp End: Case Studies in Safety Improvement." *The Milbank Quarterly* 84(1): 165–200.

McLaughlin, C.P. and A.D. Kaluzny. 1994. *Continuous Quality Improvement in Health Care: Theory, Implementation, and Applications*. Gaithersburg, MD: Aspen.

Mohr, J.J. and P.B. Batalden. 2002. "Improving Safety at the Front Lines: The Role of Clinical Microsystems." *Quality and Safety in Health Care* 11(1): 45–50.

Nabitz, U., N. Klazinga and J. Walburg. 2000. "The EFQM Excellence Model: European and Dutch Experiences with the EFQM Approach in Health Care." *International Journal for Quality in Health Care* 12(3): 191–204.

National Institute of Standards and Technology. 2007. *Frequently Asked Questions about the Malcolm Baldrige National Quality Award.* Gaithersburg, MD: Author. Retrieved March 10, 2008. <http://www.nist.gov/public_affairs/factsheet/baldfaqs.htm>

National Quality Institute. nd. *Canadian Quality Criteria for the Public Sector – Overview.* Toronto: Author. Retrieved August 15, 2006. <http://www.nqi.ca/nqistore/product_details.aspx?ID=62>

Nelson, E.C., P.B. Batalden and M. Godfrey. 2007. *Quality by Design.* San Francisco: Jossey-Bass.

O'Brien, J.L., S.M. Shortell, E.F.X. Hughes, R.W. Foster, J.M. Carman, H. Boerstler and E.J. O'Connor. 1995. "An Integrative Model for Organization-Wide Quality Improvement: Lessons from the Field." *Quality Management in Health Care* 3(4): 19–30.

Organisation for Economic Co-operation and Development. 2007. *Health at a Glance.* Paris: Author. Retrieved March 1, 2008. <http://www.oecd.org/document/11/0,3343,en_2649_37407_16502667_1_1_1_37407,00.html>

Øvretveit, J. and D. Gustafson. 2002. "Evaluation of Quality Improvement Programmes." *Quality and Safety in Health Care* 11(3): 270–275.

Reason, J. 1995. "Understanding Adverse Events: Human Factors." *Quality in Health Care* 4: 80–89.

Rogers, H. and H. Bevan. 2002. *Spreading Good Practice.* Presentation at the Cancer Services Collaborative Programme, Urology National Workshop, UK. Retrieved March 23, 2008. <www.heart.nhs.uk/serviceimprovement/1338/4647/5211/Hugh_Rogers.ppt>

Ryan, M.J. 2007. *On Becoming Exceptional: SSM Health Care's Journey to Baldrige and Beyond.* Milwaukee, WI: American Society for Quality Control.

Saltman, R.B. and J. Figueras (Eds.). 1998. *Critical Challenges for Health Reform in Europe.* Buckingham, UK: Open University Press.

Stubblefield, A. 2005. *The Baptist Health Care Journey to Excellence: Creating a Culture that WOWs!* Hoboken, NJ: John Wiley & Sons.

Walshe, K. and T. Freeman. 2002. "Effectiveness of Quality Improvement: Learning from Evaluations." *Quality and Safety in Health Care* 11(1): 85–87.

Womack, J.P., D.T. Jones and D. Roos. 1990. *The Machine That Changed the World.* New York: Rawson Associates.

2

Birmingham East and North Primary Care Trust and Heart of England Foundation Trust

Birmingham, UK

Highlights of recent achievements

- In 2005 and 2006 the Birmingham East and North Primary Care Trust (BEN PCT) was short-listed for the Health Service Journal award for Primary Care Trust of the Year (*Health Service Journal* Awards 2005, 2006).
- BEN PCT's orthopaedic triage service won the Health Service Journal's access award in 2005 for its work in managing referrals to orthopaedics in primary care settings, decreasing patient waits and increasing patient satisfaction and access (*Health Service Journal* Awards 2005).
- BEN PCT changed from the worst-performing area in the country for over-prescription of antibiotics to winning an award from the Royal Pharmaceutical Society for its achievement in reducing prescribing levels (Birmingham East and North Primary Care Trust 2006b).
- Good Hope Hospital's redesign of its vascular surgery clinic and community leg ulcer service won the National Health Service (NHS) Innovation Award for Service Delivery in 2004 and the Healthcare IT Effectiveness Award's Best Use of IT in the Health Service and Best Innovative Use of Technology awards in 2005 (Healthcare IT Effectiveness Awards 2005).

- The Heart of England Foundation Trust (HEFT) won the Acute Care Trust of the Year award in 2006 (*Health Service Journal* Awards 2006).

The system and its environment

BEN PCT is one of 152 primary care trusts (PCTs) in the NHS (see Appendix A for background information on the NHS). Responsible for improving the health of their registered populations within their geographic boundaries, PCTs commission services from providers to meet health needs following NHS service principles (i.e., universal cradle-to-grave coverage that is free at point of use). The potential providers with which they contract range from foundation trusts (hospitals) and provider trusts (district general hospitals and community services) to the voluntary and independent sectors.

Part of the West Midlands Strategic Health Authority, BEN PCT was formed in 2006 by combining the former Eastern Birmingham and Northern Birmingham PCTs. Birmingham is the second largest city in England and BEN PCT serves a diverse population of 433,000 in the eastern half of the city. The effects of socio-economic disparities in this area pose considerable healthcare challenges, with striking contrasts between the better-off Sutton wards in the north ("much more wealthy, middle class, and white" with "better infrastructure") and wards in the east that are among the "most deprived" in England (remarks from a slide presentation by the BEN PCT chief executive officer [CEO] on November 2, 2006). In the eastern wards the Southeast Asian population tends to have higher mortality and morbidity rates, such as lower life expectancy and higher cardiovascular mortality rates among males and above-average infant mortality (BEN PCT 2006). Cultural factors influence care-seeking as well as what type of care is considered culturally appropriate, needed and available in the community.

The PCT contracts for the full continuum of health services for the population within its boundaries as well as providing some services directly. The PCT also pays for independent general practitioners (GPs), dentists, pharmacists and optometrists. For BEN PCT this includes 84 GP practices (237 GPs), 46 dental practices, 95 pharmacies and 83 optometrists. According to a slide presentation by the BEN PCT CEO on November 2, 2006, the PCT has a core annual budget of £560 million ($1.28 billion CAD) and approximately 1,700 employees (BEN PCT 2007a). In addition it hosts £600 million of specialized services commissioning, covering low-volume, high-cost services for the 5 million people of the West Midlands.

BEN PCT is governed by a board composed of a chairman, seven lay members, members of the PCT executive and representatives of the PCT's professional executive committee (PEC). The PEC is the formal clinical leadership group, taking executive responsibility for clinical strategy and policy (BEN PCT 2007b).

HEFT, which includes Heartlands Hospital, Solihull Hospital and Good Hope Hospital NHS Trust, is one of the provider organizations from which BEN PCT commissions services. As a high-performance hospital trust, HEFT was granted foundation trust status in 2005, a designation that gives more autonomy and independence from government control (although HEFT is still subject to regulatory standards and review) (Department of Health 2007a).

HEFT is one of the largest trusts in England, with over 6,000 staff members treating 84,000 in-patients, over 350,000 out-patients and approximately 140,000 emergency cases each year (HEFT 2007). HEFT hospitals provide national and regional clinical services as well as specialized acute care, emergency and elective care.

As separate organizations accountable to different regulatory agencies, BEN PCT and HEFT have each developed their own successful approaches to organizational performance improvement. In addition, the extensive and unusual level of collaboration between the PCT and the foundation trust has resulted in joint programs of work to build primary care capacity and improve chronic care management. Their collaborative approach, which they call Working Together for Health, is based on values captured in three catchphrases:

- Patients as partners
- Promoting self-care
- Care in the right place

Method: Exploring a system capable of improvement

In October-November 2006 a team of researchers from the University of Toronto's Department of Health Policy, Management and Evaluation visited BEN PCT and HEFT. This site visit was part of an initiative called Quality by Design, which aims to identify and define elements of healthcare systems capable of improvement with a view to helping to inform strategic investments in improvement capability in Ontario. Quality by Design is funded primarily by the Ontario Ministry of Health and Long-Term Care in partnership with the University of Toronto's Department of Health Policy, Management and Evaluation.

BEN PCT (including HEFT) was one of five healthcare systems selected from a short list of high-performing systems nominated by a panel of international leaders and experts. In Birmingham the team met with and interviewed administrative and clinical leaders, improvement team leaders and members, as well as support staff working to make improvements. This case study highlights the findings of that site visit.

Examples of improvement initiatives

Clinical improvement projects

The following projects are examples of clinical improvement projects currently underway as part of the joint program of work between BEN PCT and HEFT (BEN PCT and HEFT 2006):

- The trusts are among the national pilot sites for the Making the Shift project, which is an initiative of the NHS Institute for Innovation and Improvement (the Institute). Making the Shift aims to move needed services from hospitals to primary care in order to better integrate access to services in the community (see Appendix A, sections 7.1 and 7.3, for more information about the Institute). Three project teams are working on lower-back pain management, heart failure and integrated continence service. They have designed clinics and care paths to coordinate care in the community by using providers from several disciplines and patient education programs as well as by decreasing wait times and unnecessary referrals to specialists.
- Assertive Case Management (see next sub-section)
- Diabetes: To deliver a community-based glucose tolerance testing service and patient education
- Chronic obstructive pulmonary disease (COPD): To identify the prevalence of COPD in the region and create a self-management pathway for the patients
- Healthy Hearts Programme: To create a clinic offering specialized treatment plans and education for those at high risk of cardiovascular disease (CVD)
- Elderly Care Assessment Unit: To further develop the unit as a rapid access assessment unit for elderly patients needing short-term medical intervention
- Hospice at Home: To improve palliative care in the home by redesigning positions for "health care assistants with specialist interest in palliative care"
- Integrating Health and Social Care: To redesign an integrated service model for day services across health and social care and the voluntary sector

Partners in Health Centre

The Partners in Health Centre is located near the HEFT Heartlands Hospital, in one of the most economically disadvantaged wards of the PCT. Opened in 2005 the building itself is "a neutral meeting space," a physical symbol of the partnership between the PCT and the foundation trust and a place where teams can collaborate on improvement and care redesign projects as part of the Working Together for Health initiative. The centre provides a focus and home for holistic, multi-provider care programs aimed at self-care and education of patients so that they can take responsibility for their own health. The programs mix clinicians from primary and secondary care (spanning both organizations) and provide support services not available in hospitals or primary care for patients with chronic conditions such as diabetes, COPD, heart failure and degenerative musculoskeletal disease. The centre also provides a base for the orthopaedic triage service.

Musculoskeletal orthopaedic triage service with choice

This award-winning service (Health Service Journal Awards 2005) is based on screening and intervention by extended scope physiotherapists who triage patients for all conditions for which a GP feels an orthopaedic consultation is required (see Appendix A, section 2.2, for more about role redesign). The service began with screening hip and knee conditions and expanded its scope in 2005 to full musculoskeletal triage. The team mapped processes across primary and secondary care, building a database for more rigorous data collection and reports on referral patterns, wait times and outcomes. Team members designed and implemented care pathways that expand primary care and incorporate alternative care choices for patients (compared to traditional surgical or medical treatment), including acupuncture, mobility groups, exercise programs, pain management clinics and expert-patient programs. The service has reduced wait times and routine referrals to orthopaedics and has resulted in improved access and patient satisfaction levels. In line with national policy directions it has also increased the choice of providers for patients (see Appendix A, section 3.2, for more about the patient choice policy).

Vascular clinic and telemedicine system

Leg ulcers are a chronic condition that benefit from careful and timely management by specialist out-patient services. In Good Hope Hospital, Simon Dodds, a vascular surgeon skilled in methods of value stream analysis and process design, led the redesign of the booking system and flow in the vascular clinic, eliminating 12 weeks of delays and adding 40% capacity (Dodds 2005, 2006). In addition, Dodds and his team designed a secure shared e-record, an electronic linkage with the PCT nurses providing wound care in the community. The system enables rapid referral, digital images and access to remote expert advice and follow-up. In a presentation on November 2, 2006, Dodds reported that changes have resulted in improved healing rates of 64% at 12 weeks (compared to studies that have shown healing rates of 22% at 12 weeks for community care and 40% with the addition of specialist out-patient care) and significantly reduced costs.

Birmingham OwnHealth®

Launched in April 2006, Birmingham OwnHealth® involves telephone-based care management in the community for over 900 patients with chronic conditions (diabetes, heart failure and coronary heart disease [CHD]). The service – commissioned by BEN PCT from NHS Direct – was developed as a partnership between the PCT, Pfizer Health Solutions and NHS Direct. It is based on an earlier Pfizer initiative called Florida: A Healthy State, which was undertaken in conjunction with the State of Florida's Agency for Health Care Administration. NHS Direct is the national 24-hour health and illness information service provided by telephone and on-line (NHS Direct 2007).

Birmingham OwnHealth® is based in one of NHS Direct's call centres and is staffed by 12 care managers who have experience in telephone nursing services and who have been trained by NHS Direct. The care managers can support up to 200 patients each, educating them about their conditions and beneficial lifestyle changes and helping them set and monitor their health status and treatment goals. The care managers' objective is to promote self-management of patients' conditions, thereby reducing avoidable morbidity and mortality as well as reliance on acute services.

Birmingham OwnHealth® is tracking outcomes, including clinical measures (e.g., blood pressure, HbA1c, body mass index, depression scores), unscheduled admissions and patient satisfaction. To measure progress toward self-care and health promotion, case managers assess the stage of change that participants have reached (i.e., pre-contemplation, contemplation, preparation, action, maintenance). After three months over 52% of patients had improved their stage of change for diet and 22% had increased their exercise levels. In just under six months Birmingham OwnHealth® has demonstrated a decrease in unscheduled care utilization (acute care admissions and accident and emergency [A&E] department and GP visits), although it should be noted that this is based on a very early-stage evaluation. Ninety percent of participants reported satisfaction with the quality of the service (Birmingham OwnHealth 2006).

Assertive case management

To better manage and prevent hospital admission for chronic diseases, clinical leaders at BEN PCT adapted Kaiser Permanente's three-level model for population management (i.e., level 1: the 70%-80% of the chronic care population that requires usual care with support; level 2: high-risk patients requiring assisted care or care management; level 3: highly complex patients requiring intensive care or case management). Launched in 2004 this model of care provides a systematic approach for prioritizing and stratifying patients according to risk and for applying a step-up and step-down approach to match skills and resources to patient need. Specifically, the model uses entry and exit criteria for three risk segments and progressive involvement and intensity of care providers with patients able to move up and down to accommodate changing clinical needs (i.e., high: district nursing teams; higher: assertive case managers; highest: advanced nurse practitioners). GPs use a validated and computerized system to routinely identify and refer patients who are appropriate for assertive case management, and specialist nurses follow up with a validated and computerized risk prediction system.

The model emphasizes cascading clinical leadership and collaboration with supervision and shared care starting from GPs. It also employs a hospital alert system to track the case-managed patients' use of hospital services. In addition, in order to build capability for this model and encourage career progression BEN PCT has integrated specialist training for case management for chronic conditions into its competency and training framework.

Among a pilot population this model has led to a 50% reduction in unplanned hospital admissions, a 55% reduction in A&E visits, a reduction in polypharmacy and an increase in patient satisfaction and compliance. Over the last year the PCT's emergency admissions to hospital were slightly reduced against a national 8% increase, and attendance at A&E stayed the same against national growth.

The strategy: Align improvement processes with system strategy, culture and operations

> *"We have to keep agile and nimble, with the right principles in mind."*
>
> – Sophia Christie, CEO of BEN PCT

Leaders in a complex change environment

The two CEOs, who have credibility, authority and very different – yet complementary – leadership styles, have played a central role in shaping the trusts' improvement journeys. The PCT CEO, Sophia Christie, recounted that as they began Working Together for Health she wanted wholesale change "yesterday," whereas the HEFT CEO, Mark Goldman, cautioned, "Steady, we *are* dealing with physicians." The Department of Health placed "incredible pressures on NHS executives; going too quickly would have destroyed the projects, yet going too slowly would have destroyed us."

The BEN PCT and HEFT CEOs worked hard with their boards to ensure they would see how their plans could be "pro-patient care," despite the financial disincentives and national policies that created obstacles. For example, the trusts are collaborating to avoid in-patient admissions by providing more comprehensive community-based services, yet the acute care trust stands to lose revenue by doing so (see Appendix A, section 3.1, for more about the payment system). In the PCT leaders decided that "even if changes we made put us financially at risk, we would do so to make sure we were providing the right services" (PCT CEO). The BEN PCT and HEFT "partnership plans were a bit contrary to the Department of Health (DOH) rules. ... When we developed the approach it was against national policy. National policy moved towards us, not the other way around!" (HEFT CEO).

There is an increasing policy emphasis in the United Kingdom (UK) on, as the BEN PCT CEO put it in a slide presentation on November 2, 2006, "providing services where they give best value." However, financial mechanisms are not aligned with this goal. The HEFT CEO stressed the difficulties encountered in his trust's "attempts to hold open the doors of the hospital to let patients go to primary care" in the face of adverse financial consequences for the hospital. When HEFT became a foundation trust in May 2005 their collaborative effort "almost came off the wheels" due to the scrutiny of Monitor (the regulatory agency for foundation trusts) and the pressure of Monitor's expectations for the trust's financial growth (see Appendix A, section 3.3, for more about Monitor).

Complicating their management responsibilities even further, significant restructuring occurred around this time in both trusts. The amalgamation of Eastern Birmingham PCT and Northern PCT raised cultural issues, the lack of a shared acute care strategy and resistance from Northern PCT to dealing with patients from the eastern wards. HEFT took over responsibility for (and has since merged with) Good Hope Hospital Trust, which had considerable financial problems. Both CEOs observed that they sacrificed progress in the trusts for which they were originally responsible as they worked to straighten out issues arising from the later additions. However, their work has proven to be part of a politically astute strategic vision for integrating care and improving patient access, outcomes and choice.

Approach to change

> *"Adapt improvement tools to use them in a situation that is already prepared."*
>
> – Sophia Christie, CEO of BEN PCT

Investment in organizational development

The Eastern Birmingham PCT had a history of investing significant time and energy in organizational development based on a "large system approach" using "whole system events" (Beedon and Christie 2006). With the assistance of an organizational development consultant the PCT CEO works in a very hands-on fashion to ensure as many staff members as possible are engaged in a meaningful way in shaping the organization. This approach has been continued successfully during the strategic integration of BEN PCT, with the involvement of large numbers of staff and stakeholders in the design process for the new organization's strategic goals and values. Participants were encouraged to come up with "great, big, hairy, audacious goals" (Collins and Poras 1994) and the CEO promised, "Whatever you come up with, we will live with and do."

This participatory process resulted in the following core purpose and goals, which are their touchstones for planning decisions, measurement and improvement efforts:

Purpose

- Working in partnership to tackle inequalities and improve the health and well-being of local people.

Goals

- To be so responsive to the population we serve that no one waits for the healthcare they need.
- That the health and well-being of the population will have improved so much that people will enjoy 10 more years of quality life.
- Our communities will be the most involved, informed and empowered in the country.
- That people regard us as the first choice organization to work with and for.

HEFT has likewise launched Moving Forward Together, a "massive, fully integrated organizational development program" (HEFT CEO). This program will develop the vision, values and behaviours of the newly merged organization as well as the skills and competencies required of staff through "skills based programs, local facilitated problem solving initiatives, and leadership development" (HEFT 2006a, 2006b).

The members of both executive teams stressed the importance of paying attention to organizational culture and preparing the organizations for change so that improvement tools and interventions can be used effectively. In the PCT CEO's words, "Adapt improvement tools to use them in a situation that is already prepared." HEFT is developing its own "Lean academy" on site and is training staff in Lean improvement methods and process mapping; however, "cascading it through will be a slow process over several years as we train people" (senior clinical leader). BEN PCT is a pilot site for the Institute's shifting care initiative; therefore, staff members involved in those projects use improvement methods adapted by the Institute.

Members of both organizations cautioned, "It is more than just a formula that you can apply from the Institute; you need the formula, but you need to adapt it and work with it" (senior leader). They observed that the former Modernisation Agency "was not successful because it focused its efforts on the improvement processes within projects led by single champions, but outside of the [organizational] culture, and it could not move the projects into the rest of the industry" (see Appendix A, section 7.1, for more about the Modernisation Agency). "The reason that we have been able to do what we have is because we have the processes – the project-level processes and improvement skills – aligned with the system, strategy and leadership" (PCT CEO).

Managing the tensions between short-term projects and long-term vision

The trusts had six or seven years of experience with earlier change efforts, which helped them to understand how to manage the tension between project-specific goals and the long-term vision. This enabled them to make the joint projects work more quickly in a short time frame. Both CEOs commented on the need for early gains through quick interventions: "We emphasize getting on with it instead of talking about it for ages. … This approach is transactional as compared to transformational. If you start with small projects and keep expanding, eventually there will be no turning back. The best way to create sustained change is to do it on this evolutionary, project-by-project, phase-by-phase approach" (HEFT CEO).

As an example of the phase-by-phase approach, the trusts started their Working Together for Health collaboration with small-scale projects in diabetes care management. A review showed that their Asian population had severe diabetes complications, yet no coordinated management program was in place for them in primary care. The PCT's director of health improvement worked on a management plan to create a community diabetes service, a link between primary care GPs and specialists. The trusts conducted a chart review to gather needed data (there had been no data collection in the past, so they were missing information on 1,000 diabetic patients). The diabetes care management program is flexible, with an aim of building capacity within primary care to handle the care provision for the target community. The service includes a consultant nurse, two specialist nurses, educators who speak more than one language and a physician consultant (a joint appointment between BEN PCT and HEFT).

A senior clinical leader noted that one of the challenges they face is "how to grow the right, skilled population of care providers; that is, taking those who are used to giving care to individual patients and turning them into consultants who advise." The interventions require extensive education, yet physicians (who often work in large, busy practices of one or two GPs) are far too busy to attend outside sessions. Trust staff therefore take these improvement programs to the practices.

Funding improvement work "is not a simple thing" (PCT CEO). The PCT has opportunities to bid for external funding, but not a lot is available; therefore, "We've dragged in money from here and there in different ways. … We have been in a good position to bid opportunistically on some opportunities because of good results and experience." Their Working Together for Health initiative is staffed by a program director, who supports its projects, attends meetings, helps with data collection when necessary and has made use of the strategic partnership with the organization development (OD) consultancy to continue developing expertise in improvement tools and cultural change.

Links with "mentor" organizations and individuals

BEN PCT and HEFT have actively sought out other organizations, both within and outside healthcare, from which they could learn. For example, BEN PCT representatives visited the Body Shop chain to learn about franchising models and then had sessions with the trust's GPs aimed at helping them to look at their practices as franchises. The knowledge – "the idea that you didn't get money for nothing, that there are standards and expectations" – made a big difference with GPs. The trust began to tie incentives to clinical practice change, for example, to encourage inclusion of smoking cessation and diet counselling as well as preventive care. This funding strategy has been broadened by the new NHS Quality and Outcomes Framework (QOF), which includes quality standards and indicators monitoring in the general and medical services' contracts for primary care (BEN PCT 2006: 35) (see Appendix A, section 3.3, for more about the QOF).

Kaiser Permanente

Perhaps the most significant external influence on Working Together for Health has been Kaiser Permanente. This large, integrated health organization and health plan from the United States (US) has played a major role as a resource that provides ongoing support and contact. "We cannot overemphasize the importance of Kaiser, the influence of seeing their plans and work and the encouragement that we could get there too, that it was possible. It was a mentorship relationship. We could not have done it without them" (senior clinical leader).

The trusts' relationship with Kaiser Permanente began in 2003, when the Department of Health offered several NHS trusts the opportunity to participate in an initiative facilitated by Professor Chris Ham of the University of Birmingham, a study tour site visit to Kaiser Permanente with the intent of working together to adapt lessons learned (Ham 2006). The PCT CEO decided to invite a multidisciplinary clinical team chosen from across the trusts to attend the first site visit. Upon the team's return, the trusts began implementing small-scale projects with GPs who were interested in doing things differently with their particular groups of patients (an "artisan approach"), with project support from the newly appointed project manager. The trusts' collaborative program, Working Together for Health, was born.

Some medical staff, as well as some community members who did not want "American healthcare," reacted negatively to the thought of adopting Kaiser Permanente's approaches, such as the view that less costly, more effective care can be delivered closer to home. Adoption of Kaiser Permanente's approaches was controversial enough that at the beginning team members were advised not to use "the K word." As a result, when they started work on their first four clinical areas (diabetes, COPD, orthopaedics and heart failure) using the Kaiser approach, members "rebadged" it to make it their own.

Later, in 2004, the two CEOs and the chair of the PEC spent four days visiting Kaiser Permanente. Both CEOs highly valued this exposure and planning time, which resulted in the agreement that they needed to make a visible commitment personally to the change initiative that their organizations had undertaken together. "We decided to stay with it until it would be unstoppable." In January 2005 they involved 26 clinicians in a week-long workshop with their Kaiser partners. Since then there have been multiple visits to Kaiser; ongoing linkages include annual meetings with Kaiser staff as well as telephone contact. Senior leaders in the PCT and HEFT described the relationship with Kaiser as "incredibly invigorating," adding, "there is a great deal of largesse about how they have related to us."

Physician leadership

Physicians hold major leadership roles in the trusts. For example, HEFT has implemented "a very medical model." The HEFT CEO, who is a surgeon by training, remarked, "We learned this from Kaiser: if you don't have the physicians on board with you, you can't succeed." One of the senior managers observed, "We have a pretty powerful clinical management system. Most of the money is in the hands of doctors."

In HEFT the three medical directors have operational line responsibility, and financial responsibility has been decentralized to these directorates. Physicians lead many of the clinical programs as well as improvement initiatives. The attitude of the nurses and allied health staff to this is quite interesting; according to several nurses in key positions, nurses are content to work alongside the physicians and behind the scenes, while letting the physicians take the lead. On the other hand, expanded roles for nurses and allied health professionals appear to be well accepted by medical staff. In addition, BEN PCT adapted the national PEC model to create clinical directors who have lead responsibility for core strategies.

Performance management: Competing demands and financial pressures

The pace and frequency of restructuring, intense scrutiny from regulatory agencies as well as the financial crisis in the NHS create a difficult working context for the trusts. Both BEN PCT and HEFT invest considerable amounts of time and resources in performance measurement and reporting. PCTs are subject to annual assessments by the Healthcare Commission against a set of core standards and targets (see Appendix A, section 4.2). BEN PCT has adapted these measures to fit their balanced scorecard (see Appendix B); each measure is discussed in detail in its performance report updates.

Although HEFT's independent status grants it more operational freedom, this freedom comes with an immense financial pressure: "As a foundation trust, you can fall over completely and no one will save you. … That has hardened our business approach; it's much more commercial" (senior leader). HEFT operates as a large healthcare enterprise, intent on expanding its market share to include more patients in the region, such as through its merger with Good Hope NHS Trust. It is also developing a range of commercial interests, such as the Heartlands Medipark, which will house a medical innovation development and research unit (MIDRU) as well as clinical and laboratory facilities.

Fiscal discipline is a hallmark of HEFT; as one senior leader commented, "We're not a toxic organization but there is accountability." This foundation trust has devised a strategy map of its high-level goals and measures (see Figure 1), which are compiled in a scorecard. All measures are tracked monthly (in some cases weekly) and published in the trust's "red book," which is its performance monitoring information pack filled with detailed tables of indicators and measures by directorate. HEFT develops RADAR plans for its indicators (HEFT 2006a). (RADAR, an action planning tool from the European Foundation for Quality Management [EFQM)], stands for "determine the *results* required; plan and develop *approaches*; *deploy* approaches; *assess* and *review*.")

Figure 1. HEFT strategy map

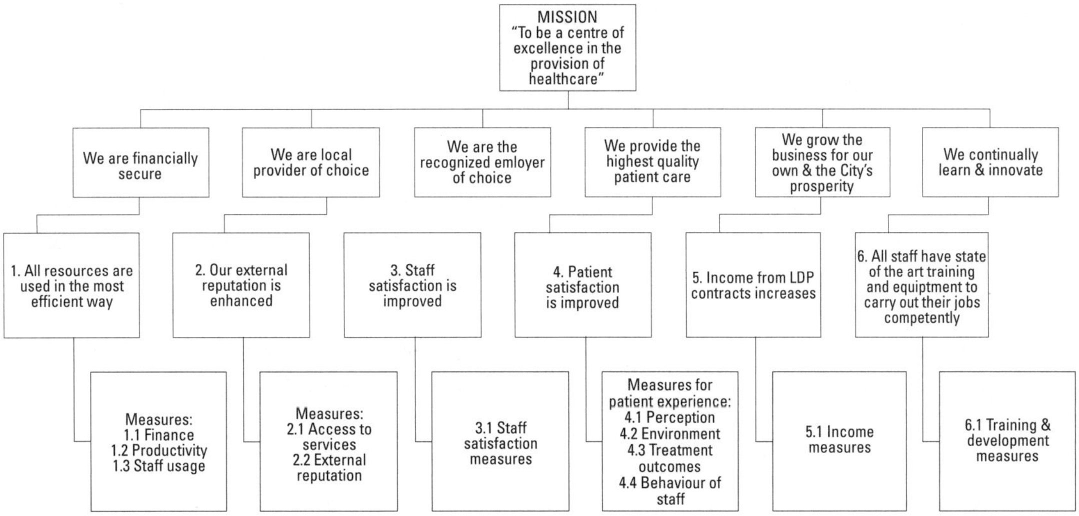

MISSION "To be a centre of excellence in the provision of healthcare"

We are financially secure
We are local provider of choice
We are the recognized emloyer of choice
We provide the highest quality patient care
We grow the business for our own & the City's prosperity
We continually learn & innovate

1. All resources are used in the most efficient way
2. Our external reputation is enhanced
3. Staff satisfaction is improved
4. Patient satisfaction is improved
5. Income from LDP contracts increases
6. All staff have state of the art training and equiptment to carry out their jobs competently

Measures: 1.1 Finance 1.2 Productivity 1.3 Staff usage
Measures: 2.1 Access to services 2.2 External reputation
3.1 Staff satisfaction measures
Measures for patient experience: 4.1 Perception 4.2 Environment 4.3 Treatment outcomes 4.4 Behaviour of staff
5.1 Income measures
6.1 Training & development measures

Source: HEFT (2006a).

Because of their contractual relationship as service commissioner and service provider, BEN PCT and HEFT also work together on performance measurement and management. The trusts, with the addition of representatives from neighbouring Solihull PCT, hold Tripartite Performance Management meetings every three weeks to review scorecard targets and action plans, assess market changes and impacts of national policies and agree on ways of implementing primary care pathways. The directors that staff the committee report directly to the CEOs. These meetings are often very challenging; as the CEO of the BEN PCT commented, “It's the edgy bit where the arguments happen.” Potentially conflicting interests arising from national policies create significant tensions; for example, an increase in hospital admissions might be positive as a revenue generator for the acute trust but is red-flagged as a cost increase for the PCT.

BEN PCT's multiple roles also contribute to the tension. As a commissioner, BEN PCT is responsible for monitoring how costs and income are managed; as a partner, for maintaining constructive relationships with providers; and, as a provider of some services in the area, for avoiding perceptions of conflict that could arise from being both fund holder and service provider. However, because the trusts have invested so much in developing their partnerships they are able to have productive discussions about the strategic issues that cut across the region, while avoiding breaching NHS rules about collusion.

Conclusion

BEN PCT and HEFT have worked hard to develop partnerships necessary for improving care in the complex UK healthcare environment (see Figure 2). Several key factors have shaped the growth of BEN PCT and HEFT as systems capable of improvement: for example, strong, capable leaders with clear vision and determination to stay the course; ongoing investment in organizational development and improvement skills that prepared the way for change; and a serendipitous learning opportunity that turned into a continuing mentoring relationship with Kaiser Permanente. The trusts have also shifted away from traditional care delivery within specialist silos in dominantly acute care settings to redesign and integrate care based on the needs of their entire population. The PCT is also working to extend its network of partnerships to include social services, a move that adds to its complex responsibilities but also offers the opportunity to integrate further services to meet population needs (see Appendix A, section 2.4, for more about health and social care integration).

To accomplish these changes the trust leaders encourage local innovation and collaboration with external resources, including industrial partners such as Pfizer Health Solutions. They have also built a robust business case for their approach to improvement, redesigning services in an effort both to meet population needs and to reduce costs in the face of the immense financial pressure felt throughout the NHS.

The trusts continue to face significant challenges in the ever-changing UK healthcare environment. The focus on financial discipline in the NHS, for example, has continued to escalate, resulting in sizeable budget challenges for the trusts and the PCT facing the need to reduce costs by £26 million in one year (a challenge it has successfully met).

The productive partnership between BEN PCT and HEFT has been shaped by the strong working relationship between their current leaders, individuals who have undertaken to stay in their roles until the improvement momentum is "unstoppable." Although one CEO commented, "We are almost there," it remains to be seen whether the cultural transformations will be sustained as leadership positions change in the future.

Figure 2. BEN PCT and HEFT: Partnership and links to national structure

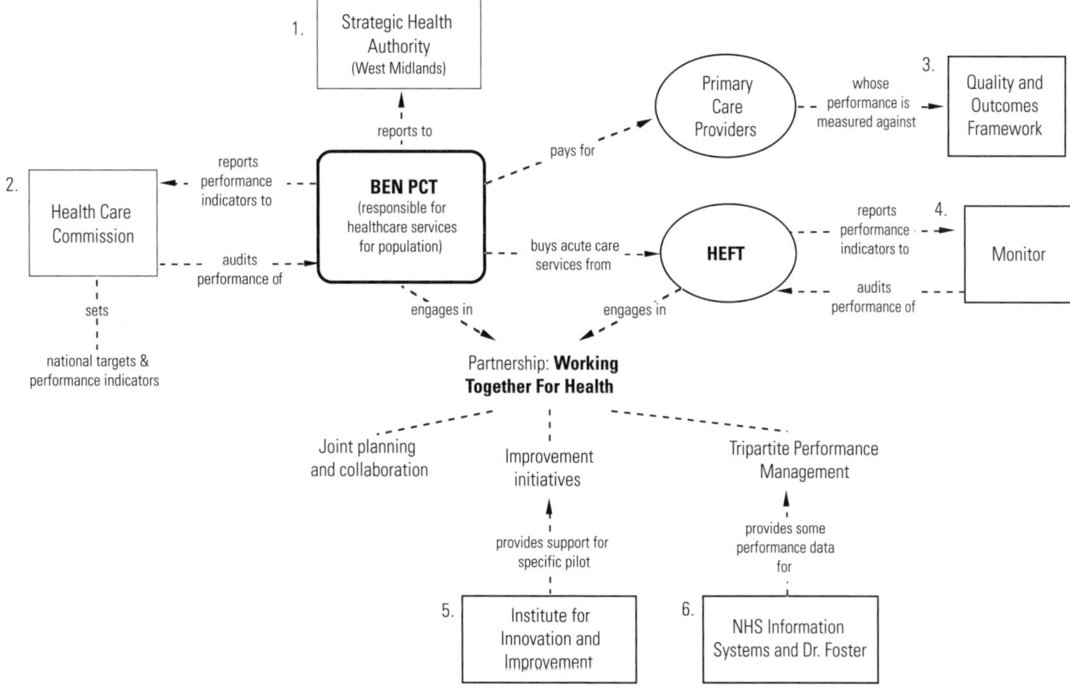

Source: HEFT (2006a).

Notes to Figure 2

For more background information about the institutions in the numbered boxes in Figure 1, see the following sections in Appendix A:

1. **Strategic Health Authority:** Section 1.0: Background; Section 5.0: Regional Accountability
2. **Healthcare Commission:** Section 4.2: Performance Reporting and External Assessment

3. **Quality and Outcomes Framework:** Section 3.3: Financial Incentives
4. **Monitor:** Section 3.3: Financial Incentives
5. **Institute for Innovation and Improvement:** Section 7.1: Modernisation Agency; Section 7.3: Institute for Innovation and Improvement
6. **NHS Information Systems and Dr. Foster:** Section 4.2: Performance Reporting and External Assessment; Section 6.0: Information Technology

Appendix A. National Health Service: Health system context

1.0. Background

Introduced in 1948 in the aftermath of the Second World War, the NHS is the UK's healthcare system and Europe's largest employer (the NHS employs 1.3 million people across England, Wales, Scotland and Northern Ireland). Financed largely from general taxation, the NHS was originally founded on the principles that healthcare is free at the point of delivery, available to all who need it and based on clinical need and not ability to pay. The Department of Health has political responsibility for the NHS, managing it at the top through policies and programs and under the leadership of the secretary of state for health. The NHS was initially structured with three arms: hospital services by regional hospital boards, primary care with GPs (dentists, opticians and pharmacists) as independent contractors and community care services managed by local authorities (for a history of the NHS, visit http://www.nhs.uk/england/aboutTheNHS/history/default.cmsx).

Today, the structure of care delivery in the NHS emphasizes local decision-making, as shown in Figure 3. PCTs – local groups of planners and providers of primary care – hold over 80% of the NHS budget. These trusts are responsible for assessing local needs, planning and commissioning both primary and secondary care services to meet these needs and providing some primary care. Hospitals, ambulances, specialist providers and providers of mental health and other health and social care are also organized into trusts that contract with PCTs. The over 150 PCTs report directly to 10 strategic health authorities (SHAs). These authorities are the key link between the NHS and the Department of Health, and are responsible for managing and monitoring the performance of local services and ensuring that these local services are aligned with national priorities.

Since its inception the NHS has evolved into a £96 billion-budget organization and has undergone several periods of reform. Following a steady pace of change, the past 15 years have brought an unprecedented scale of transformation to the structure, financing and way in which care is delivered in the NHS. For the most part "a crisis of confidence in the NHS" – and specifically in quality of care – is seen as the driver of such large-scale reform (SteelFisher 2005). The crisis in quality was illustrated by long wait times, higher than average mortality rates for key conditions and notable tragedies, such the death of 29 children at the Bristol Royal Infirmary. Observers have attributed this crisis to several factors, in particular, to an underinvestment in capacity (e.g., healthcare providers, equipment), a lack of standards and incentives for higher quality care, outdated boundaries between sectors and providers, overcentralization and disempowered patients (Enthoven 2000).

Over the past few decades the NHS's most significant transformation efforts were launched by white papers and other key consultation documents that outlined a series of interdependent reforms and priorities. Appendix A(a) describes a selection of these documents.

Figure 3. High-level structure of the NHS

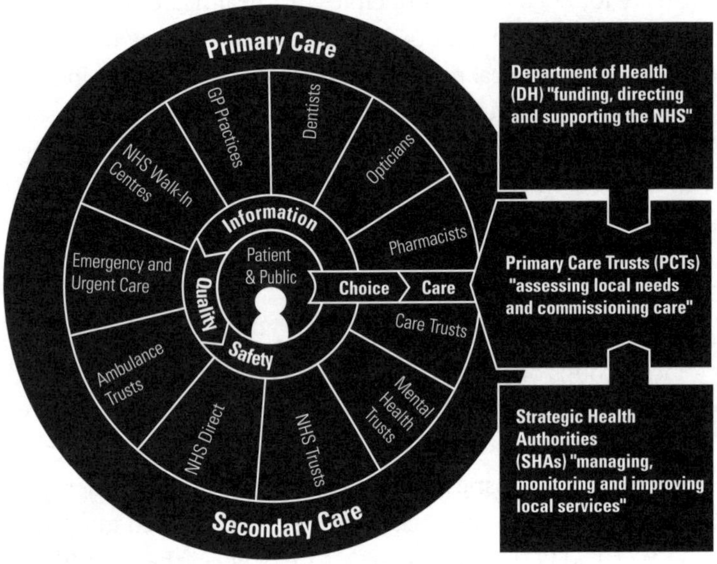

Source: NHS Choices (www.nhs.uk) copyright 2007. Used by permission.

Overall the NHS's policy context has been shaped by several key reforms. The extent to which these reforms have been levers for improving quality varies. A discussion of these reforms follows.

2.0. Supply-side reforms

2.1. Investments in capacity and a plurality of providers

Growth in funding and capacity has played a key role in the supply-side reforms of the NHS in the past two decades. To bring investment to a level equivalent with other European systems, NHS funding increased by "one half in cash terms and by one third in real terms" over five years. This increase funded investments in new NHS facilities (e.g., 100 new hospital schemes; 2,100 additional general and acute beds; 500 new primary care centres) and staff (e.g., 2,000 more GPs; 20,000 extra nurses; 1,000 more medical school places) (Department of Health 2000).

Such capacity growth was viewed as necessary but insufficient to relieve pressures on hospital beds, staff and wards, and to achieve and sustain the national targets for reducing wait times. Therefore, parallel strategies were put in place to develop a permanent increase in the volume of services delivered to patients. Typically commissioned from independent sector companies, these strategies included independent treatment centres that provide scheduled day and short-stay surgery and diagnostic procedures, overseas teams that carry out high-volume and non-complex surgery in high-pressure specialties such as orthopaedics and ophthalmology and an overseas treatment option for patients who choose to undergo orthopaedic, ophthalmological and cardiac procedures in France, Germany and Belgium (Department of Health nd a). By harnessing these strategies NHS leaders aimed to develop an independent sector that could carry out up to 15% of procedures each year for NHS patients, paid for by the NHS. To support the growth in "independent sector" options and a plurality of providers, NHS leaders also increased the number of physicians entitled to discretionary private sector payments. These independent sector options are subject to audit to ensure they provide extra capacity for care overall (rather than limiting capacity in the NHS), offer value for money and meet high clinical standards. Although there are ongoing debates about the disintegration of the NHS as a result of the growing independent sector (McGauran 2004) the NHS's success in streamlining access to care and reducing wait times is widely attributed to this strategy.

2.2. Service and role redesign

In addition to growth in actual capacity, several national reforms have focused on service and role redesign in the NHS as a means to improve productivity and, ultimately, to improve quality. One of the most profound changes is the increase in flexibility and removal of boundaries across traditional roles in primary care, especially between physicians and nurses and allied healthcare providers. Several professions have extended their scopes of practice and accompanying specialist skills training. For example, since 2005 physiotherapists, radiographers, podiatrists, optometrists and pharmacists have had prescribing authority, and some of these professionals are able to perform minor procedures previously limited to specialist physicians (Department of Health nd b).

2.3. Practice-based commissioning

Several NHS reforms have focused on developing a primary care–led system and increasingly devolving influence and control of budgets and planning to front-line healthcare providers. These reforms have included GP fundholding in the early 1990s, which was eventually abolished; commissioning by PCTs, which has remained the dominant model for the past decade; and the recently introduced policy of practice-based commissioning (PBC). PBC is currently positioned as "the engine for change" in the NHS and gives GP practices their own "notional" budgets to purchase care for their patients, including emergency care, out-patient and in-patient treatment and drugs (King's Fund 2006). This policy aims to raise GPs' awareness of the financial implications of their prescriptions and referrals and motivate them actively to redesign innovative, cost-effective and responsive services for patients.

There are examples of trusts that, by embracing PBC, have emerged as "care entrepreneurs" in the redesign of care. Such redesign includes partnering with social care and other providers to help manage chronic diseases and avoid hospital admissions by leveraging healthcare team members who have specialist training for procedures that would normally occur in hospital and by purchasing diagnostic technology for use in the community. Under this scheme, GP practices are accountable to PCTs, which directly administer funds and remain legally responsible for them as well as provide GP practices with data on their patients' utilization of services (e.g., diagnostic tests, prescribing, hospital and emergency care) and the cost of this care. Incentives are available for practices that take up commissioning, including the ability to reinvest surplus funds.

PBC has several perceived benefits, including improved coordination of primary, intermediate and community support services; clinical engagement in redesign of care and services; better collaboration between practices; more efficient and appropriate prescribing, referral and utilization of services; and care in more convenient settings for patients (Greener and Mannion 2006). However, as the Department of Health hopes to further spread and implement this policy across GP practices in the NHS there is considerable debate about whether PBC will overcome issues associated with the earlier fundholding model and whether it will be a lever to achieve change and improvement. Some observers raise concerns about the management and transactions costs. Others raise questions about whether there is sufficient evidence to support some of the key assumptions underpinning the model, including the belief that patients should choose providers (rather than commissioners) and that purchasers should commission based on population and geography (rather than individuals) (Higgins 2007).

2.4. Integration of health- and social care

With the launch of the 10-year NHS Plan in 2000, leaders articulated a vision for better-integrated health and social care (Department of Health 2000). Social care (i.e., social services) in the UK is managed by local authorities. Since the original vision was articulated several models for joining health and social care have evolved.

In 2002 the NHS piloted a new type of organization – care trusts. These bodies integrate health- and social care under a single organizational structure with multidisciplinary teams providing streamlined cross-disciplinary assessments. Conceived as a "new level" of PCT, these trusts aim to commission and deliver care to patients who require complex health- and social care in several parts of the continuum (e.g., acute, intermediate, home) and who would normally need to navigate two different systems. Patients who stand to benefit most from care trusts include those requiring mental health care, the elderly and the disabled. There are currently 10 care trusts in the NHS, fewer than initially forecasted. Observers remain divided about their value. Some see them as a structural innovation that improves access and delivers more flexible and holistic care. Others see them as an overemphasis on structural change when other partnership models would suffice (Glasby and Peck 2005).

Several other reforms are under way to help facilitate more joint commissioning of health- and social care without extensive structural integration. These include a procurement model and best-practice guidance to underpin a joint commissioning framework; streamlined budgets and planning cycles based on a shared, outcome-based performance framework; aligned performance assessment and inspection regimes; and more joint health- and social care appointments. At local levels some PCTs are now partnering with local authorities to shape the way health- and social care are delivered for patients with chronic conditions. Most recently, in an attempt to enhance patient choice in new models of health- and social care the government announced a pilot of "individual budgets." This is a scheme that would enable people needing social care to design that support and give them the power to decide the nature of the services they need (Department of Health 2006a).

3.0. Demand-side reforms

3.1. Payment by results

Historically, trusts were paid lump sums based on block contracts and locally agreed prices. Introduced in 2004 as a pilot in several trusts and expanded across the NHS for non-elective and elective care in 2006, payment by results is an activity-based payment system, adjusted for case-mix that reimburses providers with a fixed national price or tariff for each case treated. Designed to be open and transparent, and underpinned by the principle that money follows patients, the system's goal is to increase productivity, reward efficiency and support patient choice (Department of Health nd c).

Reports have shown that early implementation of the system exposed several weaknesses, including issues with data quality and accuracy of coding; inadequate involvement of clinicians in defining the tariffs, especially for complex cases and highly specialized care; and financial instability in some trusts. In addition, clinicians have expressed concern that by encouraging productivity within local organizations this system will fragment care and discourage collaboration across sectors for issues such as chronic disease prevention and management, and may lead to gaming or "upcoding" (King's Fund 2005; Dixon 2004). It is still too early to evaluate the impact of further expansion of this payment scheme.

3.2. Patient choice

In conjunction with the tariff system, patient choice has been a key part of the NHS's recent policy reforms. As of January 2006 all eligible patients across England have the right to choose where and when they get hospital treatment. Through the Choose and Book initiative patients are offered the choice of at least four hospitals or clinics for further non-emergency treatment. One of these options is a private sector provider. People are able to book the time and date of their out-patient appointments at their GPs' offices through an online system that shows where and when appointments are available. In order to inform their choices, patients are provided with information on each of the options, such as details about transportation, parking and disabled access; information about the performance of the organization on key national targets; and patient satisfaction.

Additional strategies are also under way to help support patient choice in the NHS. These include an online system called HealthSpace that allows patients to record their lifestyle and healthcare preferences on electronic medical records and an electronic prescribing service that enables patients to pick up repeat prescriptions from pharmacies of their choice (Department of Health nd d).

By enhancing patient choice in the context of money following patients, the NHS hopes to reduce variations in quality, promote faster and better access across the NHS and ensure that NHS services continue to reflect patients' needs and priorities. The extent to which choice is actually a lever for improving quality remains uncertain. There is some debate that these reforms were too narrow in their application to elective services, given their irrelevance to other significant areas of healthcare, including care for chronic conditions or emergency treatment (Appleby 2004).

3.3. Financial incentives

The Quality and Outcomes Framework (QOF) (see http://www.nhsemployers.org/primary/primary-890.cfm) is a new system of financial incentives for GP practices designed to improve GP recruitment and retention. Historically, GP practices have been paid according to the number of patients on their registers, and they were required to be available outside normal working hours. Introduced in 2004 as part of the General Medical Services (GMS) contract, the framework allows GPs to opt out of providing services after hours, rewards practices for providing high-quality care and helps to promote further investment in improvements in the delivery of care.

The QOF measures quality of practice against evidence-based national standards in four areas:

1) clinical standards linked to the care of patients with chronic conditions; 2) organizational standards relating to records and information, communicating with patients, education and training, medication management and clinical and practice management; 3) additional services covering cervical screening, child health surveillance, maternity services and contraceptive services; and 4) patient experience based on patient surveys and length of consultations.

Points and payments are awarded according to levels of achievement. QOF data are collected through patients' electronic records and fed into a national quality management database (see http://www.ic.nhs.uk/services/qof). Although participation in the QOF is voluntary, a large majority of general practices participate in the scheme. Clinicians and observers consider the framework to be a strong lever for improving quality, given its focus on rewarding general practice teamwork, allowing flexibility to choose specific targets and providing upfront funding to help raise quality standards.

In addition to GP incentives the government developed a new type of incentive for NHS trusts in 2004. Trusts that demonstrate strong performance – in particular financial performance – are invited to apply for designation as foundation trusts. These trusts are independent public benefit corporations and are free from central government control and regional performance management. Independently authorized and regulated by an organization called Monitor, foundation trusts are free to innovate for the benefit of their local communities and patients, to independently decide and make capital investments, to retain any surpluses they generate and to borrow in order to support investments (on Monitor, see http://www.monitor-nhsft.gov.uk/about.php). There are presently over 70 foundation trusts in the NHS. Current policy envisions that all hospitals will evolve to become foundation trusts.

4.0. National guidance, standards and targets

4.1. Priorities and targets

Several of the reforms outlined in this section were explicitly designed to help meet national priorities and targets, especially for wait times. In the late 1990s the government set several targets for reducing wait times: six months on in-patient lists, 13 weeks on out-patient lists, 48 hours for an appointment with a GP and four hours before being treated, admitted or discharged from A&E departments. Virtually all these targets were reached by 2005, with a new target set for 2008: 18 weeks from GP referral to visit.

While most observers agreed that wait times needed urgent attention and central investment, many now feel that some of the mechanisms for addressing these issues damaged morale and produced distortions in the system. For example, failure to meet targets led to executive replacement and, eventually, a significant turnover of leadership in the system (the link between targets and performance assessment is highlighted in the next section). In addition, the pressure to meet earlier wait time targets, which were virtually all focused on a patient's journey after diagnosis, produced longer "hidden waits," such as time to diagnosis. Clinicians and managers also worried that a disproportionate focus on wait times led to the treatment of less urgent and complex cases and a distortion of clinical priorities (King's Fund 2005b).

In its 2004 Improvement Plan the government articulated its vision of shifting away from national targets and central regulation to local target-setting and performance management and to a focus on a new set of priorities. In addition to a strong emphasis on wait times there were many other NHS standards, targets and guidance rules, elements that overwhelmed many leaders and providers. In 2004 the government announced it would reduce the number of national healthcare standards and targets from 600 or more to 24 (Frith 2004). Among the new set of national priorities was a focus on prevention and support for individuals with long-term (i.e., chronic) conditions such as diabetes, heart disease, asthma and depression.

The most recent priorities outlined in the 2007/2008 NHS operating framework (Department of Health 2007b) include the following:

- Achieving a maximum wait of 18 weeks from GP referral to start of treatment
- Reducing rates of methicillin-resistant Staphylococcus aureus (MRSA) and other healthcare-associated infections
- Reducing health inequalities and promoting health and well-being
- Achieving financial health

4.2. Performance reporting and external assessment

The national system for assessing and reporting the performance of NHS organizations evolved in conjunction with other reforms, particularly the focus on national priorities, targets and incentives. Introduced in 2001 the "star rating" system used over 50 different standards to award hospital trusts up to three stars for performance. Top-performing trusts (three stars) were awarded cash bonuses, additional freedom from central control and the option of becoming a foundation trust. Lower-performing trusts (zero stars) that did not improve over time were threatened with the replacement of their executives and other consequences.

This system of assessing and reporting performance was controversial; many observers felt it was too crude and unfairly punished hospitals and leaders. In 2004, when the Healthcare Commission for Audit and Inspection (formerly the Commission for Healthcare Improvement) – the independent inspection body for both the NHS and independent healthcare – undertook responsibility for performance assessment, it began the development of a new and more rigorous system. In March 2005 the Healthcare Commission launched the Annual Health Check. This performance assessment and reporting system measures NHS organizations against standards in seven categories: safety; clinical and cost effectiveness; governance; patient focus; accessible and responsive care; care environment and amenities; public health). In each of these areas the commission assesses and publicly reports whether organizations are meeting basic expected levels of performance and whether they are improving. In addition to developing the Annual Health Check, the commission regulates the registration of independent healthcare providers and conducts independent reviews of NHS complaints as well as value-for-money audits (Healthcare Commission 2005).

As noted earlier, Monitor independently authorizes and regulates NHS foundation trusts. Private industry in the UK is also involved in measuring and reporting the performance of healthcare in the NHS. Dr. Foster, launched in 2001, is a commercial provider of information about the performance of NHS healthcare providers, including physicians, hospitals and other care centres. While the Healthcare Commission's performance assessments are publicly available, their primary audiences are NHS providers and the government. The target audience for Dr. Foster's service guides is the general public. Dr. Foster is widely considered to be a successful endeavour.

4.3. NICE and National Service Frameworks

In 1998 *A First Class Service – Quality in the New NHS* outlined new initiatives and tools for setting, delivering and monitoring standards for a high-quality, cost-effective NHS (Department of Health 1998). The National Institute for Health and Clinical Excellence (NICE) and the National Service Frameworks (NSFs) are two successful initiatives that have emerged from the NHS's national quality agenda.

Launched in 1999 NICE uses evidence-based clinical guidelines and associated clinical audit methods to provide authoritative appraisal and national guidance on new and existing healthcare in the areas of public health, health technologies and clinical practice. In prioritizing treatments and innovations as well as in developing and disseminating guidelines, NICE considers clinical evidence, cost-effectiveness and NHS priorities (see http://www.nice.org.uk/).

Starting in 1998 a rolling program of NSFs began, focusing on priority conditions including cancer, CHD, diabetes, mental health and services for older people. NSFs provide evidence-based service models and standards that outline what care patients can expect to receive from the NHS for high-priority conditions. NSF models and standards also offer implementation strategies and support and performance measures to assess progress (Department of Health nd e). NICE and the NSFs are considered critical foundations for quality improvement and remain highly regarded by clinicians and leaders across the NHS and around the world. In large part their success is attributed to the transparency of and strong clinical and expert (including patient) engagement in their development.

5.0. Regional accountability

NHS organizations (except for foundation trusts) have regional accountability to SHAs, which play a liaison role between the organizations and the Department of Health. In 2006 the government announced a new architecture for the SHAs, reducing their number from 28 to 10. This restructuring was aimed at streamlining management and administration, redirecting resources to patient care, cutting out unnecessary bureaucracy and giving SHAs a more strategic role.

SHAs have traditionally played a central role in performance management, monitoring how well PCTs and other trusts perform and taking action to improve failing services. Given the enhanced role of the Healthcare Commission in performance management, the SHAs' role is shifting to strategic planning and support in the development of local service delivery plans and improvement. The extent to which this shift is actually occurring is unclear. Observers have reported that some SHAs are playing a critical role in ensuring the strategic integration of national and local priorities in local planning and that they have used resources to develop infrastructure to support quality improvement initiatives such as "improvement academies." Such changes, however, are occurring in only a few SHAs.

6.0. Information technology

An effort to modernize information technology (IT) in the NHS is being led by one of the world's largest IT programs. NHS Connecting for Health is the single national IT provider for the NHS, delivering an ambitious national program to create an integrated information system to connect and facilitate secure communication among providers and to provide timely decision support. The program has several components, including infrastructure to connect GPs to hospitals, universal access to information-rich resources, electronic patient records with detailed summaries of episodes of care and a lifelong summary of important information. Additional enhancements include electronic booking and prescribing services and a HealthSpace for patients (NHS Connecting for Health nd). Connecting for Health is positioned as a critical lever for improving quality in the NHS. Some sceptics are concerned about the ambitious scope of the project and the need to ensure ongoing clinical involvement in its development (Humber 2004).

7.0. Support for quality improvement

7.1. Modernisation Agency

The Modernisation Agency was established in April 2001 in order to support the NHS reforms. The agency's origins date back to 1999, when four initiatives that were struck to improve quality and efficiency in areas of national strategic priority came together: the National Patient Access Team, the National Primary Care Development Team, Action On and the Clinical Governance Support Team.

The Modernisation Agency's goals were to help enhance patient experiences and outcomes, improve access, increase local support, raise standards of care and capture and share knowledge expansively. Some of the agency's most widely recognized work is its leadership and coordination of large, multi-organization collaboratives (especially in the areas of access and wait times, and the development of some of its products, including the Leadership Guides and the *10 High-Impact Changes* document). Over a period of four years the agency grew rapidly in size, budget and scope, including over 700 improvement staff, a budget of £200 million and an aim to support a large number of NHS priorities and standards.

Despite its successes and the critical role it played to support quality improvement and provide training to enhance capacity and capability across the NHS, the Modernisation Agency came under heavy criticism. Critics pointed to its excessive bureaucracy and size. They also lamented the lack of clinical engagement or relevance in some of its activities and products, which were seen as largely management oriented, and the lack of real integration and implementation of its activities and programs into service delivery planning at the local level. As part of a review of arm's length bodies, the Modernisation Agency was abolished in 2005 (Department of Health nd f).

7.2. Clinical Governance Support Team

The Clinical Governance Support Team (CGST) was formed in 1999 by the chief medical officer in the Department of Health following the introduction of clinical governance in the Department of Health's consultation document *A First Class Service*. As of 2001 the CGST was enveloped under the Modernisation Agency. It remained in existence as its own entity following the agency's abolition in 2005.

Clinical governance is defined as a "framework through which NHS organizations are accountable for continuously improving the quality of their healthcare services and safeguarding high standards of care by creating an environment in which excellence in care can flourish" (Department of Health 1998). In an October 2006 presentation, the NHS clinical governance support team observed that, backed by a new statutory duty for quality for trusts, the clinical governance framework emphasized the need to instill quality at a local level and includes several components: patient, public and carer involvement; strategic capacity and capability; risk management; staff management and performance; education, training and continuous professional development; clinical effectiveness; information management; communication; leadership; and team and partnership working.

Over time the function of the CGST evolved, from one of supporting the development of clinical governance across the NHS through board and clinician training and other programs, to one of providing remedial support to low-performing trusts. Some observers remark that this shift in focus was underpinned by the lack of a clear mission, purpose and strategy for the CGST, especially in the context of other support resources and ongoing reforms in the NHS.

Although there are several reports of the successful implementation of aspects of clinical governance throughout the NHS, the extent to which clinical governance is still a dominant framework for improving quality across the system remains unclear. In 2006, the CGST underwent a review by the Office for Strategic Health Authorities. The CGST's future remains uncertain.

7.3. Institute for Innovation and Improvement

Following the Modernisation Agency's abolition in 2005, the Department of Health developed the Institute for Innovation and Improvement. Based at the University of Warwick, the Institute was created as a special health authority (at arm's length from government) to support the spread and uptake of new ways of working, new technology and world-class leadership in the NHS. Learning from the experience of the Modernisation Agency, the Institute operates as a compact, lean organization with 50 staff members and a budget of £80 million. It attempts to leverage the broader healthcare environment and focuses on improving outcomes on a few key national priorities that are agreed upon with the Department of Health: no delays (18-week wait), healthcare-associated infections, primary care/long-term conditions, and delivering quality and value (NHS Institute for Innovation and Improvement 2006a, 2006b).

The Institute is underpinned by specialist competencies in leadership, learning, service transformation, and technology and product innovation. Its primary work centres on identifying innovations and improvements from a number of sources and then co-designing and disseminating high-impact products to support implementation in the field. The Institute has developed a hypothesis-driven problem-solving process for all of its work in creating high-impact, innovative solutions. Figure 4 shows the four distinct phases in the Institute's work process.

Figure 4. The Institute for Innovation and Improvement's work process methodology

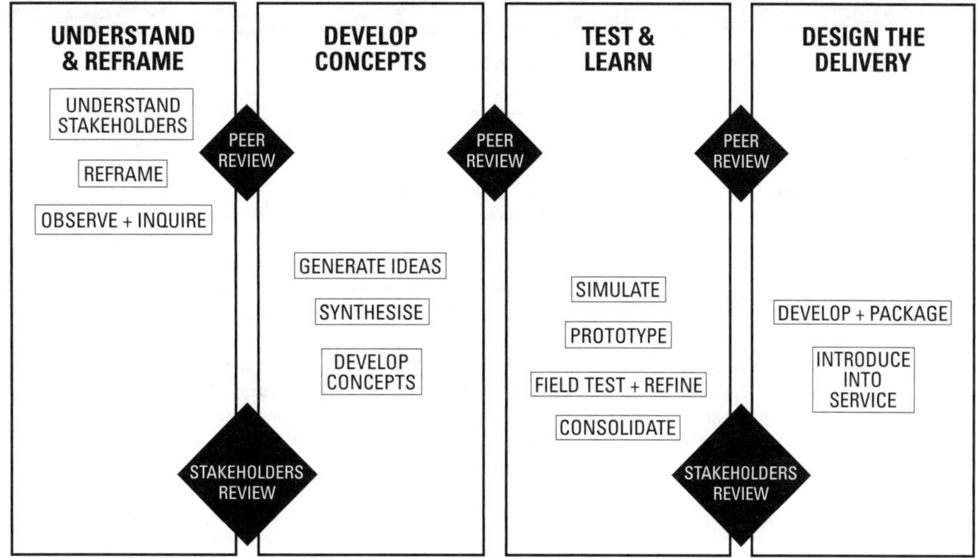

Source: NHS Institute for Innovation and Improvement (nd). Used by permission.

This design-focused role represents a shift in focus from the roles of the Modernisation Agency and the CGST by coordinating large collaborative initiatives and providing more direct support and capability for improvement. One of the initial reasons for this shift was the belief that there may now be adequate capability to facilitate uptake of such tools in the field as a result of the redistribution of former Modernisation Agency staff and funding across trusts and SHAs. Some observers, however, remain sceptical about the actual extent of improvement capability across the NHS.

Recognizing this, the Institute has begun to test strategies to better leverage and work with leaders and improvement staff across the NHS to support implementation. For example, the Institute recently engaged a former SHA CEO as a "field force" relationship manager to act as a bridge between the Institute and the field.

Appendix A(a). Key government policy papers

Year	Document	Brief Description
1989	*Working for Patients*	The Conservative government's white paper that outlines a plan to create an internal market and competition in the system through a split between purchasers and care providers and the introduction of fundholding for GPs to allow them to purchase care for their patients (NHS nd b).
1997	*The New NHS – Modern, Dependable* (Department of Health 1997)	A white paper by the new Labour government that sets out a plan to modernize the NHS. The new approach is "based on partnership and driven by performance." It preserves the principle of a primary care–led NHS but moves away from the internal market and outright competition. The paper outlines six principles underpinning this new approach, including taking quality as a driving force for decision-making at every level.
1998	*A First Class Service – Quality in the New NHS* (Department of Health 1998)	A consultation document that outlines new initiatives and tools for setting, delivering and monitoring standards for a high-quality, cost-effective NHS. These include NICE, an independent body responsible for providing authoritative appraisal and national guidance; NSFs, evidence-based service models and standards; clinical governance, a new framework backed by trusts' statutory duty for quality and through which organizations are accountable for continuously improving the quality of their healthcare services and safeguarding high standards of care; and the Commission for Healthcare Improvement (CHI), a statutory body established to provide independent scrutiny of local efforts to improve quality and report publicly on the performance of local organizations.
2000	*The NHS Plan – A Plan for Investment, A Plan for Reform* (Department of Health 2000) *Delivering the NHS Plan – Next Steps on Investment, Next Steps on Reform* (Department of Health 2002)	This ten-year plan, and its follow-up progress report, helped to bring into focus the government's strategies to modernize the NHS. The plan outlines substantial growth in the NHS budget (i.e., by one half in cash terms) and investments in capacity (e.g., facilities, staff, medical school places); an increase in the number of physicians entitled to discretionary payments in the private sector; and reforms aimed at devolving power from government to the local health service in a system of "earned autonomy." These reforms include PCTs holding the majority of the NHS budget and having the freedom to purchase care from most appropriate provider (public, private, voluntary); national targets, public performance ratings (especially for wait times) and incentives for high-performing local organizations, including administrative autonomy through designation as a foundation trust and consequences for poor-performing organizations, such as executive replacement; quality-based contracts for GPs and cash incentives to physicians for high-quality care; changes in job design, such as extended scopes of practice for nurses and therapists; a Modernisation Agency to provide technical support to spread best practices; a new hospital payment system called payment by results that uses a regional tariff or case-mix system; an integrated and modernized electronic health information system; and better integration between health and social care.

2004	*The NHS Improvement Plan: Putting People at the Heart of Public Services* (Department of Health 2004)	Building on progress to date to continue the push to meet national targets to reduce wait times, this paper outlines shifts in priorities (to 2008) toward prevention and management of chronic conditions and local target-setting and performance management, especially for high-performing trusts. In addition, this plan outlines additional priorities such as greater personal choice for non-emergency care, an electronic booking system and the right to choose from at least four or five different healthcare providers; an Expert Patients' Programme designed to help empower patients to manage their own conditions; innovations such as NHS Direct (nursing-led telephone advice); and additional IT enhancements, including electronic booking and prescribing services and a HealthSpace for patients.
2006	*Our Health, Our Care, Our Say: A New Direction for Community Services* (Department of Health 2006a)	This white paper focuses on advancing a vision for better health and social care that "puts people more in control, makes services more responsive, focuses on those with complex needs and shifts care closer to home, while achieving better value for money." Specific actions for change outlined in the paper include: PBC, which gives GPs more responsibility for local health budgets, in conjunction with individual budget pilots to test how users can take control of social care and changes to payment-by-results tariffs to support these changes; a guarantee of registration with a GP practice list and incentives for GP practices to offer convenient opening times and appointments; more care in more local and convenient settings, including the home, by working with royal colleges to define clinically safe pathways within primary care; better infrastructure to support the integrated commissioning of health and social care between PCTs and local authorities; and an increase in the quantity and quality of primary care in under-served and deprived areas, including through the removal of barriers to entry for the "third sector" as primary care providers.

Appendix B. Healthcare Commission performance indicators

Existing:	Access to a GP (not including walk-in centres) Access to a primary care practice (not including walk-in centres) All cancers: 2-week wait All cancers: 31-day diagnosis to treatment Ambulance: category A calls meeting 19-minute target Ambulance: category A calls meeting 8-minute target Ambulance: category B calls meeting 19-minute target Commissioning a comprehensive CAMHS Commissioning of crisis resolution/home treatment services Convenience and choice: facilities in place to support choice Convenience and choice: PCT booking Delayed transfers of care Diabetic retinopathy screening Number of in-patients waiting longer than the standard Number of out-patients waiting longer than the standard Patients waiting longer than 3 months for revascularization Practice-based registers: patients called for review Thrombolysis: 60 minutes call to needle time Total time in A&E: 4 hours or less
New:	Access to genito-urinary medicine clinics Access to reproductive health services Blood pressure Breast cancer screening for women aged 50–70 years Cancer: implementation of NICE IOGs CVD mortality rate (per 100,000) Cancer mortality rate (per 100,000) Childhood obesity: data quality Cholesterol levels Commissioning of assertive outreach services Community equipment Community matrons CPA 7-day follow-up Data collection: referral to treatment waiting times Data quality on ethnic group Drug misusers sustained in treatment Emergency bed days Experience of patients Four-week smoking quitters GP recording of body mass index (BMI) status Infant mortality: breastfeeding initiation rates Infant mortality: smoking during pregnancy Infection control In-patient waiting times: 18-week milestone Number of drug misusers in treatment Number of very high-intensity users Older people's mental health: assessment of needs and services Out-patient waiting times: 18-week milestone Practice-based registers Smoking status aged 15–75 years Teenage conception rates Wait times for MRI and CT scans Wait times for other diagnostic tests

BEN PCT Scorecard indicators by strategic objective

Strategic Objective	Indicator
Efficient use of resources.	Financial balance Non-elective admissions (not maternity, practice-based registers only) Out-patient GP attendances (New OP, BPR only) A&E attendance Achievement of savings plan: BEN PCT combined figure
To be so responsive to the population we serve that no one waits for the healthcare they need.	Access to a GP (not including walk-in centres) Access to a primary care practice (not including walk-in centres) Cancer wait times: 2 weeks, 1 month, 2 months Ambulance: category A calls meeting 19-minute target Ambulance: category A calls meeting 8-minute target Ambulance: category B calls meeting 19-minute target Delayed transfers of care In-patient wait times Out-patient wait times Thrombolysis: 60 minutes call to needle time Total time in A&E: 4 hours or less Patients waiting longer than 3 months for revascularization Access to genito-urinary medicine clinics Access to reproductive health services Waiting times for MRI and CT scans Waiting times for other diagnostic tests
That the health and well-being of our population will have improved so much that people will enjoy 10 more years of quality life, wherever they live.	Diabetic retinopathy screening Four-week smoking quitters Practice-based registers: patients called for review Blood pressure Cholesterol levels Infant mortality: breastfeeding initiation rates Infant mortality: smoking during pregnancy Drug misusers sustained in treatment Number of drug misusers in treatment Number of very high-intensity users Practice-based registers Smoking status aged 15–75 years Emergency bed days GP recording of BMI status
Our communities will be the most involved, informed and empowered in the country.	Number of MRSA infections (primary care) Number of MRSA infections (acute) Convenience and choice: PCT booking Community equipment Community matrons Patients with CHD, etc., who smoke, offered smoking cessation advice Percentage of population served by practices achieving 80%+ QOF points (LAA) Number of patients recruited to Expert Patients' Programme (LAA) Percentage of complaints resolved within 25 days
That people regard us as the first-choice organization to work with and for.	Achievement against HCC core and developmental standards Commissioning of crisis resolution/home treatment services Commissioning of assertive outreach services CPA 7-day follow-up Full-time equivalent staff in post (FIMS workforce return) Older people's mental health: assessment of needs and services

References

Appleby, J. and J. Dixon 2004. "Patient Choice in the NHS (Editorial)." *British Medical Journal* 329: 61–62.

Beedon, J. and S. Christie. 2006. "Bringing Multiple Competing National Health Service Organisations Together." Paper provided by authors based on chapter for B.B. Bunker and B. T. Alban, eds. 2006. *The Handbook of Large Group Methods: Creating System Change in Organizations and Communities.* San Francisco: Jossey Bass.

Birmingham East and North Primary Care Trust. 2006. *Annual Public Health Report.* Birmingham: Author.

Birmingham East and North Primary Care Trust. 2006b. "Unusual Trophy Awarded for Antibiotic Prescribing Success." *Cascade* (1): 16.

Birmingham East and North Primary Care Trust. 2007a. *About Us.* Birmingham: Author. Retrieved February 26, 2007. <http://www.benpct.nhs.uk/_aboutus_/about_objectives.aspx>

Birmingham East and North Primary Care Trust. 2007b. *PCT Structure.* Birmingham: Author. Retrieved February 26, 2007. <http://www.benpct.nhs.uk/_aboutus_/about_organisation.aspx>

Birmingham East and North Primary Care Trust and Heart of England Foundation Trust. 2006. *Accelerating the Pace of Change: Programme Progress Report.* Birmingham: Authors.

Birmingham OwnHealth. 2006. *Outcomes Report for Birmingham OwnHealth for Presentation to Birmingham East and North (BEN) PCT Professional Executive Committee.* Birmingham: Author.

Collins, J.C. and J.I. Poras. 1994. *Built to Last: Successful Habits of Visionary Companies.* New York: Harper Collins.

Department of Health. nd a. *Increased Capacity.* London: Author. Retrieved February 27, 2007. <http://www.dh.gov.uk/PolicyAndGuidance/PatientChoice/WaitingBookingChoice/WaitingBookingChoiceArticle/fs/en?CONTENT_ID=4066160&chk=CTk1dy>

Department of Health. nd b. *Service Redesign.* London: Author. Retrieved February 27, 2007. <http://www.dh.gov.uk/PolicyAndGuidance/PatientChoice/WaitingBookingChoice/WaitingBookingChoiceArticle/fs/en?CONTENT_ID=4066204&chk=efb4Jw>

Department of Health. nd c. *What Is Payment by Results?* London: Author. Retrieved February 27, 2007. <http://www.dh.gov.uk/PolicyAndGuidance/OrganisationPolicy/FinanceAndPlanning/NHSFinancialReforms/NHSFinancialReformsArticle/fs/en?CONTENT_ID=4065236&chk=/HOpHu>

Department of Health. nd d. *Choice.* London: Author. Retrieved February 27, 2007. <http://www.dh.gov.uk/PolicyAndGuidance/Patientchoice/Choice/fs/en>

Department of Health. nd e. *National Service Frameworks.* London: Author. Retrieved February 27, 2007. <http://www.dh.gov.uk/PolicyAndGuidance/HealthAndSocialCareTopics/HealthAndSocialCareArticle/fs/en?CONTENT_ID=4070951&chk=W3ar/W>

Department of Health. nd f. *Arm's Length Bodies Review.* London: Author. Retrieved April 6, 2007. <http://www.dh.gov.uk/en/Aboutus/Deliveringhealthandsocialcare/OrganisationsthatworkwithDH/Armslengthbodies/DH_4105578>

Department of Health. 1997. *The New NHS: Modern, Dependable.* London: Author. Retrieved February 27, 2007. <http://www.dh.gov.uk/PublicationsAndStatistics/Publications/PublicationsPolicyAndGuidance/PublicationsPolicyAndGuidanceArticle/fs/en?CONTENT_ID=4008869&chk=VT3hrh>

Department of Health. 1998. *A First-Class Service: Quality in the New NHS.* London: Author. Retrieved February 27, 2007. <http://www.dh.gov.uk/PublicationsAndStatistics/Publications/PublicationsPolicyAndGuidance/PublicationsPolicyAndGuidanceArticle/fs/en?CONTENT_ID=4006902&chk=j2Tt7C>

Department of Health. 2000. *The NHS Plan: A Plan for Investment, A Plan for Reform.* London: Author. Retrieved February 27, 2007. <http://www.dh.gov.uk/PublicationsAndStatistics/Publications/PublicationsPolicyAndGuidance/PublicationsPolicyAndGuidanceArticle/fs/en?CONTENT_ID=4002960&chk=07GL5R>

Department of Health. 2002. *Delivering the NHS Plan: Next Steps on Investment, Next Steps on Reform.* London: Author. Retrieved February 27, 2007. <http://www.dh.gov.uk/PublicationsAndStatistics/Publications/PublicationsPolicyAndGuidance/PublicationsPolicyAndGuidanceArticle/fs/en?CONTENT_ID=4005818&chk=zN/Moe>

Department of Health. 2004. *The NHS Improvement Plan: Putting People at the Heart of Public Services.* London: Author. Retrieved February 27, 2007. <http://www.dh.gov.uk/PublicationsAndStatistics/Publications/PublicationsPolicyAndGuidance/PublicationsPolicyAndGuidanceArticle/fs/en?CONTENT_ID=4084476&chk=i6LSYm>

Department of Health. 2006a. *Our Health, Our Care, Our Say: A New Direction for Community Services.* London: Author. <http://www.dh.gov.uk/PublicationsAndStatistics/Publications/PublicationsPolicyAndGuidance/PublicationsPolicyAndGuidanceArticle/fs/en?CONTENT_ID=4127453&chk=NXIecj>

Department of Health. 2007a. *NHS Foundation Trusts.* London: Author. Retrieved February 27, 2007. <http://www.dh.gov.uk/PolicyAndGuidance/OrganisationPolicy/SecondaryCare/NHSFoundationTrust/fs/en>

Department of Health. 2007b. *The NHS in England: Operating Framework 2007/2008.* London: Author. Retrieved February 27, 2007. <http://www.dh.gov.uk/assetRoot/04/12/11/95/04141195.pdf>

Dixon, J. 2004. "Payment by Results: New Financial Flows in the NHS (Editorial)." *British Medical Journal* 328: 969–970.

Dodds, S.R. 2005. "Designing Improved Health Care Processes Using Discrete Event Simulation." *British Journal of Healthcare Computing and Information Management* 22(5): 14–16. Retrieved February 28, 2007. <http://www.bjhc.co.uk/issues/v22-5/v22-5dodds.htm>

Dodds, S.R. 2006. "The Shared Community-Hospital Leg Ulcer and One-Stop Vascular Surgery Service." [Note: Unpublished document received from author November 2, 2007.]

Enthoven, A. 2000. "In Pursuit of an Improving NHS." *Health Affairs* 19(3): 102.

Frith, M. February 10, 2004. "NHS Targets to be Cut but Star Ratings to Stay." *The Independent.* Retrieved February 27, 2007. <http://www.findarticles.com/p/articles/mi_qn4158/is_20040210/ai_n12765572>

Glasby, J. and E. Peck. 2005. *Partnership Working between Health and Social Care: Impact of Care Trusts*. Birmingham: University of Birmingham. Retrieved February 27, 2007. <http://www.hsmc.bham.ac.uk/Programmes/JGCareTrustdispaper.pdf>

Greener, I. and R. Mannion. 2006. "Does Practice-Based Commissioning Avoid the Problems of Underfunding?" *British Medical Journal* 333: 1168–1170.

Ham, C. 2006. *Developing Integrated Care in the NHS: Adapting Lessons from Kaiser.* Birmingham: University of Birmingham. Retrieved November 12, 2007. <http://www.hsmc.bham.ac.uk/LTCnetwork/KaiserbriefingpaperMay2006.pdf>

Health Service Journal Awards 2005, 2006. Retrieved February 24, 2007. <http://www.hsjawards.co.uk/home.asp>

Healthcare Commission. 2005. *About the Healthcare Commission*. London: Author. Retrieved February 27, 2007. <http://www.healthcarecommission.org.uk/_db/_documents/04021261.pdf>

Healthcare IT Effectiveness Awards 2005. Retrieved February 26, 2007. <http://www.healthcare-computing.co.uk/hitea/index.html>

Heart of England Foundation Trust. 2006a. *Annual Performance Report, 2005-2006*. Birmingham: Author.

Heart of England Foundation Trust. 2006b. *Briefing Document Prepared for Quality by Design Project Team*. Birmingham: Author.

Heart of England Foundation Trust. 2007. *About Us*. Retrieved February 16, 2007. <http://www.heartofengland.nhs.uk/about>

Higgins, J. 2007. "Health Policy: A New Look at NHS Commissioning." *British Medical Journal* 334: 22–24.

Humber, M. 2004. "National Programme for Information Technology." *British Medical Journal* 328: 1145.

King's Fund. 2005. *Payment by Results*. London: Author. Retrieved February 27, 2007. <http://www.kingsfund.org.uk/resources/briefings/payment_by.html>

King's Fund. 2005b. *NHS Waiting Times*. London: Author. Retrieved February 27, 2007. <http://www.kingsfund.org.uk/resources/briefings/nhs_waiting.html>

King's Fund. 2006. *Practice-based Commissioning (Briefing)*. London: Author. Retrieved February 27, 2007. <http://www.kingsfund.org.uk/resources/briefings/practicebased.html>

McGauran, A. 2004. "Moving 15% of Procedures to Private Sector Will Wreck NHS." *British Medical Journal* 329: 1257.

National Health Service. nd a. *About the NHS – How the NHS Works*. London: Author. Retrieved February 27, 2007. <http://www.nhs.uk/England/AboutTheNHS/Default.cmsx>

National Health Service. nd b. *The NHS in England – History*. London: Author. Retrieved February 27, 2007. <http://www.nhs.uk/England/AboutTheNHS/History/1988To1997.cmsx>

NHS Connecting for Health. nd. *About Us*. London: Author. Retrieved February 27, 2007. <http://www.connectingforhealth.nhs.uk/about>

NHS Direct. *Home*. 2007. London: Author. Retrieved February 27, 2007. <http://www.nhsdirect.nhs.uk/>

NHS Institute for Innovation and Improvement. nd. *Prototype Work Process*. London: Author. Retrieved February 27, 2007. <http://www.institute.nhs.uk/NR/rdonlyres/34AFC44E-9C93-4AF1-955A-08EE22461BBF/0/Methodologyincludingdiagram.doc>

NHS Institute for Innovation and Improvement. 2006a. *2006/2007 Plans (2006/07 to 2008/09 Strategic Plan)*. London: Author.

NHS Institute for Innovation and Improvement. 2006b. *2006/07 Business Plan*. London: Author.

SteelFisher, G. 2005. *International Innovations in Health Care: Quality Improvements in the United Kingdom*. London: Commonwealth Fund.

Commentary: Birmingham East and North Primary Care Trust and Heart of England Foundation Trust

Murray Martin, President and Chief Executive Officer
Hamilton Health Sciences

The Birmingham East and North Primary Care Trust (BEN PCT) and Heart of England Foundation Trust (HEFT) are to be applauded for their work. Their efforts have not only tremendously benefitted their community but, indeed, inspired providers around the world. The fact that they accomplished their work not in a homogeneous, middle-class, white neighbourhood but in an urban, multicultural community with significant socio-economic disparities makes their achievements all the more remarkable. The successes of organizations such as Kaiser Permanente are often discounted because of the belief that they ensure the well-being of only a select segment of the population. A community like Birmingham, England, is truly reflective of our emerging multicultural world, thus making it a highly appropriate testing ground for new models of healthcare delivery.

The success of any group of providers in meeting community healthcare needs is clearly not just about structures and governance. Though structures and governance are important enablers for success, perhaps more significant is the alignment among providers and the leadership that is in place to make it all happen. The successes of BEN PCT and HEFT emanated from a clear alignment around the single goal of improving the health of their population. This common goal drove these organizations' priority-setting activities and their bold implementation of multiple initiatives.

Alignment is critical because every individual, no matter how humble, needs a picture of what constitutes success, and multiple leaders with unaligned notions of success are unlikely to achieve a common goal. BEN PCT and HEFT have never strayed from their vision – a vision that is clearly shared by individuals at every level of their organizations.

The relationship between BEN PCT and HEFT to some extent parallels the relationship between hospitals in Ontario and the new, evolving structure of Local Health Integration Networks (LHINs). The success of LHINs will also depend on all their constituent organizations embracing common goals and creating shared definitions of success for the LHINs' leaders. At present, a cynic might say that if success does happen, it will be by accident. A more optimistic view would be that Ontario can achieve some of the same successes realized in Birmingham, but it will take a great deal of time and may be at great financial expense.

In Canada, the issue could be that, in contrast to the National Health Service (NHS) in the United Kingdom (UK), we are too timid in our approach to breaking down the status quo. Throughout its history, the NHS has been known for its courage in making radical changes in its attempts to "get it right." How, in Ontario, can we be driven by a common goal of improving the health of our population when crucial pieces remain outside the health system? These pieces include structures such as public health and primary care. The former independently performs the vital function of monitoring the population's health status and the latter is not only outside the world of LHINs but also external to the domains of most integrated health regions across Canada.

The effective and strong working relationship between the chief executive officers (CEOs) at BEN PCT and HEFT is another factor that was paramount to the success of their ventures. Such relationships are built on trust, mutual respect and common goals. Although the two CEOs headed organizations that each played a different role within the system, the lesson to be learned is that having a common, driving and overall goal and a shared picture of success was indispensable and helped to ensure the achievability of their joint vision. The same structural and governance relationships obviously exist in other communities throughout the NHS. However, the incredible success of these two organizations clearly points to the role that their leaders played in making it happen. The case study in this volume not only highlights the strong goal orientation of the individuals who led BEN PCT and HEFT, but also the complementary nature of the styles and skill sets of those two people. For health system boards, this element highlights the fact that interpersonal compatibility is far too important to leave to chance when recruiting a new CEO into a community.

A respectful relationship is underpinned by the belief that the other individual is competent in his/her role. For several decades in the NHS, an individual's career success was defined by the ability to climb the corporate ladder within the system's regional structures. To some, the poor performance of many of the NHS's institutions was tied to the reality that the regional structures continually drained the most talented people away from those institutions. The concept of foundation trusts was established, in part, to ensure that healthcare administrators could be recognized as having successful careers by remaining in one institution and achieving success in that role. The innovation was also intended to create an incentive reward system for institutional success. One cannot help but wonder if, a decade or two down the road, Canadian provinces will take a long look at whether the concentration of senior executives in downtown office towers has had an impact on the experience and capability level of those remaining behind to lead healthcare institutions.

The creation of foundation trusts was also a clear signal by the NHS that competition is good. In the case study we read that HEFT "operates as a large healthcare enterprise, intent on expanding its market share to include more patients in the region." This phenomenon is particularly worth watching when one realizes that in a public system we have a closed, zero-sum game. If HEFT is to acquire a greater market share, this will come at the expense of the other hospital providers. The other possibility is that HEFT hopes to draw activities away from other primary trusts in the Birmingham area. This approach would be consistent with the commercial imperative that a business must always grow to remain competitive. It was most refreshing to hear about an organization that is clearly strategic in its thinking. What may be most worth watching is the impact on other weaker organizations funded by BEN PCT and their response.

The BEN PCT and HEFT case study is rich with exciting new ideas and concepts that have widespread applicability in numerous communities across Canada. I was particularly interested to note the comments regarding physician engagement. One frequently hears arguments that progress in Canada is inhibited by the fact that the vast majority of our physicians receive their compensation by way of fee-for-service payments. The case study dispels the myth that, in a salary-based system, physicians immediately buy into change. The authors make clear that in all change initiatives physicians – no matter how they are paid – must be brought in as full participants to help define the outcomes and the change process itself. I do not intend my observation here to mitigate the reality that Canadian healthcare has a long way to go to achieve alignment between the goals of practicing physicians and our healthcare system in order to achieve better overall outcomes. Indeed, the case study also emphasizes the need for long-term commitment and perseverance through the change process.

I was also interested to read of the increasing acceptance by physicians of the expanded role of other non-physician healthcare professionals within the BEN PCT and HEFT system. The UK has often been thought of as being very traditional in terms of physician tolerance for expanding the roles of other healthcare professionals. It would perhaps be useful to explore this changed reality relative to the progress that has been made in North America.

BEN PCT and HEFT have fostered learning environments and created unique settings that support the skills development of their staff members. HEFT's creation of its own "Lean academy" is indicative of the supportive environment that organization has developed in order to grow the skills its front-line staff require to lead change. The NHS is to be applauded for the ongoing refinement of the various think tanks that have been piloted in search of new best practices, the latest being the NHS Institute for Innovation and Improvement. Canada's healthcare providers would benefit from similar kinds of structures. One always wonders whether the provincial nature of healthcare delivery in Canada detracts from the ability to muster the necessary critical mass to assemble such resources. This is perhaps a role the federal ministry of health could take on and fund for the country.

All 10 BEN PCT and HEFT projects given as examples of improvement initiatives would be beneficial in almost every Canadian setting. Indeed, some Canadian jurisdictions have already undertaken initiatives similar to the ones in Birmingham. For example, BEN PCT and HEFT's focus on projects related to chronic disease management is in step with many comparable Canadian endeavours. It would be interesting to conduct an in-depth comparison between the outcomes achieved in Birmingham and those realized in similar Canadian communities. This could include projects involving chronic obstructive pulmonary disease, diabetes, home hospice services and elder care assessment.

Clearly, Kaiser Permanente played a significant support role in mentoring BEN PCT and HEFT staff members. It is heartwarming to see the strength of the bond that has grown between these organizations that are physically an ocean apart. I hope that both Birmingham organizations will now commit to mentoring others throughout the world. Their success demonstrates that the concepts that have made Kaiser so influential can be applied in other systems that have different structures, forms of compensation, kinds of governance and even political ideologies.

Again, the success of BEN PCT and HEFT must also be labelled as extraordinary, particularly in light of the reality that it occurred within one of the world's largest bureaucracies. The NHS's at-times stifling bureaucracy is legendary. The Birmingham leaders nevertheless persevered, broke the rules when needed and sometimes even got the rules changed. Most obvious of all, they remained focused on their goals and found ways to overcome the hurdles in their way. It is again a tribute to the NHS that it is emulating a learning organization and allowing its institutions to learn and change the rules. Such flexibility is seldom easy in large government bureaucracies that are all too often entrenched in regulations and red tape.

NHS organizations have had much longer experience than Canadian institutions in reporting a multitude of indicators to meet government accountability requirements. It was encouraging to read in the case study that this process is being streamlined in the UK in order to achieve purposes that are more useful and relevant at the local level. I hope that Canadian institutions will not have to endure the same arduous journey to arrive at a sensible solution.

Perhaps missing from the case study, other than brief mention among the appendices, is any reference to the use of information technology (IT) strategies as enablers in the achievement of BEN PCT and HEFT's initiatives. I expected that in lieu of discussing the purported huge investments in creating integrated IT systems, more mention would have been made of their benefits. Perhaps this has not been one of BEN PCT and HEFT's success stories.

The citizens of East and North Birmingham are obviously well served by providers who are truly committed to the goal of meeting their community's healthcare needs. They enjoy a system in which multiple providers have created an alignment of goals and in which healthcare leaders have demonstrated that they are more concerned about deliverables than protecting their turf. Staff members of both BEN PCT and HEFT truly deserve the recognition they have received for their accomplishments in healthcare delivery. There is little doubt that Canada and the world will learn a great deal from their willingness to share their experiences.

3

Veterans Affairs New England Healthcare System (Veterans Integrated Service Network 1)

New England, US

> The reengineering of the Veterans Health Administration appears to have resulted in dramatic improvements in the quality of care provided to veterans. Many of the principles adopted by the VA in its quality-improvement projects, including emphasis on the use of information technologies, performance measurement and reporting, realigned payment policies and integration of services to achieve high-quality, effective, and timely care, have been recently recommended for the health system as a whole by the Institute of Medicine. (Jha et al. 2003: 2226)

Twelve years ago the Veterans Health Administration (VHA) began the radical transformation process Jha et al. refer to above. What can we learn from the VHA's experience of becoming a high-performing healthcare system? How do the re-engineered processes and improvement efforts work at the regional and local levels?

Method: Exploring a system capable of improvement

To answer these questions, in September 2007 a team of researchers from the University of Toronto's Department of Health Policy, Management and Evaluation visited the

Veterans Affairs New England Healthcare System (VISN 1). These site visits were part of an initiative called Quality by Design, which aims to identify and define the elements of healthcare systems capable of improvement with a view to helping to inform strategic investments in improvement capability in Ontario. Quality by Design is funded primarily by the Ontario Ministry of Health and Long-Term Care in partnership with the Department of Health Policy, Management and Evaluation based at the University of Toronto.

Table 1. Abbreviations used in this case study

ACA	Advanced clinic access
CBOC	Community-based out-patient clinic
CECS	Center for the Evaluative Clinical Sciences, Dartmouth Medical School
CPG	Clinical practice guideline
ED	Emergency department
EPRP	External peer review program
IHI	Institute for Healthcare Improvement
NCPF	National Center for Patient Safety
NQSFP	National Quality Scholars Fellowship Program
PDCA	Plan-Do-Check-Act
QI	Quality improvement
QMO	Quality management officer
RCA	Root cause analysis
VA	Veterans Affairs
VAMC	Veterans Administration Medical Center
VHA	Veterans Health Administration
VISN	Veterans Integrated Service Network
WRJ	White River Junction

VISN 1 was one of five healthcare systems selected from a short list of high-performing systems nominated by a panel of international leaders and experts. The research team spent time at the VISN 1 headquarters in Bedford, Massachusetts (MA), as well as at two of the network's medical centres: the VA Boston Healthcare System (VA Boston) in West Roxbury, MA, and the VA Medical Center White River Junction (WRJ VAMC) in White River Junction, Vermont. At each site the team met with and interviewed administrative and clinical leaders, and improvement team leaders and members as well as support staff members working to make improvements. This case study highlights the findings of the site visits.

VISN 1 and its environment

VISN 1 is one of 21 Veterans Integrated Service Networks (VISNs) across the United States (US) that provide healthcare services to American veterans. Through its network of eight medical centres, more than 35 community-based out-patient clinics (CBOCs), six nursing homes and four domiciliaries (residences for sheltering homeless veterans and for the treatment and rehabilitation of veterans needing such care), VISN 1 serves over 237,000 of the 1.2 million veterans in the six New England states (see map, Figure 1). With 1,895 in-patient beds, VISN 1 handles over 23,000 hospital admissions as well as 2.4 million out-patient visits per year (US Department of Veterans Affairs 2007a). (See Table 1 for a glossary of abbreviations.)

The VHA's mission – "Honor America's veterans by providing exceptional health care that improves their health and well-being" – encompasses patient care, education of health services providers, research and support for disaster response (US Department of Veterans Affairs 2007b). This is a special patient population that evokes strong values when staff members describe their work; these people regard caring for veterans as a noble mission (VA Medical Center White River Junction 2007). As VISN 1's chief medical officer observed, "Vets are wonderful patients, very patient with teaching and the residents."

Figure 1. VA New England Healthcare System

Source: VA New England Healthcare System (2006a). Used by permission.

Staff members' positive regard appears to be reciprocated. Patient surveys reflect high satisfaction levels with the overall quality of care: in a 2006 survey, 83.6% of outpatients and 81.1% of in-patients rated overall quality as "very good" or "excellent" (VA New England Healthcare System 2006a).

The veterans present a challenging set of needs and circumstances. "We really do take care of the poor," said VISN 1's network director. Veterans' average salary is lower than that of civilians outside the VA and the military. Between 35% and 40% of the homeless in the US are veterans; consequently, the VA healthcare system often acts as a social safety net for these people (Kizer et al. 2000). How this safety net is funded and what kinds of care are covered are somewhat complicated issues and have varied over the years.

The Veterans Equitable Reimbursement Allocation (VERA) system distributes care funding to VISNs for different categories of patients. As a priority, all service- and combat-connected conditions are covered, as is the care of other enrolled veterans. If a veteran has private insurance, the VHA can bill the insurer (but not Medicare/Medicaid) for care provided for conditions not related to military service. In the past, not all potential billings were collected; centres have therefore implemented initiatives to streamline their billing processes to increase third-party billing revenue.

A proportion of the veteran population chooses to seek medical care outside the VHA. These people may, however, still take advantage of the system's drug benefits. VISNs are accountable for tracking the care and outcomes of such "co-managed patients." As a result, VA physicians are responsible for getting information about such care, data that are then entered into the VHA's electronic health records.

"A profound change": Improvement in an integrated system

VISNs were established in the mid 1990s by then–Under Secretary Kenneth Kizer, architect of the VHA's massive re-engineering (Kizer 1995, 1996). The VHA has undergone "a profound change" from being a hospital care system to becoming a *health* care system (VISN 1 chief medical officer). In other words, the VHA transformed from a very acute care–centric model dominated by individual hospitals to an integrated regional system that emphasizes primary care in the community.

Since 2000, Dr. Jeannette Chirico-Post has been VISN 1's network director (prior to that, she was its acting medical director and acting network director). Chirico-Post has been with the VA for 32 years. In the 1980s she ran VA Boston's quality program and was a member of an early VHA performance improvement committee under Kizer. Chirico-Post reflected on Kizer's style and, with a smile, recalled his "I'll give you the tools, now go away and do it" approach. The Kizer principles fit with Chirico-Post's own philosophy, for example, an emphasis on care in the community. Chirico-Post therefore started working from day one on primary care, because it offered "the biggest bang for our buck" due to duplications and gaps in care processes.

Consistent with Kizer principles emphasizing national regulations, standards and practice guidelines, VISN 1 has adopted standardization and systematization as its watchwords. Teams in the medical centres working on clinic access and patient flow processes have made strides in reducing wait times and missed appointments (see later section on the VA Boston initiatives and graphs in Appendix A). From her systems view of the network, Chirico-Post described local examples of patient access and flow problems, as well as equipment and process issues that VISN 1 continues to address – including, for example, the distances that some veterans must travel for radiation therapy.

The network structure presented opportunities to streamline and rationalize supports, including equipment, throughout all levels of care. Standardization also continues to provide several benefits; for instance, it promotes safety and saves resources. With standardized infusion pumps and defibrillators, for example, VISN 1 has to offer only one training course instead of multiple courses tailored to specific models. It is also easier and safer for staff members to move around within the system when they are familiar with the equipment. This flexibility is particularly important because the VISNs' mission also includes disaster response support in the event of local and national emergencies.

Service lines

Based on analyses of patients' needs and the services they used, care delivery was organized into five clinical service lines that are integrated across VISN 1:

- Primary care
- Specialty and acute care
- Mental health care and behavioural science
- Spinal cord injury care
- Geriatrics and extended care

Four support service lines include sensory and rehabilitation care, information management, business office and local management at the eight medical centers (Figure 2). Patients are assigned to primary care teams that coordinate their preventive care, disease management and referrals within the continuum of care, as required (VA New England Healthcare System 2007).

Within each service line, local service line managers report both to their chiefs of staff and facility directors, as well as to a network-level service line director. In-patient nurses report to facility nursing directors, while out-patient and community nurses report through their service line managers, individuals who are also responsible for day-to-day operations. Credentialing and certification of clinical competencies fall under the central nursing structure.

Figure 2. VISN 1 service lines

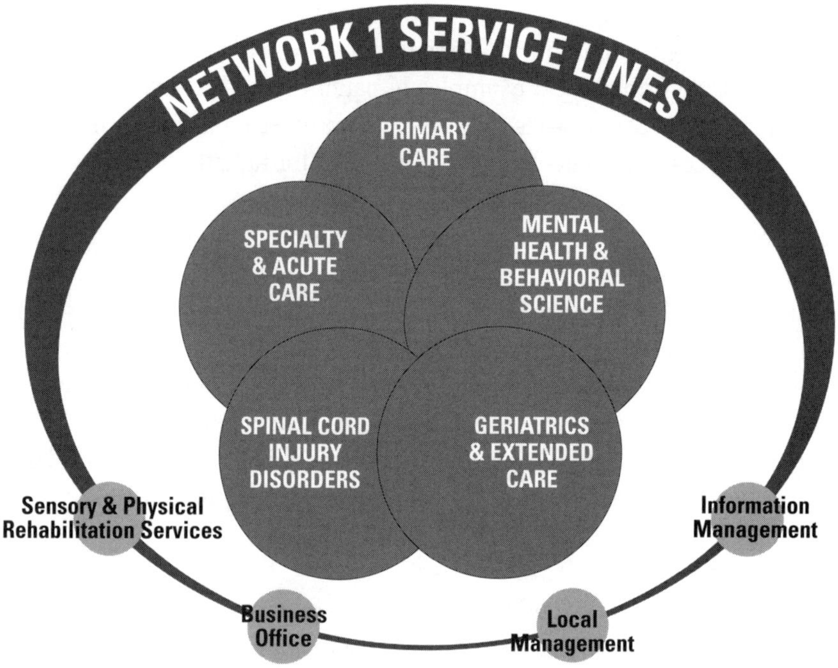

Source: Reproduced from US Department of Veterans Affairs (2007c). Used by permission.

A variety of meetings are held to facilitate communication within and between service lines. Each service line has its own executive committee and regular meetings. Service line directors, nurse executives and chiefs of staff for all eight medical centres meet monthly as the Clinical Leadership Committee (see network committee structure in Figure 3). This gives them a chance to hear presentations (e.g., about improvement initiatives) and to "rub shoulders," as VISN 1's chief medical officer explained.

Although creation of the VISNs decentralized decision-making from the national level to regional networks, VISNs also had the effect of centralizing budgets and integrating planning within the network structure. Network leaders commented that the restructuring has not always been easy and it has taken a while to develop the VISN 1 organization with roles and responsibilities matched to current needs. VISN 1's leaders undertook a year-long self-examination and realigned roles, responsibilities and power distribution in order to address more effectively the network's operating environment.

Figure 3. VISN 1 major functional committees

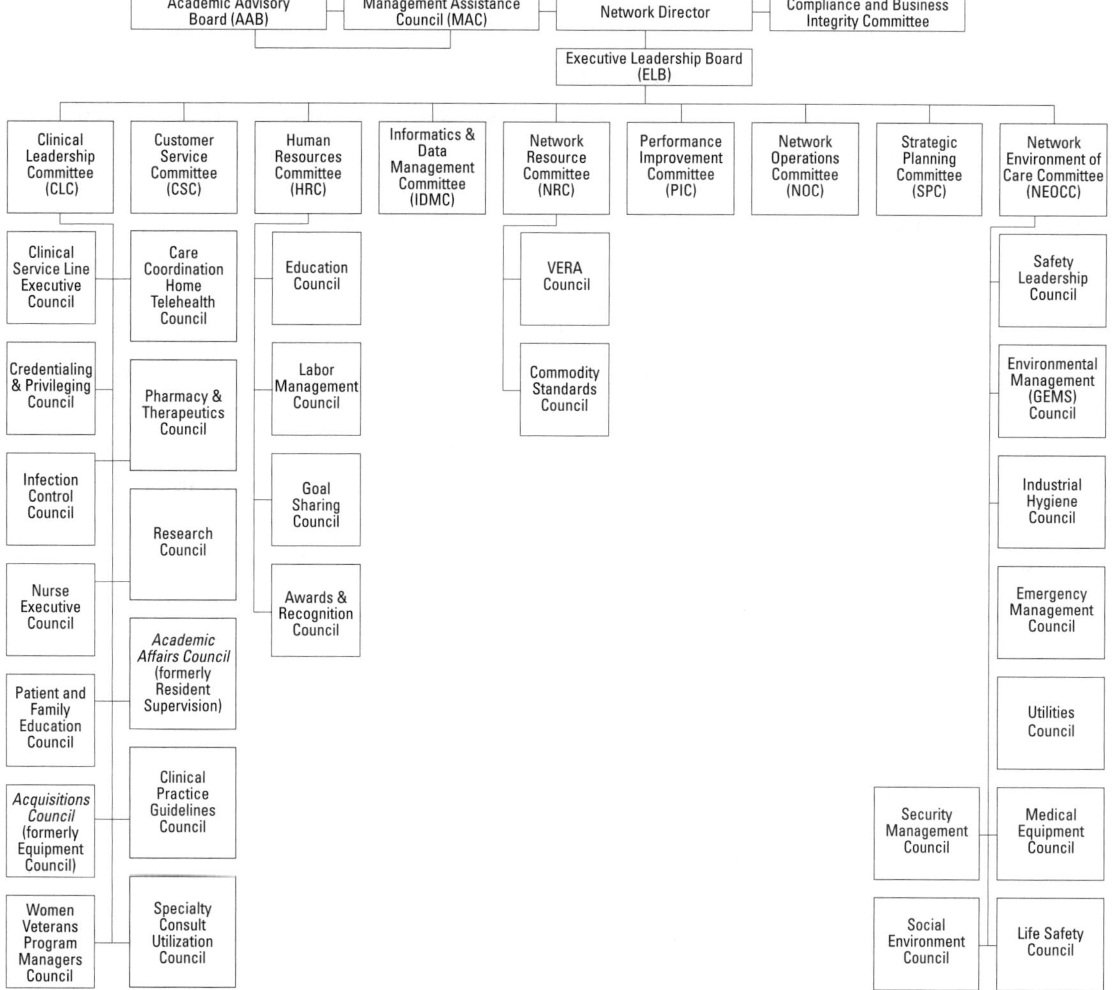

Source: VISN 1 headquarters staff on June 5, 2007. Used by permission.

Performance measurement and accountability

When he established the VISNs, Kizer also introduced stronger accountability, with an emphasis on standardizing and quantifying performance. "What Ken did for us was to ensure that from Caribou to California we were doing the same thing," observed Chirico-Post.

Kizer believed in stretch goals and setting targets for all to meet. Detailed performance contracts with agreed-upon goals and standardized measures were implemented first between VHA headquarters and the network directors and program officials. Now, there are similar contracts throughout all levels, right down to local service line managers within the facilities. Each network monitors a basic set of measures for the same elements of quality, cost and access: "We know from June '07 what the basic contract for '08 will look like" (Chirico-Post). When they began in the 1990s, they worked with 20 measures. "Now we are tracking hundreds" (Chirico-Post). The number of measures used reflects evolving views in the VHA about organizational priorities and the range of issues that can reasonably be managed.

VISN 1's quality management officer (QMO) is responsible for preparing and disseminating performance measurement data through the system. Each of the network's medical centres has a quality manager, most of whom have a nursing background. All quality managers at the centres and the network QMO have monthly conference calls and they meet face to face on a quarterly basis. VISN 1's QMO also works with a network performance improvement committee that was formed in order to track and analyze performance data more effectively and to make recommendations for actions that support the senior leadership team. As an example of its work, the performance improvement committee redesigned VISN 1's scorecard under the leadership of one of the network's service line directors. The quarterly reports include an array of in-patient and out-patient clinical, process and satisfaction measures (see Appendix B). Approximately one third of these measures relates to wait times and missed appointments, indicators that are linked to national access goals.

Indicators are derived from data collected from chart audits carried out by the VHA External Peer Review Program (EPRP) (US Department of Veterans Affairs 2001) (see Figure 4). Through the national EPRP, third-party reviewers audit a monthly sample of electronic and paper records in all VA medical centres. These reviewers scrutinize preventive indicators and clinical practice guideline compliance, such as HbA1c control in diabetes management or timing of prophylactic antibiotic administration in surgery (see examples of results in Appendix C). VISN 1 has a full-time analyst who prepares the reports (not all networks have invested in such a support position). In addition to the VISN scorecard, each service line has standardized monthly reports that focus on a "vital few measures" relating to quality, revenue and cost. They also include a description of what the service line is doing to add value to the service line and for its affiliates. The power of the service line structure, VISN 1's chief medical officer said, "is that it allows clinical disciplines to be focused and develop metrics of excellence specific to the service line."

The performance measurement system figures dominantly in any conversation about quality and improvement in VISN 1. Discussion invariably circles back to performance review of the measures and targets on the quarterly comparative scorecard, the "Christmas tree report," a nickname derived from the gold, green and red flags for scores that exceed, meet or fail to meet targets. The VHA's national office sets performance targets for all the performance measures. In addition, it establishes a "floor." If any facility does not meet the "floor" target, the network fails the measures.

Figure 4. VHA: Linkages among performance measurement, accountability and improvement

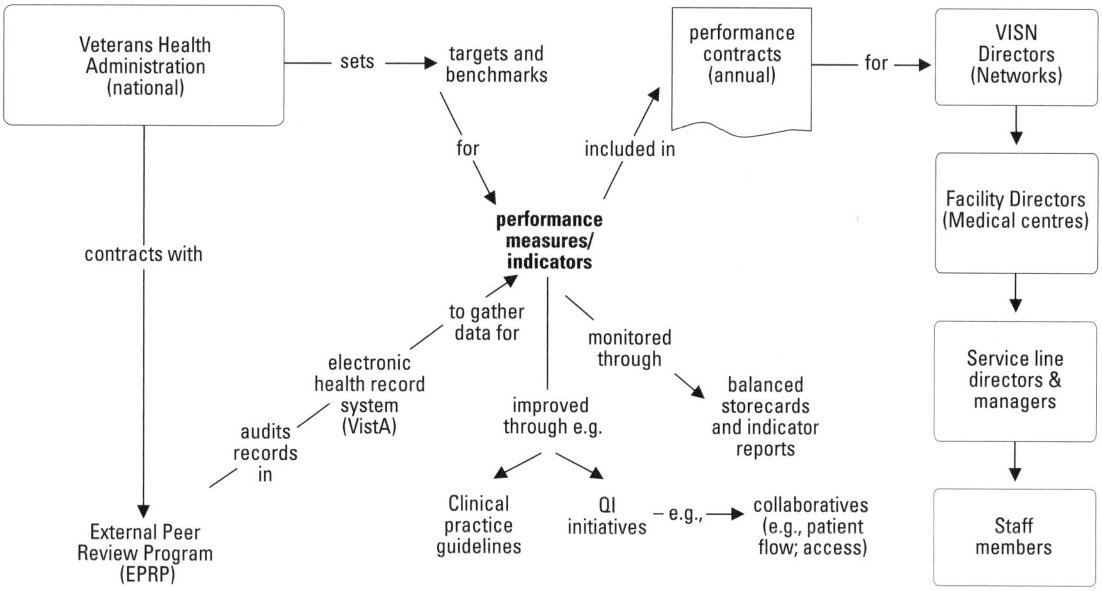

Source: US Department of Veterans Affairs (2001). Used by permission.

VISN 1's director and QMO meet quarterly with facility directors to go over their Christmas tree reports. The QMO emphasizes improvement over compliance in discussions of action plans. He finds out from high-performers what they are doing well and generates a lessons-learned list that he circulates across the network. "My concern," he reported, "is improving. How do we get to the *next* level of performance?"

The VISN 1 service lines also conduct quarterly reviews with the intent of discussing and capturing improvement opportunities arising from the reports. The QMO noted that "the point is that any measurement system needs to focus on meeting the target as a marker of good clinical care. It should be about the care, not about the numbers."

VISN 1's service line directors use the quarterly reports to review the performance of all local service line managers. Outstanding performance is defined as being better than the national and the VISN average. A facility director can overrule the performance review decisions of the service line directors; however, that rarely happens. One service line director noted, "You have to make the metric. ... The metric part of the job is not negotiable." Service line directors hold monthly meetings with managers and telephone conversations with each one individually. Near the end of 2007, one service line director explained that he was focusing on measures that were close to the target (one percentage point away) because he could "push those over the edge." He said he had deferred working on tobacco counselling, for example, because he could not influence the more than 20% gain that would be required by year-end. However, he was working on the system issues behind that measure, discussing with managers what was going on and how to fix the process during the upcoming reporting year.

About 60% of the indicators are new each year and/or targets are changed. Some measures count for the whole year and some relate only to a specific quarter, such as immunization rates in the winter quarter.

Information technology: Electronic medical records and clinical reminders

The VHA is a recognized leader in the implementation of information technology that has enabled both indicator measurement systems and coordinated patient care management. Nationally, the VHA's clinical patient record system (VistA) won the 2006 Innovations in American Government Award presented by the Ash Institute in Harvard University's Kennedy School of Government (US Department of Veterans Affairs 2006e, 2006f).

Setting the same standards and using electronic health records have been central to integration throughout the VISNs. In VISN 1, for example, early in her tenure Chirico-Post recognized the importance of standardizing information technology across the network. As a result, between $25 million and $30 million were set aside for new computers, which enabled the move to electronic health record-keeping. There was some initial resistance to mandatory electronic charting; however, VISN 1 staff members did make the switch, although dictation of operative notes and discharge notes is still allowed.

The VHA's electronic record system made possible the implementation of clinical practice guidelines (CPGs) and clinical reminders, which are mandated for primary care by the CPG committee and reminders subcommittee. The same requirement was then applied to mental health and specialty and acute care (e.g., for acute myocardial infarctions). The VHA's Office of Quality and Performance develops clinical practice guidelines for the system (US Department of Veterans Affairs 2006d, 2007d; see Appendix

D for a description of their functions). In VISN 1, the goals are to standardize reminders across the eight sites and to reduce reminder overload. A service line sponsor and subject matter expert is assigned for each reminder that is developed. The system can produce reminder reports by provider within each facility and make comparisons across centres. The reminders and positive feedback help to improve clinical care. They also encourage a bit of "healthy competition," the program manager noted, because no one wants to be seen as not responding to reminders.

The reminder system is so well advanced that the VISN has reached a saturation point, prompting the need to explore new approaches to continue to improve compliance with guidelines. For example, the VISN is considering use of support staff rather than physicians to carry out preventive care with patients, such as checking immunization status. The reminder program has been very successful: since the inception of the program in 2004, VISN 1 has been first or second in the VHA primary care performance measures.

Electronic medical records and physician accountability

The use of electronic medical records is an important factor facilitating physician accountability. "Our ability to do performance measurement, monitoring, physician accountability [and] workload measurement is all grounded in the electronic medical record. How you would do this without it, I don't know," commented one service line director. "If it's not all integrated it loses a lot of its power. … The clinical information system can produce information that the decision support system can't."

The VHA has developed a standardized staffing model for all primary care clinics. A VHA advisory group on physician productivity and staffing (chaired by VISN 1's chief medical officer) developed strict business model guidelines for and definitions of what constitutes a patient panel, and used a combination of number of exam rooms, number and types of support staff and patient mix to determine expected or model panel sizes. It is now possible to carry out sophisticated studies of the relationships between panel size, quality, access and patient satisfaction. This innovation also helps to reduce variation.

Most VISN 1 physicians are salaried employees, although some are on contract and may be paid on a fee-for-service basis, especially in scarce specialties such as neurosurgery, obstetrics and gynaecology. An element of pay-for-performance is included in the physician reimbursement plan if a physician meets performance targets, such as quality measures or access. The incorporation of pay-for-performance is seen as only part of the solution to improved performance.

Clear goals and performance measures

Chirico-Post summed up VISN 1's improved performance thus: "My legacy: when we started we met one third of the performance measures. Now we are in the top tier of percentage met."

VISN 1's leaders emphasized the importance of articulating clear goals. Early on, the senior leadership team set a goal of clinical and research excellence, wanting to be number one. "We wanted to be the leading academic network in the country, measured by the number and value of research grants," the chief medical officer noted. "We are a leading academic program in spinal cord injury and we are a leader in mental health." This position helps with staff recruitment because it draws top investigators and clinicians to the network.

How do local centres deal with national and network expectations? Implementation tensions and adjustments

While VISN 1 has demonstrated significant gains, there are tensions inherent in how integration, standardization and performance measurement have unfolded within the system. VISN medical centres are by no means homogeneous; neither are their approaches to improvement. Individual centres have had their own struggles with how to implement the nationally mandated performance measures and standards. The experiences of VA Boston and WRJ VAMC illustrate these challenges. As part of a large, complex, hierarchical system, their facilities' leaders have found ways of adapting the system's requirements to fit with strategies they believe are needed to meet local population needs. With characteristic good humour, WRJ VAMC Director Gary De Gasta summarized the challenge: "How do we do what we need to do in the context of a national organization where we do share the same goals, but where we sometimes need to do something a bit different – and not get into trouble!"

VA Boston

VA Boston, the largest consolidated facility in VISN 1, encompasses three main campuses and six out-patient clinics within a 40-mile radius of the greater Boston area. The consolidated facility consists of the Jamaica Plain Campus, the West Roxbury Campus and the Brockton Campus (US Department of Veterans Affairs 2007e). VA Boston grew out of the integration of two large centres in 2000: Jamaica Plain and West Roxbury/Brockton (the latter the result of an earlier merger in 1983). "At integration it was really hard; we started from zero because we didn't have common quality programs," commented the associate director of nursing. "We needed to rethink two very different sets of organizations, processes and cultures," said the quality manager.

VA Boston's current approach to improvement incorporates the VHA and VISN performance measurement system. It also includes formal change initiatives, such as participation in collaboratives run by the Institute for Healthcare Improvement (IHI).

Performance measurement

VA Boston is responsible for the same basic mix of population health measures as other VISN 1 facilities, including immunization rates and percentage of patients who smoke, as well as clinical process, access and patient satisfaction measures. Director Michael Lawson asserted, "You need some mandatory measures and to hold people accountable for them."

But use of the measures and other means to stimulate performance have changed over time, as the organization has come to understand better what motivates its employees. For example, VA Boston leaders debated the merits of financial rewards for compliance with the required measures. The chief of staff argued that reimbursement mechanisms can be a powerful incentive. In the last year, the centre introduced an element of pay-for-performance for physicians, a $1,500 bonus for meeting some percentage targets. Director Lawson did not see money as the only motivator: "If the only leverage you have is money, you are in a very difficult situation. … *Culture* is important – pride in doing things well." The chief of staff concurred, "It is the performance measures *and* the information and feedback to people in the right culture, where people care." He continued, "The Hawthorne effect is very important; when you measure something, people pay attention." However, the performance measure review at the local level can, one senior leader noted, generate "pressure and competitiveness; no one wants to be on the lowest rung." Lawson said, meanwhile, "We know who is number one and where we are; we are very competitive and we want to do better and be the best."

With regard to the development of the measures themselves, the chief of staff commented that most staff members understand intuitively the literature and evidence behind the measures. Some disagreements do arise: for example, the monotherapy guideline for hypertension was not perceived to be correct (some patients and physicians were reluctant to add a medication if a patient's blood pressure was stable) and an antibiotic guideline for patients presenting with pneumonia was not seen to be working; as a result, these guidelines will be reviewed.

Evidence-based reviews and the flexibility to re-examine performance measures over time are important factors that have encouraged acceptance of performance measures. Centrally developed evidence-based directives must be locally adapted for implementation. "It is 10 years into performance measurement and we are still getting to agreement," summed up one senior leader. VISN 1's QMO noted that "the overarching issue is for the organization to achieve balance between the art and science of medicine; some measures … will … have more evidence than others and some patients' conditions are complex enough to not fully match a given guideline. Also, there are technicalities with how measures are defined, gathered, etc., so that a couple to a few each year get pulled or modified to work out details."

The measures continue to evolve, expanding to include development of nursing-specific indicators. VA Boston is a pilot site for the VA Nursing Outcomes database. The system will, for example, soon provide national comparative data on decubitus ulcers, medication issues and falls. Currently, unit managers have a quarterly report card with these measures reported by unit, which they review with their staff members (see Appendix E). The nursing measures are reported to VA Boston's quality manager as part of its quality improvement (QI) plan.

Implementing changes

Adaptation, monitoring and review of the measures are preliminary steps in the performance measurement system; changes must be implemented to achieve improvement. VA Boston leaders invest to make changes when services or clinics demonstrate need based on the measures. For example, the dermatology clinic management staff and clinical leaders maximized process improvements to reduce wait times, which allowed for a more accurate supply and demand analysis that demonstrated the need for more staff members (who were subsequently hired).

VA Boston follows systematic processes to implement changes and make improvements. Teams apply an evidence-based approach, noted the associate director of nursing: "We make changes based on what is in the research literature." According to the quality manager, "The big change in approach that allowed improvement in the performance measures was assigning teams and supporting them, and the encouragement." The VA Boston system pays a lot of attention to how teams and committees operate in order to promote efficient and productive meetings that make good use of staff time and enthusiasm. The need for staff involvement is discussed with managers in advance to ensure their understanding and support for staff participants before projects are launched. Four different nursing unions represent VA Boston staff, a situation that can present challenges for improvement efforts. Earlier, unions required that changes to work processes that were perceived to affect job responsibilities be negotiated in advance before the changes were even tested; however, this has become less of an issue over time.

"We are very thoughtful about who we select for physician leaders and participants, and we are also very clear about endpoints and expectations. We are very clear about who we want, why we want them and what we want them to do," the quality manager commented. Most physicians are employees and are part of the system, which sometimes makes a difference in physician engagement, but the issue is not payment structures alone. "Some of my most enthusiastic members are fee-for-service [physicians] ... who see where the improvements can be made."

Project team processes are designed to respect staff members' time and to use their talents; this design encourages participation. The chief of staff (or associate) and the quality manager meet once a year with each committee chair to find out how things are going, whether there are any issues and how they can support the committees' work.

Lawson advised, "Pick demonstration projects and start where there is some promise." He cautioned that implementing best practices may be problematic, as changes have to be tailored locally. "What works in Boston may not have a chance in Maine."

Participation in IHI improvement collaboratives

VA Boston's formal change efforts include multi-centre collaborative improvement projects. The centre has a long history of participating in IHI Breakthrough Series collaboratives. VA Boston teams have participated in the access collaboratives since 1999 and have engaged in several each year for the past five years, including collaboratives on flow, patient medication safety and transforming bedside care.

The influence of the IHI methods and the rapid cycle model for improvement are pervasive in the centre, which emphasizes interdisciplinary teams and action plans. "It's always 'What are you going to do by next Tuesday?' (an improvement mantra derived from a talk by Don Berwick). Rapid cycle methodology made so much sense and was intuitively appealing to the front-line staff and teams," the quality manager said. All management team members (i.e., service chiefs and senior leaders) have been trained in rapid cycle methods, change concepts and improvement strategies. Team members are taught how to map their current processes and the concepts of value stream mapping. They use rapid cycle improvement methods, planning and testing change cycles. The goal is to have the actual teams do the work; they therefore emphasize short meetings or 15-minute huddles and do as much as possible by e-mail.

Although many network facilities participate in IHI collaboratives, the extent of VA Boston's involvement in IHI initiatives is somewhat unusual within VISN 1. This is a strategic investment and significant commitment due to the cost of IHI collaboratives, which average $20,000 a year plus travel per team. As the quality manager commented, "We always take our whole team to the collaborative meetings, plus the leadership sponsor; it signals the importance [of the initiatives]."

Access collaborative

In 1999 the VHA began a major national initiative with the IHI to improve patients' access to out-patient clinics by reducing wait times for appointments (Institute for Healthcare Improvement nd; Parlier 2003). "It took about a year before we saw dramatic results locally. … Within two years we were at the top of our VISN and within three years we were in the top three nationally. … At the start our actual [performance] was 60 to 90 days, and our current is 14 days and we are working towards open access," recollected the out-patient access coordinator.

The VA Boston access coordinator is the medical centre's local point of contact with the national advanced clinic access (ACA) initiative. She works alongside physician champions with the centre's ACA steering committee and participates in VISN-wide meetings. Their work with specialist clinics has been a success. In the access coordinator's words, "Even in orientation, new medical staff are told what the expectations [on access] are, and that delays are not acceptable."

The access team identified an initial list of about 10 high-volume, high-priority clinics, such as primary care, cardiology, audiology, surgical, mental health and orthopaedics. Based on that experience, the team is now expanding the initiative to the top 50 clinics. A clinical champion and an expert in advanced clinic access were identified for each clinic, and the committee set an access goal that patients will have an appointment to be seen within 30 days.

By focusing on what can be done, staff members become more engaged in accomplishing goals. If staff members say, "'No, we can't do that,' we ask, 'Okay, what can you do?'" said the access coordinator. The team also pairs similar clinics so they can learn from the experience of the ones who have been successful. "The whole VHA system is open to sharing accomplishments and tools," and because they share components of the information systems teams "do not have to start from scratch."

VA Boston's access collaborative teams follow the IHI Breakthrough Series model, especially its data requirements, although the data and information commitment can be very demanding. Over time, local data systems have become more flexible, reducing the need for "stubby pencil" work. "It can be hard to get the team members to stop and gather the data and measure and huddle, but once they see results it helps," noted the access coordinator.

Across the 21 VISNs there have been national-, network- and local-level collaboratives on access. By meeting together on a network-wide basis, audiologists, for example, were able to share ideas for changing the design of their audiology clinic processes.

Improving patient flow

VA Boston is one of the most successful participants in the IHI Breakthrough Series flow collaborative. As the largest acute care centre for VISN 1, VA Boston was under pressure to improve patient flow; the centre therefore joined the IHI initiative in 2002. Currently, VA Boston has flow teams working on in-patient, operating room, emergency department (ED) and long-term care flow issues.

Among VA Boston's West Roxbury units, the ED was one of the first areas to start and has also been the most successful. Their results:

- No ambulance diversions in 16 months
- Less than 1% of patients leave without being seen
- Average wait from triage to disposition: 2 hours and 53 minutes
- Exceed the IHI goal of less than one hour from decision to admit to admission to an in-patient bed

The West Roxbury units achieved these results by developing standardized order sets and implementing a fast-track system to handle less complicated patients. Initially, not all the changes were readily accepted: "Redesign was vigorously resisted where it was seen to interfere with clinical autonomy," noted the ED medical director. The ED information system provides the data needed to monitor productivity; West Roxbury's leaders were therefore able to show staff that changes were leading to improvement. As the nurse manager commented, "Data speaks volumes" and was sufficient to persuade most staff members. Even at that, some among the medical staff did not immediately recognize the benefit of seeing the fast-track patients, preferring not to interrupt their focus on the more acute patients. The ED flow team moved the fast-track room to the front of the computer terminals as a way to heighten awareness of the fast-track patients and their needs. In addition, staff members call the few patients who leave without being seen the next morning; patients are pleased and surprised by this attention.

The ED leaders commented that the flow team has made a real difference in ED culture. ED staff members brainstorm ideas, develop implementation plans and try them out the next day. Everyone involved has a say and all staff members vote on priorities, based on the ideas that are within their control to implement and that are a priority for their patients.

The in-patient flow coordinator and the out-patient access coordinator are looking at forming a joint steering committee to focus on the linkage and coordination of in-patient and out-patient flow and access issues and changes. This will create a more comprehensive system redesign committee.

Patient safety

VA Boston has been involved in a variety of patient safety initiatives for some time. "We have been ahead of the curve because we started in advance voluntarily, before we were required to," noted the Patient Safety Committee chair, a cardiovascular surgeon. Boston was a pilot site for medical team training and briefings designed by the National Center for Patient Safety, as well as IHI's perioperative safety program.

The Patient Safety Committee also oversees the implementation of the IHI 100k Lives initiatives, which have presented a variety of challenges. "None of this was easy," observed a cardiologist member of the team. The physician leaders emphasize the importance of letting everyone discuss proposed changes, noting "eventually you have to move on and implement." The Patient Safety Committee chair recounted the example of glucose control for surgery patients, saying it took a year to implement a modified Portland protocol. "You can't eliminate individual variation and *make* everyone follow one protocol." Data on the Portland outcomes were stressed as important. All involved staff members were part of the change process, and some variation was allowed in how they got there. Now glucose levels are controlled for 94% of in-patients.

Participants emphasized that, at times, the improvement work could be very challenging and taxing for everyone involved. "The changes were not all smooth. There were a lot of blood, sweat, and tears," laughed the patient safety coordinator. "But now people say 'may as well do it because it will be required in a few years.' That's a real change."

Resident training: Patient safety and QI rotation

VA Boston is affiliated with both Boston and Harvard universities' medical schools and 500 to 600 residents per year complete six-week clinical rotations at the centre's facilities. In 2006 VA Boston's General Internal Medicine program started a new patient safety and QI rotation as an optional elective open to approximately 12 third-year residents per year. The hospitalist who designed the program with the patient safety coordinator commented that physicians tend to be trained in individual decision-making as opposed to systems thinking, noting that, "It's not fair to expect people to be involved in quality and patient safety if we don't train them in it."

The one-month rotation integrates patient safety and QI education with clinical time in subspecialty clinics. Residents review charts of in-patients for whom they have cared prior to starting the elective, tracking their post-discharge care to look for any iatrogenic complications and care issues as well as changes they could make to their own practices. As an example, the in-patient discharge record was changed to record impending issues. Residents participate in root cause analysis (RCA) reviews and patient safety meetings and also learn about the Joint Commission national patient safety goals and healthcare failure modes and effects analysis.

Staff and patient satisfaction

According to the quality manager, "We spend a lot of time and effort working on staff satisfaction. … We have very high staff and patient satisfaction. VA Boston was second in the All Employee Survey results for VISN 1, "which is huge, because we were at the bottom seven years ago. In nursing, we are one of the best in the nation," observed the associate director nursing/patient services.

There is a strong emphasis on customer service at VA Boston, spearheaded by the efforts of the Customer Service Committee, formed in 2004 based on needs staff members identified during annual priority planning. The committee has worked on a variety of issues, ranging from improving signage and directions for patients and visitors to arranging for beepers for patients with prolonged care or clinic delays. Committee members review patient satisfaction survey results and patient complaints, and canvas staff for suggestions. There is also an ambassadorship program in which patients are met and greeted in waiting areas. In the past three years, all VA Boston employees have been required to go through customer service training based on a standard program provided by the VISN. In recognition of these efforts, the centre won the 2007 VHA Comprehensive Facility Customer Service Program Award.

White River Junction VA Medical Center, Vermont: A strategic approach to improvement

The WRJ VAMC is a rural, 60-bed primary and secondary care medical centre affiliated with the medical schools at Dartmouth College and the University of Vermont (US Department of Veterans Affairs 2007f). Under Gary De Gasta's leadership it has forged a strategy-driven path to improvement developed over almost 20 years.

In 1994, in a move that predated the VHA's re-engineering initiatives, De Gasta invited Dr. Paul Batalden to help the senior leadership team develop a strategic framework to guide the organization. Batalden is an internationally respected expert in improvement who leads the Health Care Improvement Leadership Development group in the Dartmouth Medical School's Institute for Health Policy and Clinical Practice (formerly Center for the Evaluative Clinical Sciences [CECS]) (Dartmouth College 2002a). Monthly working sessions took place for over two years, building insights that resulted in a profound understanding of White River Junction as a system capable of improvement (Batalden and Mohr 1997; VA Medical Center White River Junction 2007). Batalden insisted that each of the facility's leaders had to take ownership of and personally lead one of the four strategic themes that were identified. Despite initial resistance, WRJ VAMC's senior leadership team took on that task, demonstrating strong constancy of purpose over the years in the face of continuous changes in their environment. "It has created a frame to allow the conversation about quality to happen, and Gary has sustained the focus and the interest in that," Batalden noted.

The conception of WRJ VAMC as a system capable of improvement is compatible with business excellence frameworks such as the Baldrige National Quality Program (2007). The VA's Robert W. Carey Performance Excellence Program, based on the Baldrige criteria, was established to

> recognize organizations that have implemented exemplary approaches to systems management that achieve excellent results for America's veterans. The foundation for the awards is the Malcolm Baldrige Criteria for Performance Excellence. These criteria are designed to help organizations use an integrated approach to organizational performance management that results in:
>
> - Delivery of ever-improving value to customers and stakeholders, contributing to organizational stability;
> - Improvement of overall effectiveness and capabilities; and
> - Organizational and personal learning.
>
> (US Department of Veterans Affairs 2006c: 3)

Not surprisingly, therefore, embarking on the Carey self-assessment process was a logical next step in WRJ VAMC's growth as a learning organization. By 2002 the centre had conducted its first Carey Program organizational assessment and received its first Carey Achievement Award. That experience has formed the foundation of a continuous cycle of self-assessment and recognition:

2003: 2nd Carey Award and Vermont Governor's Award
2004: Carey Trophy Award and 1st Baldrige site visit
2005: First VA Circle of Excellence Award and 2nd Baldrige site visit
2006: Second VA Circle of Excellence Award

In 2007, WRJ VAMC completed its 11th and 12th cycles of Carey and Baldrige applications. "I think it gives us a structure in an environment in a constant state of flux. We have no consistency, so this is the one consistency," remarked De Gasta. "It *all* fits: the six process chapters and the one results chapter. ... Baldrige involvement has been a big contributor to our financial solvency," he added. However, De Gasta explained, there is a cost to the work involved and the resulting feedback process: "It is so painful to get the feedback report that we ask ourselves every year should we do this. But the opportunities for improvement [identified by the examiners] are rarely a surprise. Two thirds are things we knew about and one third are things we failed to communicate well enough."

A service line director also emphasized the continuity provided by the strategic frameworks:

> Adopting the one approach started with Batalden and now continued with Baldrige has been important. ... Over the years we have continued to grow this one process, this pathway. ... During turbulent times we didn't change our process, we stayed with it. We've tried lots of new things, but we put it in that same framework. You start to see that there are places for the entire organization in the Baldrige criteria; by the time you get to chapter seven, you see how it all contributes to quality. ... We've learned that you don't implement a change today and see results tomorrow; it's been a long process for us, over 10 years.

The "turbulent times" referred to by several staff members included a period from 1997 to 1999, when the quality of WRJ VAMC's surgical services was called into question. While an external review showed that the quality was good, the next challenge asserted that it would be less expensive to contract out the services (another external consultant study showed that this was not the case). These challenges were traumatic for the centre and provoked an exodus of medical staff members, from which it took several years to recover.

It is relatively more difficult for an entire network (than a single facility) to be successful in these award review processes. VISN 1 has also adopted the Baldrige framework and uses the principles as the model for its governance committees (VA New England Healthcare System 2006a). The network won a VHA Kizer Quality Achievement Recognition Grant in 2004–2005 and used the award money to fund improvement initiatives in the network facilities (US Department of Veterans Affairs 2006b). Medical centres and community-based out-patient clinics submitted project applications to VISN 1 headquarters, and Dr. Chirico-Post decided to fund all 31 projects by supplementing the Kizer award funds. Although VISN 1 submitted another application in 2007, the network did not advance to be considered for the Carey awards.

Local versus national performance measurement

WRJ VAMC leaders have had to translate the VHA performance measures to fit the Baldrige/Carey framework. The centre balances the expectations and structure of the national/VISN performance measures against its own organizational strategic theme-driven measures and reports. WRJ VAMC has been obliged to manage the national performance measurement system to some degree, while managing by its own report card process. "Performance improvement really came into play when Ken Kizer said, 'No, *show* us how you are doing.' … His efforts really changed the face of the VA," noted De Gasta. "'BK' (before Kizer) we had no measures; we said we were good but we didn't really know. 'AK' (after Kizer), we have lots of measures, but we are still not there yet."

De Gasta observed that WRJ VAMC had developed its own performance measures and "stoplight report" before the VA "kicked up the performance measures and we got a lot more." Now it is responsible for hundreds of measures, an obligation that some leaders find difficult to manage. WRJ VAMC therefore developed a strategic themes stoplight report to focus on the important clinical, financial and satisfaction measures (Figure 5). For example, the centre's quality manager noted that on the VISN Christmas tree report there are no employee-related measures, which WRJ VAMC leaders felt were critical. Spurred on by the Baldrige criteria, they added position vacancy and injury rates as measures. Likewise, neither the Christmas tree nor the national performance reports contain measures of ethical performance or community image; therefore, the quality manager said, "we took on more measures over and above those required of us." WRJ VAMC decides which of the 20 to 30 measures in each category are important in relation to the strategic themes. (Each theme includes five or six sub-themes, and some sub-themes are a combination of multiple measures.) The governing board's executive committee then decides which measures are the most critical. "Each year we tweak the list of measures at our annual retreat," reported the quality manager. The goal for WRJ VAMC leaders is to complement the national measure set and align it with local priorities.

Several years ago WRJ VAMC was at the bottom of the VISN Christmas tree report, which required that centres meet at least 80% of all VISN measures. WRJ VAMC executives began a First Friday meeting to discuss with all process owners how the organization was doing and what could be done to improve. Staff members attend these meetings with Plan-Do-Check-Act (PDCA)-type action plans and give progress updates. The chief of staff commented on the collaborative nature of the discussions, noting that "The interdisciplinary discussion of the measures across service lines is valuable." For example, the director supported a system change idea (appointing a new case manager) to help the centre meet multiple performance measure requirements for in-patients, such as smoking cessation counselling and primary care prevention. Measures are also discussed with front-line staff members at staff meetings.

"We were pretty well prepared when the focus on measurement came down from the VA," the WRJ VAMC chief of staff remarked. "The philosophy of support from leadership has been key." He recounted how he had "put a team together for every single

Figure 5. WRJ VAMC stoplight report

STRATEGIC THEME	1st			2nd			3rd			4th			
	OCT	NOV	DEC	JAN	FEB	MAR	APR	MAY	JUN	JUL	AUG	SEP	
INDICATORS													**Final**
Excellence in Clinical Care and Scholarship													
1. Coordination of Care	✖	→	✖	→	→	✖	→	→	✖				
2. Technical Quality	→	→	✖	→	→	✖	→	→	✖				
3. Patient Safety	→	→	✔	→	→	❍	→	→	❍				
4. Patient Satisfaction	✔	❍	✔	✔	✔	✔	✔						
4a. OEF/IEF	✔	✔	✔	✔	✔	✔	✔	✔	✔	✔			
5. Knowledge Management	→	→	❍	→	→	→	→	✔					
Community Stewardship													
1. Ethics: Respecting Pt. Rights	✔	✔	✔	✔	✔	❍	✔	❍	✔				
2. Environmental Protection	✔	✔	✔	✔	✔	✔	✔	✔	✔				
3. Emergency Preparedness	→	→	✖	→	→	✔	→	→	✔				
4. Public Image		✔	❍	✔	✔	✔	✔	✔	✔	✔			
5. Clinical Education	→	→	→	→	→	→	→	→	→	→	→	Collected at EOY	
6. Strategic Partnering	✔	✔	✔	✔	✔	✔	✔	✔	✔				
Maximizing Financial Resources													
1. Cost of Care	✔	✔	✔	✔	✔	✔	❍	✖					
2. Financial Index	✔	❍	❍	✔	❍	✔	✔	✔	✔	✔			
3. Coding Accuracy	✔	✔	✔	✔	✔	✔	✔	✔	✔				
4. Non-appropriated Revenue	✔	✔	✔	✔	✔	❍	✔	❍					
5. Capital Spending									✖				
6. Space Planning									✔				
Preserving and Promoting a Healthy Workforce and Work Environment													
1. Staff Safety & Wellness	✖	✔	✖	✔	✔	✔	✔	✔	✔				
2. Recruitment	✔	✖	✖	✖	✖	✖	✖	✖	✖	✖			
3. Employee Satisfaction							❍						❍
4. Retention	✔	✔	✔	✔	✔	✔	✔	✔	✔				
5. Labor Relations	✔	✔	✔	✔	✔	✔	✔	✔	✖	✖			

✔ Meets or exceeds target: 100% of target or greater ❍ May need attention: 80% of target ✖ Not meeting target: less than 80% of target

Source: Adapted from version provided by quality manager, WRJ VAMC, on September 25, 2007. Used by permission.
Note: The original version included red, green and yellow symbols, hence the name "stoplight report."

measure we were responsible for, whether we were doing well or not. I didn't trust the data, so I thought it was safer to work on everything to improve." WRJ VAMC has a mix of more formal project teams; however, QI is integrated into day-to-day operations. "Primary care is probably our most mature, established product line and we have spent a long time trying to do that one thing the best we can. Lots of improvements and standardization have taken place." Examples of other local improvement initiatives include the Care Coordination Home Telehealth program and the Stop Workforce Accidents Team (SWAT) (see Appendix F).

"Over the years we have moved up in the VISN Christmas tree so that we are in the middle and achieve over 80%," reported WRJ VAMC's quality manager. "The difference between a number-one VISN and number eight may be miniscule, but in the eyes of the VHA, if you are number one [in the performance measures], you are number one," said De Gasta. "Would I like us to be number one in those measures? Yes, but I am not going to give up doing [other] things that I believe we need to do in order to accomplish that."

The role of WRJ VAMC's leadership is to balance the needs and priorities of the whole organization. Batalden endorsed De Gasta's approach: "Gary has this right; he preserves the space to work on improvement." Support, attention and time for improvement work are critical. As the union local president pointed out, "You need to be actively involved in a QI process. You can be mandated to collect measures but what will you do with them when you have them?"

"We've had challenges with our performance measures," De Gasta remarked. "We are much more expansive here than just the national quality measures. If you look at the quality measures we're not the star there." "Depends which quarter!" the quality manager countered, suggesting that results need to be looked at over time as opposed to one reporting period when judging performance.

Measurement challenges

"You can argue about the measures, but if you don't meet them and others do you have to ask how come?" commented De Gasta, adding, "It's hard to dink the numbers when you've got outside people gathering the data." (The indicators are based on monthly random samples of charts abstracted through the VHA External Peer Review Program [US Department of Veterans Affairs 2001].)

WRJ VAMC's chief of staff commented that it is hard to argue with the clinical measures, given the good intentions with regard to outcomes. He explained, "For me the issue with the performance measures is sometimes how the results are interpreted, because of the confidence intervals and the sample sizes. For example, the smoking cessation counselling [measure] can be based on six or eight of 27,000 patients." However, increased data pulls are being considered for 2008 and "there are lots of ways to mine the e-records to look at whole panels of patients by provider and their entire course of care, so you don't have to worry so much about sample sizes or confidence intervals."

"We were perceived as close to the worst, now we are perceived as close to the best, and neither is completely true because of difficulties with measurement," cautioned a WRJ VAMC clinician researcher concerned about the dangers inherent in making global judgments of care based on just a few measures. When the VISN focuses on certain measures, there is a strong emphasis on improving those measures, but at what cost? Attention is distracted from elsewhere. "What is the unit of analysis? That is the heart of the issue," the clinician remarked. On this view, there is a bit of a danger in moving to outcomes measures because it has the potential to create perverse incentives. For example, he noted, it is important to focus on how well blood pressure is being controlled in the severely diabetic population, which can be hard to manage. But the easiest way to improve the diabetic measures is to diagnose more diabetics so that fewer sick patients are included in the population. It can also be difficult to create good measures for certain diagnoses, such as psychiatric patient populations, where measures of functional status and an emphasis on recovery models would be needed. Developing information that is "good enough" to guide the organization is still a critical issue for the VA.

E-health record and information system

"You can't do what we do without electronic medical records," observed the chief of staff. WRJ VAMC clinicians participated in a state-wide diabetic collaborative and it took only 10 minutes to identify all their diabetic patients, compared to other organizations for which the process has posed a major challenge. The e-records form an extensive database that can be mined for clinical comparisons. "We are a bit unusual here; we give out comparative information on a provider-specific basis to all physicians, with their names on," said the chief of staff, something that is not done uniformly across the VA or even across VISN 1. This includes detailed information about how physicians are doing on key measures such as HgA1c or lipid levels for their panels of patients. As one clinician remarked, "I like that kind of feedback … it's a real quantum leap."

Electronic medical records can also be adapted to improve care processes. For example, based on an idea from a national primary care consultant, the chief of staff plans to add a low density lipoprotein (LDL) algorithm with a list of steps and drugs and "one click to the doses." This innovation will encourage staff members to consider multi-therapy for such patients. The system supports WRJ VAMC's extensive use of clinical reminders and, while there is "some reminder fatigue," the chief of staff said, a review showed that they were all important, "so we kept them all."

Clinicians spoke favourably about WRJ VAMC's e-health record system: "It makes a big difference. ... It was such an incredible shift for me to be able to see all the meds a patient is on."

WRJ VAMC and Dartmouth Medical School: "A symbiotic relationship"

WRJ VAMC has ongoing affiliations with 25 to 35 academic organizations, although it can be argued that the influence of contacts with Dartmouth Medical School have been the most significant. The centre has benefited greatly from its relationships with members of Batalden's Healthcare Improvement Leadership Development group, several of whom are based at WRJ VAMC. "We have a symbiotic relationship with Dartmouth Medical School. They need us because we are their primary clinical site," De Gasta said. WRJ VAMC can focus more on teaching than is possible at Dartmouth Hitchcock Medical Center (DHMC) because the clinical productivity pressures may not be as great. (DHMC is the other major teaching hospital associated with Dartmouth Medical School.) A large number of WRJ VAMC medical staff members teach at Dartmouth.

Although it is a relatively small organization, WRJ VAMC hosts a number of national research initiatives. "We have to be innovative and creative," notes De Gasta. "That's why we have that group [of research and national centres leaders] – and it's like herding cats!" Researchers involved in the organization provide benefits because they are, in De Gasta's words, "questioners who throw bombs at the status quo." The research programs, which include the VA Outcomes Group Research Enhancement Award Program, the National Center for Post-Traumatic Stress Disorder and the field office of the VA's National Center for Patient Safety, have \$6.0 million annual funding from the VA and the National Institutes of Health. Clinical researchers based at the centre described the VA as a supportive place for clinicians who want to do research and for researchers who want to keep their hand in clinical work.

WRJ VAMC's symbiotic relationship with Dartmouth has produced some remarkable programs and initiatives, including the following:

The VA National Quality Scholars Program

Sponsored by the Office of Academic Affiliations, Department of Veterans Affairs (VA), the VA National Quality Scholars Fellowship Program (NQSFP) is a two-year post-residency QI training program developed and run by Dartmouth's Institute for Health

Policy and Clinical Practice. Two fellows at each of six sites across the US are linked electronically for academic and research efforts. Based at one of the six sites, fellows work with senior quality scholars (program directors) and faculty at their site and with the Institute's faculty leaders. The curriculum includes QI theory and research methods as well as completion and publication of clinical QI projects (Dartmouth College 2002b).

WRJ VAMC is the program's lead site. The centre's advanced clinic access in mental health is an example of an idea that began as a quality scholar's project and evolved into an award-winning redesign.

Advanced clinic access in mental health

By embracing an open-access approach and revamping its processes for patient referral, intake and assessment, the WRJ VAMC's mental health clinic has achieved impressive results. While clinic volumes have increased, the wait times to see a mental health specialist have dropped from 33 days to 16.9 *minutes*, and there are no longer any no-shows. The clinic, which opened in 2004, is located in a primary care clinic; primary care providers are thereby able to bring patients directly to the mental health clinic, with no bookings required. A clerk registers patients and they complete four assessment instruments using touch pads. The data are reviewed by a psychiatrist, the patients are screened to see if any basic tests have been missed (e.g., thyroid) and they have psychosocial interviews with therapists. Upon a patient's first visit, a treatment plan is initiated and, if necessary, a referral is made to the in-patient service.

This collaborative care clinic design is known nationwide as the "White River Model." It has won awards from the VA and the American Psychiatric Association.

VA National Center for Patient Safety field office

WRJ VAMC is a field site for the VA's highly regarded National Center for Patient Safety (NCPS), based in Ann Arbor, Michigan (US Department of Veterans Affairs 2007g). Root causes analysis (RCA) reports from all VHA facilities are forwarded to the NCPS database and are analyzed by a WRJ VAMC physician researcher who heads up the field office and his/her team. The team looks for trends and system vulnerabilities so that action can be taken to mitigate risks. Team members prepare reports and publish their research nationally.

Analyses have identified events that are rare on an institution-specific basis, yet show a pattern when aggregated in the database. For example, a series of near misses with pacemakers was identified across the US; patients were thereupon able to return to have the problem corrected. RCAs are time-consuming to perform, report and analyze, and there has been variation in reporting across the VHA. Because RCAs are valuable for learning, the VHA has implemented a new rule that each facility must annually do four individual RCAs and four aggregate reviews (e.g., of falls or medication errors).

WRJ VAMC is also the hub site for the new VA Interprofessional Fellowship Program in Patient Safety. This program will train two fellows in each of six sites across the US each year (US Department of Veterans Affairs 2006a.)

Leadership in an improvement culture

When listening to WRJ VAMC staff talk about their organization, interesting facets of the organizational culture become evident. In general, it appears to possess an informal, positive and collaborative interpersonal style, yet be driven when it comes to improvement and innovation. "The director is 'Gary'; his first name is known and used by everyone. We are very laid-back here. … The director is very engaged and interested in what the front line are doing," said the service line director. As an example of this, De Gasta has borrowed an approach from the Marriott corporation, making appointments with randomly selected front-line staff to spend time getting to know what's happening with them. In addition, the entire executive staff has adopted an open-door policy. At the same time, the billings manager commented that "WRJ has a type-A personality; lots of innovation going on."

Systematizing improvement and innovation required an attitudinal shift. "Paul Batalden asked us 'what did you have to unlearn to do Baldrige?' We had to stop being victims. Stop finding excuses," De Gasta remarked. As a humorous reminder, leaders imposed a requirement on themselves to pay a dollar penalty for negative comments: "You have to put a dollar in the pot [at meetings] if you make excuses about not meeting the measures!" De Gasta noted. The chief of staff, meanwhile, said, "I think it is important to break down your processes and understand the parts, but focusing only on negatives makes you think that you are doing really poorly. I tend to an appreciative inquiry approach." He explained how they do medical student reviews, discussing those who are doing poorly first, but ending with those who are doing really well. "I use it more informally; it's more of a psychology of trying to be more positive."

When asked whether the improvement focus would survive the impending turnover in senior leadership positions, a service line director responded, "Try and beat it out of us, good luck! It's part of who we are here … so embedded in what we do." "Quality improvement is pervasive around here; it's our culture," affirmed the chief of staff.

"We have a collaborative approach here, get the right people involved," but "it has been years of cycles of refinement to get to this point," observed a service line director. Collaboration includes the unions: "The unions are involved in everything," noted the union local president, a WRJ VAMC staff member who is a trained Carey Award examiner. He does presentations about the importance of union involvement in QI. "If you look at a sample of award-winning organizations, you would see that a key to success is strong labour-management relations," he continued. There are now measurable results included in the performance review process for staff, which creates a connection between the system's QI processes and the front-line staff.

A service line director observed,

> One of the challenges is to show front-line staff that the little process improvement project that they are doing contributes to the bigger picture. It may be partly a language issue; it's really an education process. The way we get staff engaged is to get them to understand that they can make changes at the lowest level and see results, to be able to see that immediate improvement. When staff say they have no time to participate I say you are already doing it, but not in a systematic way or documenting it, so you're not getting credit.

"You need to show staff that showcase of awards in the hall," said the union local president. Doing so, he claimed, symbolizes the cumulative accomplishment of all the front-line improvement efforts.

Training and education

Building improvement capacity requires ongoing education and skills training. VHA employees have extensive training and leadership development opportunities. Employee and leadership development is crucial for succession planning, because 60% of all managers are eligible to retire by 2008 and 70% of dental staff by 2009 (VISN 1 education services director).

Eight core competencies are expected of all VHA staff:

- Systems thinking
- Organizational stewardship
- Technical competency
- Service
- Interpersonal effectiveness
- Creative thinking
- Flexibility/adaptability
- Personal mastery

These national expectations are used to frame all training efforts, which also include mandatory training in organizational ethics, cyber security and information security in research. WRJ VAMC has developed a diagram and explanatory table (see Figure 6) documenting its "corporate DNA" to show staff members how the individual core competencies relate to organizational competencies.

Figure 6. "What Makes WRJ Excellent: Our Corporate DNA"

<table>
<tr><th>Critical Success Factors
"Those capabilities and resources that absolutely have to be in place if you want to succeed over the long haul."</th><th>Strategic Theme</th><th>Individual (HPDM) Core Competencies</th><th>Organizational Core Competencies
"What are the most important capabilities and resources that 'create' the marketplace advantages."</th><th>Marketplace Competitive Advantages
"What are the most important things we do that consistently meet or exceed the marketplace customer expectations or 'competitors' performance."</th></tr>
<tr><td>• Safe, competent care for the veteran population throughout the continuum</td><td>• Excellence in Clinical Care and Scholarship</td><td rowspan="4">• Creative Thinking
• Customer Service
• Flexibility
• Interpersonal Effectiveness
• Organizational Stewardship
• Personal Mastery
• Systems Thinking
• Technical Skills</td><td>• Clinical Expertise (chronic disease management, mental health, patient safety, non-institutional care)
• Health Care Teaching and Research</td><td>• Excellent Clinical Quality Outcomes
• Outstanding Patient and other Stakeholder Satisfaction
• Clinical Affiliations
• National Role Model Electronic Medical Record</td></tr>
<tr><td>• Fiscal Solvency</td><td>• Maximizing Financial Resources</td><td>• Cost Savings (bulk purchasing, product standardization)
• Revenue Generation (MCCF, Sharing Agreements)</td><td>• Mitigation of out-of-pocket expenses for patients</td></tr>
<tr><td>• Workforce Engagement</td><td>• Preserving & Promoting a Healthy Workforce & Work Environment</td><td>• Federal Employment Package
• Provision of a safe stable work environment (strong Union partnership; family/group culture; research & education opportunities)</td><td>• Noble Mission
• Substantial employee satisfaction and support</td></tr>
<tr><td>• VHA Mission and Vision
• WRJ Credo</td><td>• Community Stewardship</td><td>• Education and Research
• Visionary Leadership
• Entrepreneurial/Innovative Culture
• Information Technology</td><td>• Contributions to community health and body of knowledge
• Performance Excellence Role Model
• World-class information systems</td></tr>
</table>

Source: Quality manager, WRJ VAMC, on September 25, 2007. Used by permission.

Although there are national QI education programs available (e.g., Quality 101 and a coaches college), as well as network- and facility-specific training opportunities, improvement training is not standardized across the facilities. VISN 1 network director Chirico-Post cautioned, "You have to be careful about the ice cream flavour of the month." VISN 1's quality management officer added, "We impart the concepts of Lean and Six Sigma, but without the language. All service line directors and many managers have had advanced clinic access training based on IHI's program. The network's education services department has given facilitator training for years, with some overlap between facilitation and improvement tools.

WRJ VAMC leaders have emphasized the importance of continuing education and training to support improvement efforts within their strategic frameworks. According to one service line director, "Senior leaders saw value in training as a Carey examiner, to learn about the Baldrige criteria and process improvement. Now that lots of leadership positions are trained we are starting with the staff." Within the centre, the Future Emerging Leaders (FUEL) program curriculum also includes the Carey/Baldrige criteria and process improvement.

Continuing challenges: Balancing improvement with accountability and compliance in a shifting – and political – environment

VISN 1 has made significant efforts to standardize care processes and performance measurement in order to become a high-performing system. Enabled by the VHA's electronic health records system, the network has implemented numerous CPGs backed by electronic reminders. Processes are monitored through rigorous review of performance measures in quarterly scorecards and reports. Teams from the facilities participating in numerous improvement collaboratives have made gains in patients' access to care, patient safety and preventive measures in primary care.

VISN 1 and its facilities, however, face continuing challenges in their improvement efforts. These challenges arise from various factors:

- Operating in the context of a large, complex national government agency
- A detailed accountability framework
- A shifting patient care environment, including the pressures created by a growing number of veterans from the conflicts in Iraq and Afghanistan

Government rules and relationships

Being part of an immense government bureaucracy entails balancing central "rules" with local autonomy. VISN 1's annual budget is $1.5 billion, yet the network director is accountable to a national-level administrator for $1,000 allocated for training for four new positions.

Relationships with various levels of elected members of government also must be managed. "Congress really are friends of the vets and want to do what's best for them," Chirico-Post noted. As a local example, in this highly politicized environment congressional members (as well as New Hampshire's governor) are considered to be WRJ VAMC stakeholders, and that organization's senior leaders conduct quarterly briefing meetings with them to discuss issues facing the medical centre. Equipment and program placement can be deeply political decisions because congressional members favour local facilities in the areas that they represent.

Budget appropriations can also be affected by issues that reach the national press. The highly publicized problems at the army's Walter Reed Army Medical Center, for example, have brought money from Congress for infrastructural improvements. In contrast to hiring freezes and deficits with which the medical centres have had to deal, they are now faced with having to decide quickly how to spend the unexpected funds, but with restrictions on how the money may be used.

With changes in national policy decisions, benefits entitlement and coverage of particular veteran groups have often tended to transform over the years. These shifts have had consequences for VISN 1's planning and care delivery. For example, since entitlement to drug benefits was opened to all veterans, many patients have opted to get their medications from the VHA system; these same people, however, also seek care outside the system. Approximately 40% of VHA patients are co-managed with private sector providers, from whom they may receive various high-tech procedures. This situation can create safety issues related to medication monitoring and adjustment, for example, when veterans get their post-transplant drugs from the VHA yet their transplant care is delivered elsewhere.

"What is critical to acknowledge is that we operate in a political environment; we have to sing the political song," says De Gasta. An advantage of being part of the network is that while the VISN 1 is accountable for local medical centres' performance, it also recognizes the unique identities of each. The network acts as a buffer between the national level and the local organizations, allowing some latitude for local initiatives and innovation. While all VA medical centres are accountable for their performance on common measures, WRJ VAMC's smaller size and location may also make it easier for it to be something of a maverick. "White River Junction is little enough that they can permit more flexibility compared to larger centres; to let White River Junction run on a longer leash is less risky," Batalden suggested.[1] De Gasta also described his role as a senior leader as being, in part, to protect staff members and help them make sense of national initiatives and changes. Indicative of the frequency of changes his organization confronts, De Gasta commented, "I have a magnetic organization chart board so it can be changed each week instead of paying $400 each time to reprint it when the government changes things!"

Standardization and performance measurement – improvement or compliance?

Across VISN 1 there has been strong emphasis on standardization – of equipment, processes and procedures. However, Chirico-Post noted that this is also a continuing challenge: "How to get what is left in those facilities to a standardized approach?" She also mused about the limitations of performance measurement and the difficulty of knowing how well the network's eight facilities execute care. Because the spinal cord program is so focused, there is relatively good information about how well it is performing; however, in some other service lines (e.g., geriatrics) the measures are not so clear. Despite the emphasis on uniform performance measurement and standardization both nationally and within VISN 1, there are still variations in processes, structures and cultures across its constituent organizations. "If you've seen one network, you've seen one network," Chirico-Post noted.

The strong pressure to meet performance measure targets can stimulate compliance lectures as well as improvement activities. Several VISN 1 staff members commented that preoccupation with the focused set of measures can distract attention from other important issues. A number also said that it can be difficult to keep up with the moving targets.

Aging and decreasing patient population

VISN 1 and its medical centres face numerous pressures in a changing landscape. Between 2007 and 2013, the number of veterans over age 85 in VISN 1 is projected to increase by 47%, while the overall number of veterans in New England is projected to decrease by 42% by 2023 (VA New England Healthcare System 2006c). An aging population requires more intensive and costly services, which increase pressure on the system. WRJ VAMC also faces resource challenges; for example, transportation issues are harder to resolve because it is a rural centre. De Gasta asserted, "The Kizer model assumed there would be cost savings in the shift from acute to primary care, but the resources are not there. We still have to deliver specialty and acute care and we are see-

[1] After reviewing the case study, VHA officials noted that, while each facility has a unique identity, all its centres are accountable and all must comply with required rules, regulations, directives, guidance and standardization.

ing twice as many patients now." At the same time, the declining population of veterans has prompted discussions about the very future of the VHA system.

Leadership and staff turnover

VISN 1's organizations have benefited from stability and long tenure of leadership positions; however, a number of staff members are eligible to retire in the short term. Succession planning and ensuring that new leaders are developing in the ranks have been intensifying as network priorities. WRJ VAMC's chief of staff noted, for instance, "Normally we've had very little turnover, but people with long institutional memory are retiring." While recruitment may be challenging, WRJ VAMC has been successful in certain areas; for instance, in attracting primary care physicians.

The turnover of leaders and staff will test both VISN 1 generally and WRJ VAMC in particular (Chirico-Post retired in March 2008 and De Gasta retired at the end of 2007). Has the network's improvement culture permeated its organizations or will the long institutional memory leave with key individuals?

In little more than a decade, the VHA has been transformed from an organization under fire for deficiencies in the quality and safety of its care to a high-performing organization that has demonstrated better outcomes than those delivered in non-VA facilities. These achievements commenced with policy initiatives that shifted the VA away from its focus on in-patient care in largely independent facilities with limited accountability for results. The new VA became a results-focused system that has made access to care a priority and that has integrated services across the continuum. The challenges to maintaining improvement in this highly complex service delivery system will require continued strong leadership.

References

Baldrige National Quality Program. 2007. National Institute of Standards and Technology. Gaithersburg, MD: Author. Retrieved November 4, 2007. <http://baldrige.nist.gov/>

Batalden, P.B. and J.J. Mohr. 1997. "Building Knowledge of Healthcare as a System." *Quality Management in Health Care* 5(3): 1–12.

Dartmouth College. 2002a. *Health Care Improvement Leadership Development.* Hanover, NH: Author. Retrieved October 7, 2007. <http://www.dartmouth.edu/~cecs/hcild/hcild.html>

Dartmouth College. 2002b. *VA National Quality Scholars Program.* Hanover, NH: Author. Retrieved October 7, 2007. <http://www.dartmouth.edu/~cecs/fellowships/vaqs.html>

Institute for Healthcare Improvement. nd. *Reducing Waiting Times: Veterans Health Administration.* Boston: Author. Retrieved October 8, 2007. <http://www.ihi.org/IHI/Topics/OfficePractices/Access/ImprovementStories/ReducingWaitingTimesVeteransHealthAdministration.htm>

Jha, A.K., J.B. Perlin, K.W. Kizer and R.A. Dudley. 2003. "Effect of Transformation of the Veterans Affairs Health Care System on the Quality of Care." *New England Journal of Medicine* 348: 2218–2227.

Kizer, K.W. 1995. *Vision for Change: A Plan to Restructure the Veterans Health Administration.* Washington, DC: US Department of Veterans Affairs. Retrieved October 20, 2007. <http://www1.va.gov/vhareorg/VISION/2CHAP1.pdf>

Kizer, K.W. 1996. *Prescription for Change: The Guiding Principles and Strategic Objectives Underlying the Transformation of the Veterans Healthcare System.* Washington, DC: US Department of Veterans Affairs. Retrieved October 20, 2007. <http://www1.va.gov/vhareorg/rxweb.pdf>

Kizer, K.W., J.G. Demakis and J. R. Feussner. 2000. "Reinventing VA Health Care: Systematizing Quality Improvement and Quality Innovation." *Medical Care* 38(6): I7–I16.

Parlier, R.L. 2003. *Improvement Report: Advanced Clinic Access Initiative.* Boston: Institute for Healthcare Improvement. Retrieved October 8, 2007. <http://www.ihi.org/IHI/Topics/OfficePractices/Access/ImprovementStories/MemberReportAdvancedClinicAccessInitiative.htm>

US Department of Veterans Affairs. 2001. *Veterans Health Administration. VHA Directive 2001-015, External Peer Review Program.* Washington, DC: Author. Retrieved October 20, 2007. <http://www1.va.gov/vhapublications/ViewPublication.asp?pub_ID=103>

US Department of Veterans Affairs. 2006a. *Office of Academic Affiliations. VA Interprofessional Fellowship Program in Patient Safety.* Washington, DC: Author. Retrieved October 8, 2007. <http://www.va.gov/oaa/specialfellows/programs/SF_patient_safety.asp?p=17>

US Department of Veterans Affairs. 2006b. *VISN 1 Announces Kizer Award Grants Selected for Funding.* Washington, DC: Author. Retrieved October 17, 2007. <http://www.va.gov/VISN1/news/docs/NewsGlance06_11.asp>

US Department of Veterans Affairs. 2006c. *VA Office of Policy and Planning. Desk Guides, Training, and Technical Assistance. Robert W. Carey Performance Excellence Award. Judge's Desk Guide.* Washington, DC: Author. Retrieved November 4, 2007. <http://www1.va.gov/op3/page.cfm?pg=46>

US Department of Veterans Affairs. 2006d. *Office of Quality and Performance. VA/DOD Clinical Practice Guidelines.* Washington, DC: Author. Retrieved October 20, 2007. <http://www.oqp.med.va.gov/cpg/cpg.htm>

US Department of Veterans Affairs. 2006e. *VA VistA Innovations Award.* Washington, DC: Author. Retrieved October 10, 2007. <http://www.innovations.va.gov/>

US Department of Veterans Affairs. 2006f. *VistA, Winner of the 2006 Innovations in American Government Award.* Washington, DC: Author. Retrieved October 8, 2007. <http://www.innovations.va.gov/innovations/docs/InnovationsVistAInfoPackage.pdf>

US Department of Veterans Affairs. 2007a. *VA New England Healthcare System. About Us.* Washington, DC: Author. Retrieved October 8, 2007. <http://www.visn1.med.va.gov/network/index.asp>

US Department of Veterans Affairs. 2007b. *VA New England Healthcare System. Mission, Vision, and Values.* Washington, DC: Author. Retrieved October 8, 2007. <http://www.visn1.med.va.gov/network/mission.asp>

US Department of Veterans Affairs. 2007c. *VA New England Healthcare System. Service Lines.* Washington, DC: Author. Retrieved October 7, 2007. <http://www.visn1.med.va.gov/service-lines/>

US Department of Veterans Affairs. 2007d. *Office of Quality and Performance. About Us.* Washington, DC: Author. Retrieved October 20, 2007. <http://www.oqp.med.va.gov/general/about_us.asp>

US Department of Veterans Affairs. 2007e. *VA Boston Healthcare System.* Washington, DC: Author. Retrieved October 7, 2007. <http://www.boston.va.gov/>

US Department of Veterans Affairs. 2007f. *VAMC White River Junction, VT.* Washington, DC: Author. Retrieved October 8, 2007. <http://www.whiteriver.va.gov/about/index.asp>

US Department of Veterans Affairs. 2007g. *VA National Center for Patient Safety.* Washington, DC: Author. Retrieved October 7, 2007. <http://www.va.gov/NCPS/>

VA Medical Center White River Junction. 2007. *Malcolm Baldrige Award Application.* White River Junction, VT: Author. (Document provided by WRJMC staff on September 12, 2007.)

VA New England Healthcare System. 2006a. *Annual Report 2006.* Bedford, MA: Author. Document provided by VISN 1 headquarters staff on September 11, 2007.

VA New England Healthcare System. 2006b. *Care Coordination Home Telehealth Program: Performance Improvement Utilization Report Presented August 2006, OCC Conditions of Participation Review.* Bedford, MA: Author. PowerPoint slides provided by program manager on September 12, 2007.

VA New England Healthcare System. 2006c. *Stage 2: Strategic Plan for FY 2006-2010.* Bedford, MA: Author. Document provided by VISN 1 headquarters staff on September 11, 2007.

VA New England Healthcare System. 2007. *The Secretary's Robert W. Carey Performance Excellence Awards. 2007 Application.* Bedford, MA: Author. Document provided by VISN 1 headquarters staff on September 11, 2007.

Appendix A. VISN 1 Patient wait times for clinic appointments – examples of measures and results

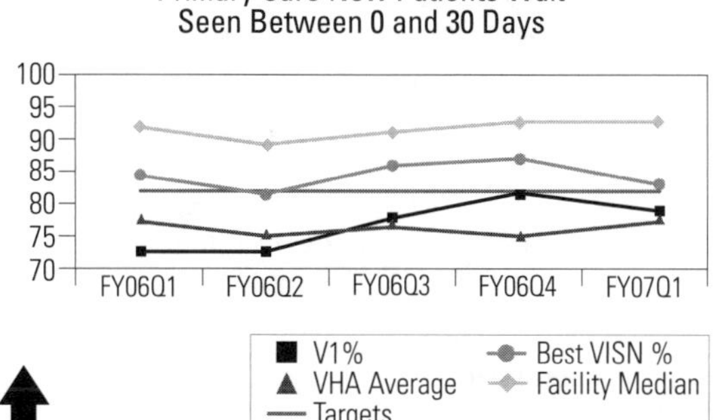

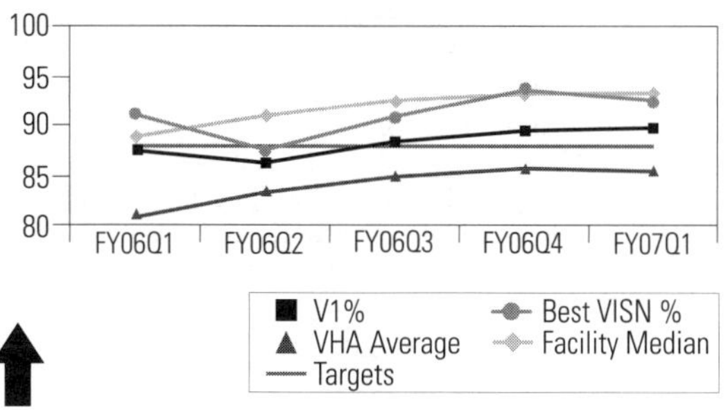

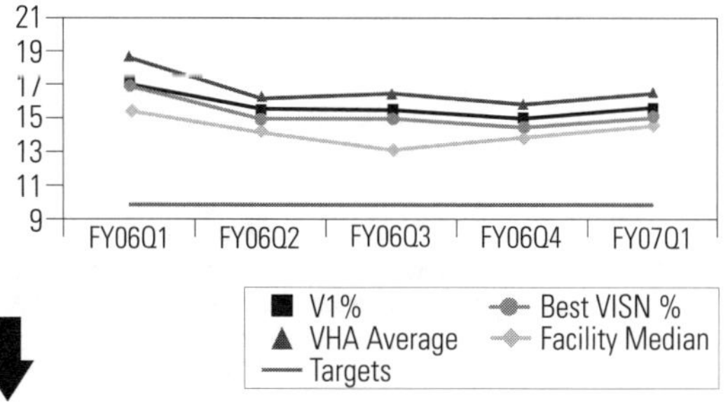

Source: VA New England Healthcare System (2007). Used by permission.

Appendix B. VISN 1 performance measures – 2007

(Note: "Missed Opportunities" = missed appointments)

Business Office:	Reducing AR > 90 Days old (lower better) Financial Index Revenue - Collections % of Goal
Geriatrics and Extended Care:	Non-institutionalized Care Target ADC Non-institutionalized Care Telehealth Census
Local Management:	SHEP Satisfaction Overall - Outpatient SHEP Satisfaction Overall - Inpatient Waiting Times - Provider C&P Exam Report Quality Transition Coordination - OEF/OIF Contacts HR - Work Force Planning
Mental Health:	Homeless Contact access to MH/SUD Tobacco Cessation Offered Meds Homeless Program access to Eval & Mgmt SMI - MHICM Capacity Homeless Program F/u in MH/SUD CBOC - % MH specialty access Waiting Times - Established Patients - Mental Health Homeless Program access to MH/SUD Waiting Times - New Patients - Mental Health Substance Use Disorder - Continuity of Care Missed Opportunities - Mental Health (Lower Better) New DX of Depression - Medication Coverage Tob - Used Tobacco past 12 mos (Lower Better) New DX of Depression - Provider Follow-up Tobacco Counseling w/ Referral
Primary Care:	Tobacco Cessation Offered Meds DM - BP </= 140/90 Cervical CA Screening IHD - LDL-C<100 & Full Lipid Profile last 2 yrs SHEP Wait Time - New Patients Perceptions SHEP Wait Time - Established Patients Perceptions Waiting Times - Established Patients - Primary Care Colon CA Screening IHD - LDL-C >/= 120 (Lower Better) DM-BP>/=160/100 not done (Lower Better) DM - LDL-C < 120 & Full Lipid Profile in 2 years HTN - BP </= 140/90 Breast CA Screening Missed Opportunities - Primary Care (Lower Better) HTN-BP>/=160/100 or not done (Lower Better) Tob - Used Tobacco past 12 mos (Lower Better) Waiting Times - New Patients - Primary Care HTN - Mono-therapy receiving thiazide HTN - Multi-therapy receiving thiazide Tobacco Counseling w/ Referral Influenza Immunization Alcohol Screen - AUDIT-C with doc responses PTSD Screen - with doc responses MDD Screen - PH-Q2 - with doc responses

Sensory and Physical Rehabilitation:	Waiting Times - Established Patients - Audiology Missed Opportunities - Audiology (Lower Better) Waiting Times - New Patients - Audiology
Specialty and Acute Care:	Surg Pts w/ Appropriate Pre-op Hair Removal Waiting Times - New Patients - Orthopedic Resident Supervision - Timely Admit Note - Surg Cardiac-controlled serum glucose-POD1 & POD2 SIP - Correct antibiotic given Waiting Times - Established Patients - Eye Care Waiting Times - Established Patients - Orthopedic Waiting Times - Established Patients - Podiatry IP HF - Rec Discharge Instructions (JCAHO Core) Prophylactic antibiotic Began Timely Waiting Times - New Patients - Podiatry Waiting Times - Established Patients - Dermatology Waiting Times - Established Patients - Urology Missed Opportunities - Dermatology (Lower Better) SIP - Prophylactic Antibiotic Discontinued Timely Waiting Times - Established Patients - GI ACS - LDL Cholesterol Assessment Missed Opportunities - Eye Care (Lower Better) Missed Opportunities - Orthopedic (Lower Better) Missed Opportunities - Podiatry (Lower Better) ACS - Cardiology involvement in 24 hrs ACS - Troponin returned in 60 min of order PN - Blood Cultures before antibiotic dose Waiting Times - Established Patients - Cardiology Waiting Times - New Patients - Cardiology Missed Opportunities - Urology (Lower Better) PN - Antibiotic first dose in 4 hours of Arrival Radiology Reports Verified in 2 Days Waiting Times - New Patients - GI Missed Opportunities - Cardiology (Lower Better) Missed Opportunities - GI (Lower Better) ACS - ECG in 10 min of arrival or 15 min prior. Waiting Times - New Patients - Dermatology Waiting Times - New Patients - Eye Care Waiting Times - New Patients - Urology Colorectal-Post-op Normothermia in 10 min ACS - LDL Lipid Lowering Therapy at Discharge ACS - Reperfusion intervention as Appropriate ACS - Reperfusion - PCI in 90 min. ACS - Reperfusion Thrombolytic Rx in 30 min.
Spinal Cord Injury:	Pneumococcal Immunization Tob - Used Tobacco in past 12 mos (Lower Better) DM - BP </= 140/90 Tobacco Cessation Offered Meds DM-BP>/=160/100 not done (Lower Better) DM - LDL-C < 120 & Full Lipid Profile in 2 years DM - Retinal Eye Exam Tobacco Counseling w/ Referral Influenza Immunization

Source: VISN 1 headquarters staff on September 11, 2007. Used by permission.

Appendix C. VISN 1 examples of results for clinical performance measures

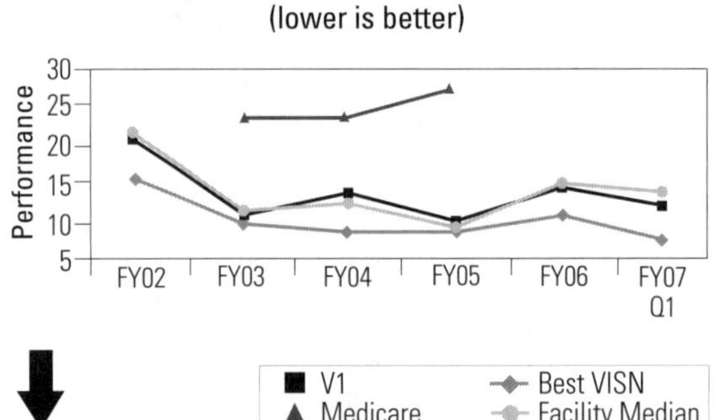

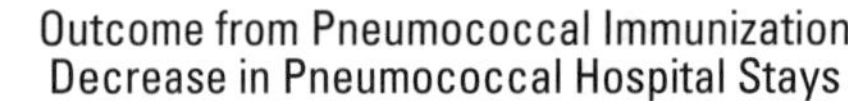

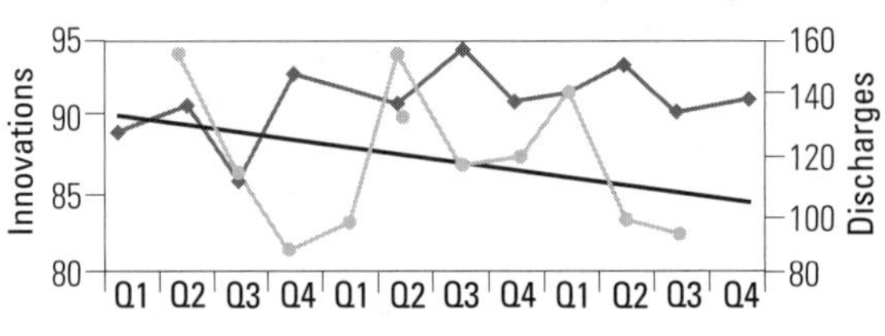

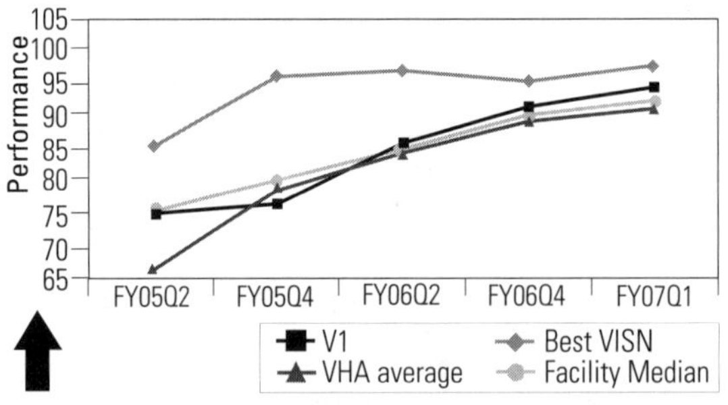

Source: VA New England Healthcare System (2007). Used by permission.

Appendix D. VHA Office of Quality and Performance – April 2001

The mission of the Office of Quality and Performance (OQP) is to support clinicians, managers and employees in providing the highest quality of care for veterans. Specific areas of service include:

- Performance Measurement Program (all "Value-Domains")
  - Objectives
    - Assess the process and outcomes of care provided to patients
    - Provide an accountability framework for assessing the performance of the leaders, clinicians and managers in VHA
    - Link VA/VHA strategies with accountability measures to support improvement
  - Data Sources
    - Large administrative data-set analysis (links with HCFA)
    - Massive chart review (EPRP)
- Clinical Practice Guideline Development
  - To improve care by reducing variation in practice and systematizing "best practices"
- Accreditation (JCAHO, CARF, NCQA)
  - Objective: To provide external validation of quality systems
- Credentialing (VetPro)
  - Objective: To verify that practitioners' training and certification is consistent with the defined requirements of their clinical appointments, that their licensure is current and unrestricted and that any history of adverse judgments can be identified for further review, thereby improving patient safety
- Patient Satisfaction (Durham)
  - Objective: To understand patient perceptions with respect to Veteran Service Standard (VSS) commitments in the areas of access, coordination, courtesy, education, emotional support, involvement of family and friends, physical comfort, patient preference, transition, continuity, pharmacy and specialist care
  - Patient satisfaction "computers" to support employees
- Functional Status
  - Objective: To assess and improve the functional status of veterans
- Performance Analysis Center for Excellence (PACE)
  - Objective: To provide data feedback, satisfaction surveying and other work, but expanding existing functions to emphasize the provision of clinically appropriate and operationally sensitive data interpretation that documents performance, describes effective approaches to improvement opportunities and provides guidance that supports efficient implementation of those approaches
- Internal Baldrige-based Awards Programs with USH, VHA, PQA

  - Objective: Identify unmet patient needs and improve the organization to better address those needs; identify gaps in supporting best outcomes
- Linkages with Quality Scholars Program
- Linkages with National Center for Patient Safety
- Linkages with HSR&D (QUERI); co-funds translation health systems research
- External interfaces related to Quality (e.g., QuIC, NCQA, NQF)

Source: US Department of Veterans Affairs (2007a). Used by permission.

Appendix E. VA Boston Healthcare System nursing report card measures

Restraints:	% restraint free rate
Height and weight:	% height in VS package % weight in VS package on admission/monthly
Pain:	% pain score in VS package % pain qualified as acceptable or unacceptable % unacceptable pain with detailed assessment
PRN effectiveness:	% PRN effectiveness % pain PRN effectiveness documented w/in 30-240 minutes % pain PRN effectiveness documented w/acceptability
Documentation:	% Morse tallied % at risk for fall with plan % Braden tallied % at risk for breakdown with plan % completed Audit-C in admission assessment (AC & MH) % completed monthly summary note (MH) % competed safety intervention section on admission assessment (MH)
Verification of orders:	% orders verified by RN % chart reviewed
Incidence:	# medication errors Assault rate Fall rate Fall w/injury rate # hospital-acquired pressure ulcers

Source: Document provided by associate director of nursing, VA Boston Healthcare System, on September 10, 2007. Used by permission.

Appendix F. Examples of other improvement initiatives at WRJ VAMC

Care Coordination Home Telehealth program

In 2005 WRJ VAMC began a home telehealth monitoring program for heart failure patients who used text messaging to communicate daily with specialized care coordinators. The program now uses a mix of technology – including videophones and "health buddies" (a device programmed with a condition-specific dialogue that prompts patients to enter data) – to allow patients to send in clinical information and status updates. Care coordinators review the updates, discuss care issues with the patients and consult with other providers as needed. About 100 patients participate in the program, including patients with diabetes, hepatitis C, hypertension and spinal cord injuries, as well as those in palliative care. A six-month pre- and post-implementation program review showed that ED visits and in-patient admissions were 25% and 35% lower for this population and that 30-day readmission rates had dropped by 67% (VA New England Healthcare System 2006b).

Stop Workforce Accidents Team (SWAT)

In addition to clinical improvements, WRJ VAMC is participating in a national VHA initiative to develop minimal-manual lift environments to avoid injuries to staff members and patients. An interdisciplinary SWAT team has implemented ergonomic technologies and practices, as well as after-action reviews of accidents and near-miss reviews. As a result, in 2006–2007 WRJ VAMC had only one minor injury reported and no work-days lost to injuries experienced while handling patients. "It just snowballed; staff got involved because of positive results" (SWAT team leader).

Commentary: Veterans Affairs New England Healthcare System (VISN 1)

David Levine, President and Chief Executive Officer
Montreal Health and Social Service Agency

Introduction

As president and chief executive officer of the Montreal Health and Social Service Agency (the agency), I am responsible for ensuring that health and social services on the island of Montreal are safe, efficient and meet the needs of the population. Quebec's minister of health and social services has charged me with planning healthcare services, signing performance contracts with all centres that receive funding from the agency and ensuring that performance targets are met. Many of my colleagues in similar positions across Canada have the same mandate, and some are responsible for the direct operations of their organizations.

My main approach to improving performance involves developing integrated networks. I was therefore very interested to read about the success of the Veterans Affairs New England Healthcare System (VISN 1). I have reviewed the case study from the point of view of a health systems manager and I have considered how VISN 1's experience can be adapted to the Quebec and Canadian contexts.

In 2005, the Quebec government established 12 integrated health services networks to serve Montreal's 1.8 million people. Prior to these mergers, each institution had a specific mandate, was preoccupied with its own growth and functioned largely in a silo. Each of the new networks was formed through the merger of a community hospital, rehabilitation centre, long-term care centres, home care organizations and primary care institutions into a new body responsible for the care of the population in a designated area. The networks have three principal objectives:

- To develop multidisciplinary primary care teams
- To monitor and improve the health of their populations
- To ensure timely access to care

The first two years following the mergers were mainly dedicated to creating the new institutions' administrative and organizational structures and protocols. The focus now is on the implementation of integrated services along clinical lines. The challenges facing this task are enormous because professionals are being asked to work in ways that differ markedly from how they have performed their roles for most of their careers.

The VISN 1 example allows us to look at 10 years of experience and at what has worked and not worked in New England. It is important to take into account the differences between our jurisdictions' care models in order to understand more clearly what can be applied in the Quebec and Canadian contexts.

Developing service lines

The organization of services along clinical service lines and support service lines is an excellent approach to managed care that can ensure the smooth, continuous flow of patients through a healthcare system. Optimal patient flow can be achieved more easily in an integrated model in which all services fall under one central authority. It is not impossible when there is a multitude of different providers, but certainly it is far more difficult. The key elements of standardization and systemization are much more difficult to implement in a non-integrated network. In an integrated network, meanwhile, the use of clinical protocols is simplified and it is much easier to get consensus among physicians in the same organization.

One major distinction must be made between VISN 1 and the Canadian system. In Canada almost all physicians are not employees of their organizations. They are paid by government bodies on a fee-for-service basis and have privileges to work in their various institutions. Primary care physicians do not belong to any institutions and they work out of private offices on a fee-for-service basis. The greatest challenges facing Canada's healthcare system are how to connect the primary care physicians with the rest of the system and how to develop multidisciplinary primary care teams that collaborate with other providers in a seamless care process.

Performance measurement and accountability

The performance contract used in VISN 1 as a basis for measuring and tracking patient care and each organization's clinical and administrative performance has clearly been demonstrated as the tool of choice in an integrated network. VISN 1's commitment to performance measurement and the strong support from all levels of management are essential to implementation and adherence both by clinicians and staff members.

Once again, the fact that Canadian physicians are independent, autonomous professionals adds many challenges to developing standardized clinical performance measures. There is a growing consensus that the increasing availability of clinical data will make it easier to track the provision of care and its outcomes. As a result, it stands to reason that clinicians will be drawn to a more evidence-based approach and to using more standardized protocols.

VISN 1's development of standardized staffing and productivity models for physicians has had a positive impact on that network's physicians and should be introduced into the Canadian system. In Montreal we are setting up network clinics and must decide on panel size and physician support so that appropriate funding can be provided to the primary care teams. This approach has already produced some positive results; for instance, 40 clinics have signed contracts with the island's 12 local networks and are providing greater accessibility as well as more continuous care. Each clinic has also been provided with support resources and at least two nurses to begin helping physicians manage their patients.

Electronic medical records

VISN 1's implementation over a 10-year period of a home-grown electronic medical record system has been a key ingredient in the network's success. The Canadian system is certainly lagging behind in this area. However, a combined federal and provincial effort has recently been set in motion aimed at creating the data warehouse necessary to provide clinicians throughout regions and provinces with the data they need to treat their patients. Organizing the electronic medical records at the local institutional level has been left to each province or region to implement.

Realizing the importance of a more uniform and standardized approach in Montreal, the 12 CEOs and the non-integrated teaching hospitals decided to piggyback on the electronic record that the city's two major teaching hospitals chose for their institutions. This approach means that all physicians and other professionals in their institutions or private offices will eventually be using the same software to generate and maintain their patients' medical records. This standardization will allow for much easier transfer of patient data and offer a common way of viewing records and reading files.

Performance measurement at the national level

The Veterans Health Administration (VHA) has developed nationwide standards. Each of the system's networks, however, has the opportunity to develop its own strategies and implementation processes.

In Canada the development of sets of performance measures, either clinical or administrative, should be mandated to a national organization. The measures should then be validated and provided to the provinces and territories for adaptation to each jurisdiction's unique needs. The Canadian Institute for Health Information (CIHI) would be an ideal organization for carrying out this mandate because the agency already collects healthcare data across the country. VISN 1's experience has shown that performance comparison and transparency are critical for driving change. CIHI has the knowledge and credibility in Canada to carry out this vital work.

Levers of change and the importance of leadership in a performance culture

The VA Boston Healthcare System (VA Boston) realized that money was not the only – and in most cases, not the most important – lever for ensuring high-quality performance. Culture and pride in performing well became the key catalysts for change.

VA Boston's success demonstrates that implementing change is crucial to improving performance. How should we implement such cultural changes in the Canadian context? The use of clinical care indicators and individual physician and team performance have been shown to be the most effective drivers of change. Leadership, especially medical leadership, is a factor of prime consideration, and developing clinical leadership must be part of the process.

VA Boston's experience shows that ongoing training of service chiefs and senior leaders supports cultural change and that the involvement of organizations in the Institute for Healthcare Improvement (IHI) Breakthrough Series provides the structures and processes to bring about positive change. Improving access to primary or specialized care, managing emergency departments more efficiently and effectively, redesigning the use of operating rooms and implementing managed care models are all helped by implementing processes that have demonstrated positive results. Establishing a Canadian collaborative in a more structured form than is presently the case could greatly assist our emerging networks.

The case study documenting VISN 1's transformation illuminates the importance of the actors involved – in particular, their leadership, insight and commitment to a culture of performance. This is the same message that emerges from a study of the Kaiser managed care model in California. The need to be the best and to be recognized as the leader in a field is a powerful driver in cultural change. The question, therefore, is how to instill the desire to be the best.

First, as VISN 1's experience suggests, it is important to stop finding excuses. This involves an attitude change that is led by people who believe in themselves and their capabilities – people who are driven to excellence because they believe excellence is possible. Leaders must be able to show this possibility to their teams through their personal beliefs, knowledge and commitment to the services being offered.

Leaders must infuse throughout their organizations the belief that "We sell health and ours is the best product on the market." It's the Ken Kizer in each of us that we need to bring out if we want to introduce a high-performing culture. Systematized processes, along with clear, measurable goals and rigorous feedback processes are essential tools; however, their users must also be believers. In Montreal, as in much of the rest of Canada, we are now at the interface between the science and art of management. I am convinced that the art must come first.

Conclusion

The VISN 1 case study offers an excellent description of what was done in the VA model of healthcare and allows us to glimpse some of the strategies we can adopt in the Canadian healthcare system. I have highlighted some of the differences between the two systems, but the essential issues that led to the success of the VA model are highly pertinent to our own experience. Standardizing processes and performance measurement are the key ingredients to creating a high-performing system. It takes, however, the right leadership to make it happen.

4

Jönköping County Council

Småland, Sweden

Highlights of recent achievements

"Jönköping County opens the minds of their peers and offers hope, encouragement, and new ideas. Their superb teamwork and organization have helped us all to think more clearly and to act more boldly."

– Donald Berwick (quoted in Institute for Healthcare Improvement nd a)

For the past decade Jönköping County Council – a county council in southern Sweden serving a population of less than 340,000 – has gained national and international recognition for making and sustaining large-scale improvements in healthcare. For many international leaders in the field of quality improvement, Jönköping exemplifies the innovation, strong and stable performance and social values on which Swedish healthcare was founded, and provides a model of healthcare system transformation that ranks among the best in the world. While Jönköping was a well-kept secret for some time, it has become a popular site to visit for healthcare leaders eager to learn more.

Figure 1 shows that compared to the other 20 county councils in Sweden, Jönköping achieves the best overall ranking on indicators across Sweden's six goals for quality:

efficiency, timeliness, safety, patient centredness, equity and effectiveness (Jönköping County Council 2005).

Figure 1. Summary of county councils' performance

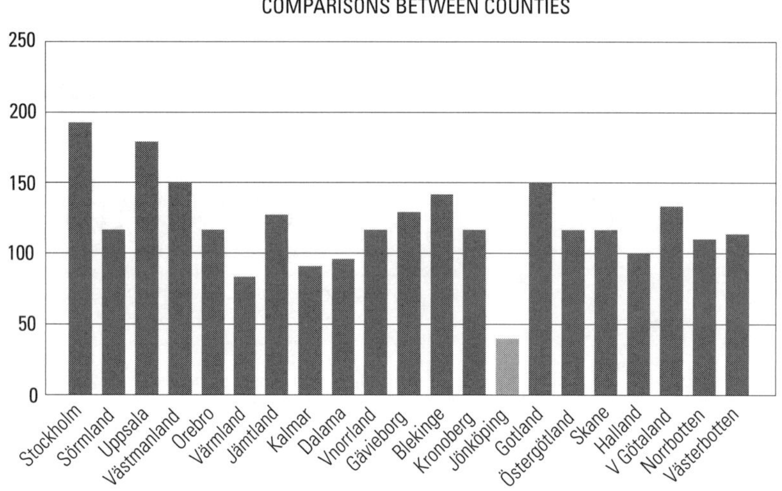

A. Cost for healthcare, excluding dental, per inhabitant, 2003
B. The relationship between real cost for healthcare and cost according to the Swedish adjustment system (healthcare model and countryside) indexed per inhabitant (average = 100)
C. Consumed care visits per 1000 inhabitants – real value and standardized by age
D. Number of physicians' appointments, per inhabitant, 2003
E. Appointments at other providers of care, excluding doctors, per inhabitant, 2003
F. Share of patients who have been admitted within 7 days, Oct., 2004
G. Case mix – 2003 – consumption
H. Share of caesarean sections per all delivering women, 2003
I. Share of patients, affected by stroke, who feel their health is bad or really bad, 3 months after being ill, 2003
J. Share of patients, affected by stroke, who often or constantly feel depressed, 2003
K. Share of patients readmitted into inpatient care, 2003 and 2002

Points (Note: Points assigned based on A to K criteria. Lower score = Better performance)

Used by permission.

Jönköping has dramatically reduced its rates of sepsis and made impressive measurable gains in chronic disease management while reducing staff absenteeism and turnover. The council estimates that its work on efficiencies has led to 80 million SKr savings ($13.5M CAN), or 2% of its net costs (Jönköping County Council 2005). Jönköping has won national recognition by the Swedish quality award for healthcare – Qvalitet, Utveckling, Ledarskap (QUL) – on multiple occasions over the last decade. This award is often referred to as the Swedish Malcolm Baldrige award.

Two initiatives stand out among Jönköping County Council's achievements:

Esther

Esther is a persona that clinicians in Jönköping invented to help them improve patient flow and coordination for seniors in six of the county's municipalities. Care for the elderly is a critical issue in Sweden, a country that has the world's oldest population (18% are aged 65 or over). Esther is an 88-year-old Swedish woman who continues to live alone in the community but has a chronic condition and occasional acute needs. Beginning in late 1998 Jönköping clinicians and leaders came together to map Esther's movements through the complex network of care settings and providers. In addition, interviews were conducted with patients like Esther and clinicians who provide care for her across the system.

This exercise provided a starting point for identifying and working on improvements in the way patients flow through the care system. Much work was done to align capacity with demand and to strength coordination and communication among providers. Examples of changes made included a redesigned intake and transfer process across the continuum of care, open access scheduling, team-based telephone consultation, integrated documentation and communication processes and an explicit strategy to educate patients in self-management skills. The Esther project yielded impressive improvements over a three- to five-year period, including an overall reduction in hospital admissions by over 20% (9,300 to 7,300) and a redeployment of resources to the community, a reduction in hospital days for heart failure by 30% (from 3,500 days per year to 2,500) and a reduction by more than 30 days of wait times for referral appointments with specialists such as neurologists (Institute for Healthcare Improvement nd b).

Pursuing Perfection

Pursuing Perfection was an ambitious project funded by the Robert Wood Johnson Foundation and directed by the Institute for Healthcare Improvement (IHI) in the United States (US). The goal was to create system transformation across all major healthcare processes. Seven successful US health system applicants received over $2 million each through a competitive process to participate in this initiative. Jönköping (and several other international health systems) participated without this funding.

Jönköping County Council leaders considered their Pursuing Perfection efforts to be an investment that built on the Esther initiative and helped to transform the way care is provided. Top managers wondered whether it would be possible to develop "a Toyota in healthcare." Their efforts focused on developing new ways of working and tools at three levels: leadership, new designs and innovations, and front-line results. Jönköping leaders and clinicians focused their efforts on systems thinking at all levels (i.e., macro, meso and micro) in several areas, including achieving access in every office, improving patient flow, asthma care, elder care, partnerships for children's services in the county, prevention of influenza and patient safety.

This work led to substantial streamlining of processes and cost savings across the system, including in surgical units and orthopaedic clinics. Key changes included role redesign with occupational therapists and nurse practitioners having more enhanced roles in doing follow-up exams. By bringing together all providers and resources for children with asthma in the county and by mapping and improving processes, Jönköping reduced the number of hospitalizations for pediatric asthma to 7 per 10,000 (Jönköping formerly had 22 hospitalizations per 10,000; the US national average is 30 hospitalizations per 10,000). Jönköping's rate of influenza vaccination increased by 30% (over four years), translating into substantial reductions in acute care hospital admission as well as in morbidity and mortality among the elderly population. Jönköping County was considered the highest performing of all Pursuing Perfection sites, financially and clinically, thereby demonstrating "that gains are possible when innovative design meets rational resourcing" (Institute for Healthcare Improvement nd a).

Setting an example

It is uncommon to be publicly praised and held up as an example to peers in Sweden, where unity, modesty and equality are strongly valued. That is no longer the case for Jönköping County Council. In a report published by Sweden's Department of Finance in 2005, Jane Cederqvist urged other county councils to build on Jönköping's successes in transforming its system and noted the resulting possibility of realizing cost savings across the country:

> We have done some calculations, and our evaluation of the counties in Sweden shows that it is possible to save at least 30,000 million SKr [$5 billion Canadian] in a 10 year period. ... It would be very good for Swedish health care if we can start a Pursuing Perfection project in Sweden based on the successes the County Council of Jönköping have achieved in their care. This should develop all of Swedish healthcare a lot, and offer us new learning and the inspiration needed for tomorrow's work in healthcare. (Jane Cederqvist; qtd. in Berwick 2006: 54)

These results are impressive. But beyond what is published in facts and figures – comparative county-level performance rankings, awards, key improvement initiatives and results – little is known about *how* Jönköping developed into a system capable of improvement.

Method: Exploring a system capable of improvement

In June 2006 a team of researchers from the University of Toronto's Department of

Health Policy, Management and Evaluation visited Sweden. This site visit was part of an initiative called Quality by Design, which aims to identify and define elements of healthcare systems capable of improvement with a view to helping to inform strategic investments in improvement capability in Ontario. Quality by Design is funded primarily by the Ontario Ministry of Health and Long-Term Care in partnership with the University of Toronto's Department of Health Policy, Management and Evaluation.

Jönköping County Council was one of five healthcare systems selected from a short list of high-performing systems nominated by a panel of international leaders and experts. In Sweden the team met with and interviewed administrative and clinical leaders, support staff and front-line staff working to make improvements at regional and organizational levels in Jönköping, and leaders and stakeholders in Stockholm at the healthcare system's national level. These interviews helped to provide a balanced and detailed perspective of the evolution of Jönköping County Council's investments in improvement capability, and the strategic drivers of sustained improvement at Jönköping, including the role of national-level or external influences. This case study highlights the findings of this site visit.

The System and its environment

Sweden

Sweden's healthcare system is a publicly funded comprehensive system with an international reputation for strong performance, equity and innovation. In the early 1970s Sweden was among the first countries to recognize the limits of hospital care and to make a national commitment to primary care and preventive services (Glenngård et al. 2005). Compared to systems in other industrialized countries and international standards, the Swedish system manages to balance superior access and medical outcomes with moderate resource and cost levels (Organisation for Economic Co-operation and Development 2005). Rooted in a social ethic of participation and partnership, the Swedish system is highly decentralized and aims to achieve its objectives through public ownership as well as local and regional democracy, operation and accountability.

Since 1982 regionally elected political bodies called county councils, which typically include several municipalities, have been funding, planning and delivering healthcare services. They base their work on broad principles that guide planning and delivery as well as on goals for quality established by the central government. Healthcare is a dominant focus for county councils, comprising over 70% of their resources (other responsibilities include cultural activities, public transportation and regional development). County councils finance their healthcare expenditures by levying proportional income taxes (in addition to taxation revenue, healthcare financing is supplemented by state grants and user charges). They plan and allocate resources to healthcare, dental care, education and research for their jurisdictions, own and operate all their healthcare facilities and contract with healthcare providers. The councils employ salaried, community-based primary care physicians. Hospitals, which are owned and operated by the county councils, employ salaried, hospital-based physicians (Glenngärd et al. 2005).

Other national organizations that influence healthcare in Sweden include the National Board of Health and Welfare, which sets standards for patient safety, performance assessment and practitioner licensing. The Swedish Association for Local Authorities and Regions (SALAR), a result of a recent merger of the Federations of County Councils and Local Authorities, is the county councils' membership organization. The SALAR advocates for county councils and regions in government and reports publicly on their performance, supports quality improvement and oversees relations with labour unions (Stenberg nd). Appendix A lists the SALAR's priorities for the near future.

Jönköping County Council

Jönköping County is located 330 km southwest of Stockholm in the southern province of Småland. It has three hospitals and 34 care centres (including primary care clinics, specialized medical services, rehabilitation facilities and pharmacies), with a combined workforce of over 9,900 across 13 municipalities (Bojestig, Henriks and Karlsson 2006). Many people consider Jönköping County to be both the spiritual and entrepreneurial centre of Sweden: it is home to the country's largest number of religious establishments (leading to references to its status as "Sweden's bible belt"), while Småland is the origin of Ingvar Kamprad, the founder of IKEA.

Jönköping County Council is proud of its strong connection to its communities. The council's vision – "For a good life in an attractive county" – was developed after 400 hours of dialogue with leaders and stakeholders across the region. This vision, which resonates with Swedish values, has remained constant for more than a decade.

A system capable of improvement

> You have to be sure about what problems you can solve and what problems you cannot solve with organizational charts and structural changes. ... Traditional ways of thinking and behavior patterns are hardly going to transform because of organizational changes. (Bojestig, Henriks and Nolan 2006: 17)

Continuous and effective leadership and governance

Leadership has been key to the achievements of Jönköping County Council and its ability to make and sustain improvements in quality. Over the past 18 years Sven-Olof

Karlsson, the council's chief executive officer (CEO), has led the council's single management system. This is the longest tenure of any county council CEO in Sweden.

In addition to continuous leadership at the chief executive level, there has been (until recently) a stable majority of politicians elected to the council's assembly, led by the same chair, throughout Karlsson's tenure. Functioning like a board of directors, Jönköping's assembly is made up of 81 politicians elected every four years. As a governance body the assembly holds public meetings four times a year to set and monitor the council's strategic plan and to make decisions about the tax rate, often with members of the opposition sitting at the same table (Bojestig, Henriks and Karlsson 2006). In fact, Jönköping's board chair is from the Social Democratic Party, which is in opposition to Jönköping's political majority, the Christian Democratic Party.

A frequent challenge with this politically driven, large-size governance structure is the change in power every four years and the unwillingness of board members to maintain an arm's length distance from day-to-day operations. In counties across Sweden, CEOs often struggle with board members' meddling with their front-line workforce (board members visit healthcare facilities to lobby for votes and influence specific decisions). This was not the case in Jönköping. Over time Karlsson and his board chair, Lars Isaksson, developed a sound working relationship underpinned by trust. By engaging the board in open, consensus-based decision-making, by clarifying roles and mutual expectations for board members and leaders and by demonstrating strong performance for the system, Karlsson and his chair gained other board members' confidence. Continuity, transparency and trust won over political partisanship, and board interference in day-to-day operations is virtually non-existent in Jönköping.

A commitment to financial discipline and quality improvement in a crisis

Formerly the county council's chief financial officer, Karlsson has been credited with developing and reinforcing Jönköping's culture of financial discipline and the region's spirit of open dialogue. During the past decade Karlsson and his senior team have paired Jönköping's long-standing commitment to strong financial performance with a strategic focus on quality improvement. Two key members of Karlsson's senior team – physician leader Mats Bojestig and learning and innovation leader Göran Henriks – have been particularly instrumental to this evolution, which began in the early 1990s.

In the early 1990s the Swedish healthcare system was in a state of economic crisis, which was reported as the worst in Europe. Access was a major problem; wait times, particularly for elective procedures, were at an all-time high and increasing; the quality of home care was poor; and community services were underutilized (Stenberg nd). In addition, the number of elderly people was rising quickly, contributing substantially to healthcare costs and worsening budget deficits across county councils. By the mid 1990s the Swedish government enacted policies designed to address the crisis, including a Wait Times Guarantee (Stenberg nd). County councils at the same time shifted into a mode of cost containment.

Although Jönköping had a foundation of strong financial performance and open dialogue, the county started to feel the effects of the economic downturn. By 1995-1996, tensions among politicians and leaders were rising. In addition, feeling the pressure of the guarantees, healthcare facilities across the county were asking and competing for increased capacity (i.e., more beds, clinicians and space) to help them deal with issues of access. Around that time two members of Karlsson's senior team, Bojestig and Henriks, had become increasingly familiar with various frameworks and tools, such as the Malcolm Baldrige quality award criteria, audit and measurement tools and principles of total quality management. Bojestig, an internist/endocrinologist at Höglandet Hospital since 1984, had become involved in a national effort to develop QUL, Sweden's version of the Baldrige criteria. Henriks, a former Swedish National Basketball coach who had held various roles in education and quality at Jönköping since 1982, deeply understood process and systems thinking (using strategic measurement to monitor and plan different dimensions of performance) and the importance of learning better habits for change and improvement. Henriks saw healthcare workers as knowledge workers.

In the midst of the national crisis Karlsson and his senior team began actively to use frameworks and tools, particularly those introduced by Bojestig and Henriks, to provide an objective picture of performance and to guide decision-making. Karlsson was worried that efforts to make changes to contain costs would harm patients. He wanted more and better information and an even more open dialogue with leaders, politicians, staff and patients. Management and measurement tools such as audit instruments (e.g., Audit Group for Medical Evaluation, Swedish Organizations Granskning) and the Balanced Scorecard helped Jönköping's leaders use numerical data to measure and understand their performance across parts of the county on different dimensions and over time (Jönköping County Council 2005). This information was included in a new annual report that went to stakeholders and became central to Jönköping's "dialogue" as a system.

Communicating objective information that showed widening variations in efficiency (beds and staff per capita), costs and quality across the county and over time helped to convince board members and county leaders that adding capacity was not an effective solution. Furthermore, interviews with patients and clinicians confirmed that integration and coordination of care were significant issues, especially for the aging population. In the short term this exercise led to the initiation of projects designed to improve integration and continuity of care (e.g., Esther). In the long term it led to a more balanced and data-driven approach to strategic and budget planning for the council. Karlsson began to establish a closer linkage between finance and quality, homing in on value for patients instead of just costs and maintaining an ongoing strategy of making modest capital expenditures, removing waste and improving quality as a means of cost reduction. As he noted, "Work on quality does not mean a distraction from a focus on finance – it is an expectation that healthcare areas maintain and reduce costs." Through a self-assessment using the Swedish Baldrige/QUL criteria and an introduction to the principles of total quality management, Karlsson and his senior team began to use these as a framework for developing a more central and strategic focus on quality.

A common vision for system-level investment in improvement capability

Bojestig, Henriks and others knew that while the use of new tools had helped to move Karlsson and Jönköping's senior team beyond a focus on finance, new ideas and frameworks for planning at a senior level were "not going to be enough to improve the system." Initiatives to improve quality were being led by a few champions in three disparate parts of the county and were not yet yielding major system-wide improvements. There was a need for more strategic guidance, support and coordination of these initiatives. It was also critically important that management and front-line staff become better oriented toward process and systems thinking in their everyday work and learn how to systematically test changes in process on a small scale. At the time Henriks asked, "How can we really help people optimize their work?"

Although Karlsson had been intrigued by and began to use tools for total quality management, he was still uncertain of the need for more significant investment in improvement skills and capability. After all, at the time Jönköping was already conducting more improvement initiatives and consistently performing in the top quartile of county councils on all cost and quality indicators.

Henriks and Bojestig had attended the IHI forum in the US for several years, experienced intense learning and received inspiration from leaders in high-performing improvement-focused systems: they knew what was possible. After a few unsuccessful attempts, Henriks and Bojestig convinced Karlsson to join them at the annual IHI forum. In agreeing to attend, Karlsson articulated one caveat: the team was to "work together to prepare beforehand, while at the forum and upon their return" in order to harvest all relevant learning that would add value to the work Jönköping County Council was undertaking. In 1998, after meetings to prepare, select sessions and establish learning objectives, Karlsson and his entire senior team attended the IHI forum in New Orleans. The experience of attending as a team led by the CEO, of explicit planning and debriefing and of hearing the same ideas and stories about improvement were important catalysts at Jönköping. Karlsson and his team began to develop more detailed knowledge of improvement methods and they began to understand issues of performance as being process- and systems-related. They also came to recognize the methods and context needed for change and improvement and the importance of investing in educating their workforce in the skills and knowledge associated with improvement.

One of the most important methods was a simple yet powerful tool for action-oriented learning called the Model for Improvement. This model asks three fundamental questions to help teams set aims (What are we trying to accomplish?), establish measures (How will we know a change is an improvement?) and select changes (What changes can we make that will result in improvement?). The model also includes the Plan-Do-Study-Act (PDSA) cycle that guides the testing and implementation of changes in a real work setting and accelerates improvement (Langley et al. 1996).

A changing quality agenda at the national level

This knowledge acquisition by Jönköping's senior leadership coincided with two national-level developments. First, in 1994 the National Board of Health and Welfare developed a series of regulations on quality issues. These regulations, which were reworked in 1997, state that all health services in Sweden must include a system for continuous quality improvement. The revised version shifts the emphasis from quality assurance (defined as monitoring and improving technical measures of quality) to quality improvement (continuous, target-oriented development focusing on the people for whom health services are intended) (The Swedish Institute, 2003). Second, the Federation of County Councils, which eventually merged with the Federation of Local Authorities to become the Swedish Association for Local Authorities and Regions, had started to provide central support for improvement by organizing an annual Quality Conference, the QUL award and Breakthrough Series modelled after the IHI's approach. The approach is an action-based learning series that brings together teams working collaboratively toward a common improvement aim. Breakthrough Series collaboratives attempt to spread and adapt existing content knowledge through the development and use of improvement knowledge and to create opportunities to share progress and ideas across teams. The goal is to achieve significant and rapid changes that produce breakthrough results.

The Federation also began to fund demonstration projects and develop a leadership network for improvement. A group working at a national level within the Federation had also begun to develop a quality agenda with a focus on improvement. This group, led by leaders such as Margareta Palmberg and Michael Bergstrom, had undergone its own evolution in terms of developing improvement knowledge and an enhanced understanding of the importance of a strategic focus on improvement in order to generate a sustainable healthcare system. Furthermore, this group had begun to develop an informal relationship with IHI, attending conferences and courses and engaging Paul Batalden, the physician and improvement scholar at Dartmouth Medical School in New Hampshire. Batalden's expertise, particularly in systems thinking, was considered instrumental in contributing to some of these national-level developments.

While Jönköping County Council participated in the Federation-led Breakthrough Series and other activities, it was already further ahead than most other counties in making process and patient-focused improvements. The council had also already adapted the Breakthrough Series model to suit its own needs (e.g., placing a greater emphasis on developing process knowledge at the outset; focusing on teamwork and organizational development). While the Leadership Network provided a venue for dialogue and sharing among CEOs and other decision-makers, Jönköping had already started to invest locally in leadership development and education across various council levels.

Although the growing quality agenda and activities at the national level began to assist other county councils that were motivated to improve but needed guidance, support and momentum began to wane. Nationally, leaders were increasingly focused on other issues (e.g., rising unemployment in some areas of Sweden), and views diverged on the importance of process-oriented quality improvement as opposed to other approaches, such as standards-oriented technology assessment. Leaders saw more important and urgent alternatives for the use of funds. As a result, money originally earmarked for the quality improvement agenda was directed to human resources planning, with a parallel turnover of some of those involved in pioneering the improvement agenda at a national level. According to some observers, "This was a lack of senior leadership vision."

A strategy of complementary leadership skills

By 1997 Karlsson was committed to developing Jönköping as a system capable of improvement, and he understood more about what was required to make that happen. Karlsson began by making a few key strategic changes to his leadership team. In 1997 a new position was developed for Henriks, who became chief of learning and innovation. While the pairing of clinical and executive leadership is common in most counties, Karlsson's emphasis on developing and providing time, resources and decision-making ability to a leader who championed quality, learning and coaching process improvement was uncommon. This unique set of complementary skills and roles at a senior level set the stage for a more system-level approach to investing in improvement capability and to shifting improvement from a series of projects to a way of leading and working. More recently, in 2006 Bojestig was named chief medical officer and planning director. These changes have supported Jönköping's transformation into a healthcare system driven by leadership and focused on clinical results.

Widespread learning about how to change and improve processes for patients

In the initial wave of county council–wide education that took place from 1997 through 1999, senior leaders, managers and front-line teams learned they had two jobs: "to do what they do (i.e., manage, provide care) and to improve what they do." They learned about the values of the Malcolm Baldrige/QUL quality award and how those values were critical for improving patient care at Jönköping at all levels. They also learned about the Balanced Scorecard and the importance of paying attention to multiple dimensions of performance simultaneously: units and programs across Jönköping developed their own scorecards and used them for planning and monitoring. Participants were taught a common improvement language, methods and tools, and particularly the Model for Improvement and the PDSA cycle, so as to better understand and map change processes on a small scale in order to improve care and create value for their patients. They also learned about thinking reflectively about their work, teamwork, the interdependencies of their work and managing change.

Management was also restructured to align with this learning. Managers and clinicians who were working on improving common or linked processes across the council came together regularly to share ideas and progress, and managers and clinicians were assigned as process leaders. Over time this effort led to the education of large numbers of staff, the start of a redesign of 53 processes and was critical to the success of initiatives such as Esther (Jönköping County Council 2005).

Karlsson reflected on the council's strategy during those years:

> Our strategy was like an old military strategy. ... [We] involve employees in lots of quality improvement projects and help them learn how to make change and let them define how to create results using learning and innovation. …
>
> Results across the small parts of the system create big results for the system … and lots of winners. ... Big, high-risk projects and changing structures in a traditional way, buying and selling and depending on the market, creates losers.

The impact of this strategy was visible across Jönköping County. For example, staff at the Vaggeryd Primary Care Centre began to measure their performance regularly and to test changes in process using daily huddles and active data walls. The clinic management and staff documented a new set of "ground rules" for working at the Centre, stating that all staff would be responsible for improving work, that a culture of continuous improvement would be built together by seeking the wisdom of all staff members and that information and results would be transparent (Jönköping County Council 2004).

Establishing Qulturum – a centralized "quality" house

At the same time the Office for Learning and Innovation, and most of the early quality education, had been physically situated at Ryhov Hospital, Jönköping's largest. Despite strong leadership support and expectations to participate, front-line staff members found it challenging to avoid day-to-day distractions, especially if they were working at Ryhov Hospital. Furthermore, this arrangement made it more difficult for the Office to be a visible support for learning and improvement across the entire region.

Leaders at Jönköping County Council established the Qulturum learning centre in 1999 in response to these challenges. The centre is a standalone building located on the central campus of the council's healthcare facilities. Funded by 0.03% of Jönköping's annual budget and a partnership with the Swedish Pharmacy Association, Qulturum, which means "meeting place for quality and culture," was carefully designed. Its physical structure and layout allow small and large groups to meet and learn together in open dialogue or "learning arenas," using technology when necessary. Even the aesthetics of the rooms are designed to stimulate thought and learning. Qulturum also provides a common language for all staff: Henriks calls Qulturum an "institute for language" that links staff members together on common ground because their own "languages (e.g., finance, clinical) are still so different." Henriks leads Qulturum and has strong support from Karlsson and other senior leaders who regularly interact with the staff and participate in teaching and learning.

Qulturum has an explicit strategy for staff recruitment and development. Personnel are carefully selected from among the county's front-line champions. Many staff members were nursing, medical or allied health workers. Specialist skills that are sought and further developed include front-line team facilitation, project management, leadership development, improvement methods, data collection and measurement for improvement, process mapping and patient-safety-related methods such as root-cause analysis.

Supported by Qulturum, Jönköping County Council reports having made over 800 measurable improvements. These encompass all seven of the council's strategic aims: good stewardship, medication, learning and renewal, safety, access, flow/co-operation and clinical improvement.

Unlike many other systems that have emphasized "practical" improvement methods rather than ones based in theory, Qulturum attempts to bridge this divide. The key principles for the support and training Qulturum provides are its alignment with the council's strategic aims, its link to action and its grounding in improvement theory. Qulturum provides support for system-wide and unit-based projects using a modified version of IHI's Breakthrough collaborative model to ensure ongoing learning and support for staff and leaders as they make changes to care processes. Integrated into learning sessions are the theories of Senge, Juran, Deming and others, as well as the use of rapid-cycle methods, the Clinical Value Compass and other tools. To date, 4,000 of the 9,000 staff members and leaders across the system have received such theory-based and action-oriented quality improvement training at Qulturum.

This centralized investment in a long-term strategy of developing internal expertise and the capacity for internal skill and knowledge development counters a common habit of making externally driven investments in improvement knowledge and skills and only limited investments in the education of front-line staff and managers. Ironically, this investment in Qulturum has also meant that Jönköping's senior leaders can continue to maintain financial discipline and a policy of "no new money" for improvement for individual organizations and programs (aside from specific capital projects). Programs and teams have access to improvement support and facilitation from Qulturum staff, and they fund changes through process improvement.

Harvesting ideas and approaches from elsewhere

An important feature of improvement at Jönköping is the strategic harvesting and adapting of ideas from international training programs, centres and experts. Henriks and others at Qulturum carefully screen new ideas and tools and adapt and introduce only those that will help Jönköping to advance.

Henriks and his colleagues are also careful to ensure that any external relationships they forge to train, learn or harvest ideas are developed at the interface between coaches and trainers and not at the front lines: "We have a rule of not bringing in consultants to solve our problems. ... We are of the mindset of see one, do one, teach 500." They regard this approach as an efficient way of learning from others and building internal capacity/capability as well as corporate memory, habits and ways of working. For example, by 2003 patient safety had become a strategic priority at Jönköping. By 2005 two Qulturum staff members had participated in the IHI's Patient Safety Officer program. By 2006 that program had been adapted to meet Jönköping's needs in patient safety knowledge and skills, aligned to the learning model used at Qulturum and implemented for staff across the Jönköping region.

At a conference in 2004 Qulturum staff heard about the work of the United Kingdom's National Primary Care Development Trust to engage patients in self-management using improvement methods. Given Jönköping County Council's focus on care for seniors in the community, a focus that includes chronic disease management, preventive health and strong community connections, the council adapted this concept to launch the

Passion for Life initiative. This initiative uses a version of the Breakthrough Series model to teach seniors to use improvement methods and measurement to learn about and test changes in their diet, occupational safety and other care areas. The initiative also provides seniors with an enhanced social network and access to a primary care physician on an occasional basis. Funded through a partnership with the SALAR, and supported in particular by Michael Bergstrom at the SALAR, this initiative is spreading across Sweden and has generated momentum for patient-led improvements at Jönköping. Qulturum staff members working on the initiative say that "patients are now our teachers." Seniors identified as champions from the Passion for Life initiative visit clinical units to share their knowledge and use of the PDSA cycle with nurses.

More recently, Henriks and his colleagues learned from experts in the US about ways of transforming care by working at the level of clinical microsystems (i.e., teams working at the front line of service delivery) (Nelson et al. 2002). This is a current and growing focus for Qulturum and Jönköping County Council.

To help systematically manage the selection, introduction and spread of new tools and approaches Henriks and other leaders have recently begun to use a three-stage method involving testing, piloting and prototyping. In the test stage the tool or approach is introduced to and discussed with staff at Qulturum; in the pilot stage units across Jönköping are introduced to and invited to use the tool or approach and common measures are established; in the prototype stage the tool or approach becomes embedded in work and improvement (Jönköping County Council 2005).

Integrating improvement knowledge and skills into clinical education

Despite the participation of physicians in education at Qulturum, Jönköping's leaders realized they needed a parallel approach in order to introduce improvement to the next generation of clinicians. To integrate clinicians' learning of improvement methods earlier and in conjunction with their learning of content knowledge, Jönköping initiated a partnership with a medical school and other health professions, programs in Sweden (Bergstrom and Thorne nd). Karin Thorne, a Jönköping-based physician working with Futurum (a new research-focused arm of Qulturum), led this partnership. One of the early accomplishments of this work has been the development of a network of medical residency supervisors trained at Qulturum and the creation of modules these supervisors can use for just-in-time training of physicians and other professionals on the units. As Thorne noted, "The learning has been very powerful. ... Clinicians are educated in the biological context and [yet] much more is needed for effective problem-solving." This work has developed into a national-level initiative supported by Bergstrom at the SALAR and has spread across four Swedish universities.

Putting quality at the centre of strategic and business planning

By the late 1990s Jönköping County Council (with Qulturum as the primary engine) had made significant investments in improvement capability, in particular, the widespread development of enhanced knowledge and skills. Although improvements were being made and sustained, there were gaps in understanding how improvement at the team level contributed to system-level enhancement. A Jönköping manager recalled that "people sometimes felt as though they were not part of the strategic discussion." In a spirit of continuous learning at the senior level, Karlsson and other leaders reflected on the need to ensure that the Jönköping system maintained a strategic focus on improvement and ensured value for these investments. According to Boel Andersson-Gare, the chief of pediatrics at Jönköping County Council, "We have always had activities that have delivered good results, but no one took the responsibility for the entirety (Jönköping County Council 2005)."

By 2001 Jönköping's leaders had tested a new approach for putting quality planning at the centre of business and strategic planning for the county council. Called Big Group Healthcare, this approach is a meeting of all executive, clinical and quality leaders and managers across the system over five days throughout the year. During these meetings leaders and managers gather in "circles of learning and open dialogue" to report on their progress in achieving strategic aims and to discuss how quality improvement initiatives are (or are not) contributing to these in measurable ways. Attendees use this opportunity to learn from their peers, to understand more about how the system is performing as a whole and to get involved in co-designing the plan for the health system.

Big Group Healthcare has strengthened the ability of Jönköping's senior leadership team to create a context for system-wide improvement. It has also created a more explicit link between strategy, quality and finance and a tangible way to bring together learning and improvement (Qulturum), strategic aims and measures for the system and Balanced Scorecard results. Karlsson estimates that less than 40%–50% of the discussion in these meetings focuses on finance, a fact that makes it possible to focus on quality improvement. Much of Big Group Healthcare discussion focuses on considering the value that Jönköping is creating for its patients. As a result of Big Group Healthcare, leaders and managers at Jönköping created the "diamond picture" to show how learning and innovation drives improvement across the strategic themes and that quality improvement, in turn, drives improved finance and reliability (see Figure 2) (Jönköping County Council 2005).

Jönköping leaders and managers also redeveloped their annual budget plan and performance reporting to support and reflect these linkages. Results of Big Group Healthcare meetings are documented in a newsletter that is disseminated to staff across the system.

According to the County Council's senior leaders, "People have a better understanding of the system and this has decreased the rumours that developed when they did not." Staff at different levels of and in different parts of the system are familiar with the diamond picture and with the business strategy as a whole (see Appendix B). Jönköping's leaders share their commitment to embedding these ideas in the system and its work: "We never change our pictures."

Figure 2. Jönköping County Council's "diamond picture"

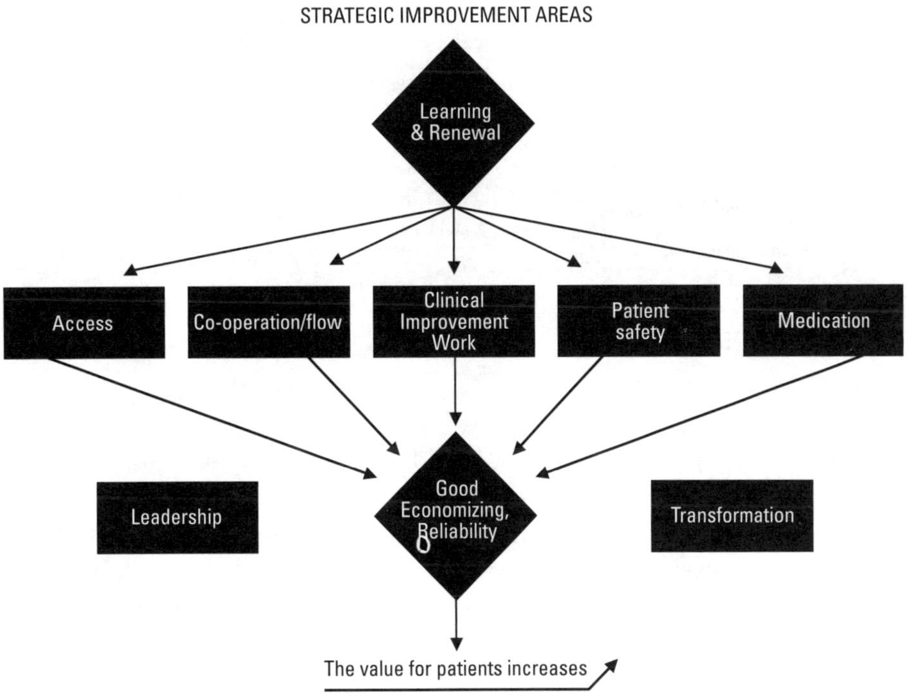

STRATEGIC IMPROVEMENT AREAS

Learning & Renewal

Access

Co-operation/flow

Clinical Improvement Work

Patient safety

Medication

Leadership

Good Economizing, Reliability

Transformation

The value for patients increases

Used by permission.

Removing disincentives for improvement

In conjunction with Big Group Healthcare, the three hospital CEOs began to receive limited incentives (5% of salary) for demonstrating Baldrige-type values in their leadership. In addition to these incentives for leaders, Karlsson focused on removing typical disincentives for improvement across the system. For example, instead of reclaiming cost savings in the global budget, organizations and units that realize cost savings as a result of improvement are able to reinvest all of these funds. This continues to be an effective way to keep managers and staff focused on lean consumption and process optimization.

Pushing beyond improvement to system transformation

Jönköping County Council depicts its improvement journey as a development stair (see Figure 3) (Jönköping County Council 2005). The next step in its evolution – the step at the top of the stairs – is Pursuing Perfection.

Figure 3. Jönköping County Council's development stair

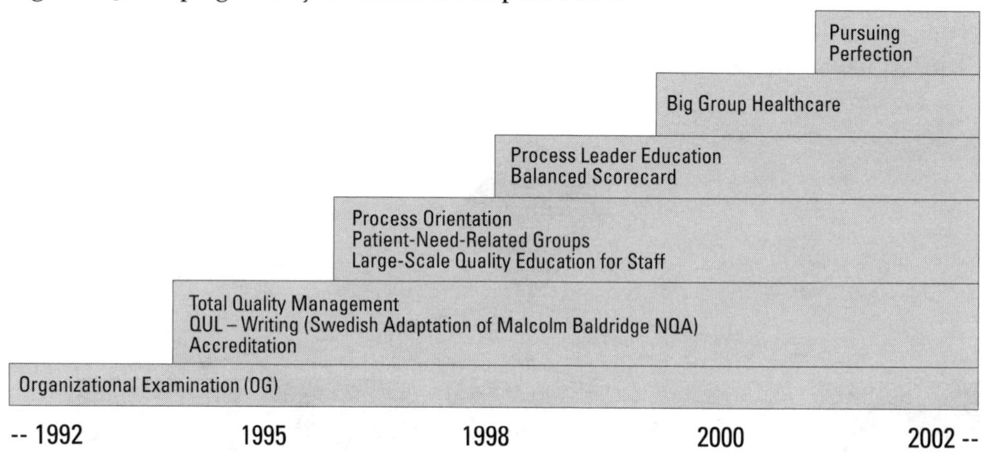

Used by permission.

Big Group Healthcare exposed the system, including its imperfections, to Jönköping's leaders. As they continued to work to create and establish conditions that would allow change, Jönköping's leaders saw Pursuing Perfection as an opportunity to redefine and transform their system even beyond the goals that had already been accomplished: "We realized that the learning and work that would be most strategically important for our system was ahead of us."

As we noted in the introduction to this case study, Jönköping County Council funded its own participation in Pursuing Perfection and received coaching and mentoring from US improvement experts such as Tom Nolan, Jim Reinertsen and Cliff Norman. Rather than seeing these efforts as an expanded group of projects, the Pursuing Perfection work and the advice of external experts pushed Jönköping and its leaders to redefine its entire system. In doing so they came to understand better the linkages among drivers such as leadership and learning and support functions such as finance and human resources, as well as how these could optimally support the mainstay of patient care (see Figure 4) (Jönköping County Council 2005).

This new perspective helped leaders and staff to appreciate their roles more fully and to recognize the interdependencies throughout the system and the opportunities they had to transform it. Pursuing Perfection pushed Jönköping beyond rapid cycle change to whole-system redesign. As noted above, this process included the redesign of roles and information systems that yielded more dramatic clinical and financial improvements than ever before.

Figure 4. System view of Jönköping County Council

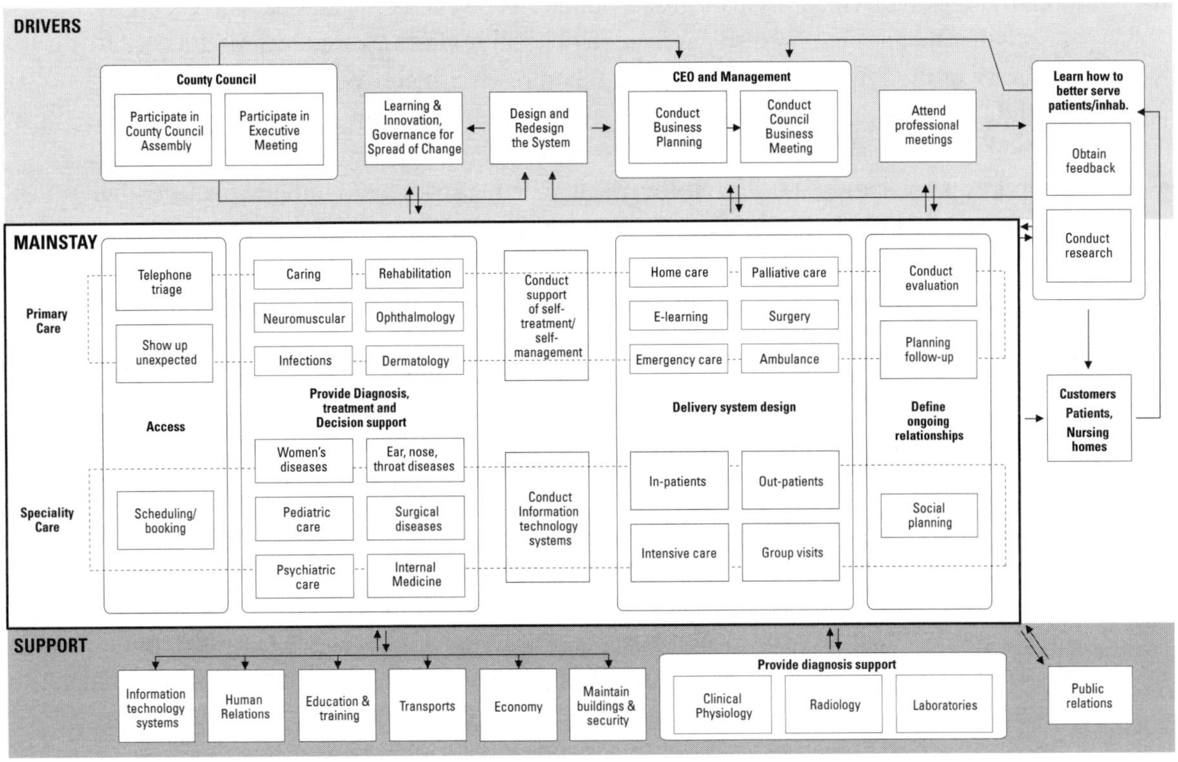

Used by permission.

Maintaining momentum and challenges for the next generation

Jönköping County Council's investment in improvement capability has been characterized by a constancy of purpose for achieving quality in the context of financial discipline, strong and stable leadership and a steady learning journey for the entire system. As Karlsson and his colleagues approach two decades of leadership, they continue to learn and prepare for the next generation of improvement. To create leadership at the microsystem level with the new generation of front-line managers, Karlsson and Henriks are leading a 21-day leadership development program and Deming Days, which provide education about Deming's Theory of Profound Knowledge across the county. Bojestig has been named chief planning officer and is in charge of the new electronic health record and information system.

Jönköping had developed an early warning system of monthly measures using a combination of administrative databases and manually collected data. The county is now attempting to move beyond this approach to a true decision-support system that will facilitate bedside improvement. Bojestig and his colleagues are striving to ensure this system will be integrated into normal workflow and will facilitate ongoing outcomes measurement.

Jönköping's involvement in managing a number of Sweden's 57 national clinical registries is also increasing (Swedish Association of Local Authorities and Regions 2005). An initiative of the SALAR and the National Board of Health and Welfare, these registries include patient-level data on diagnoses, interventions and outcomes. They are considered to be one of the few major, long-standing and successful national efforts that support a knowledge base for improvement. The registries were initially managed by researchers and used mostly for research. County councils now play a more dominant role in their management, resulting in the more widespread use of the data for improvement. Among Sweden's county councils Jönköping was one of the earliest to use the registry data for improvement. The increased use of these data and recent involvement in managing three of the registries emerged from Jönköping's need for better quality and more timely information on clinical outcomes, a need that was particularly evident in the Pursuing Perfection initiative.

Despite this progress several uncertainties loom on the horizon. Jönköping's leaders have always prided themselves on "doing it all ... we change everything at the same time." However, Qulturum's staff is beginning to feel overwhelmed: "We are going to burst" is a sentiment shared by some key support staff. Qulturum's staff faces increasing pressure to meet the ongoing facilitation and support needs of quality improvement staff in the hospitals and care centres and must also provide organized training for teams. At the same time, staff members are starting to develop informal networks with key support personnel in other organizations and to attempt to use the train-the-trainer model more actively; however, they are uncertain whether these initiatives will be sufficient. Clinical leaders expressed the need to be more focused and evidence-based in the application of improvement work to clinical groups, for example, using epidemiological data to determine priorities. Can Jönköping move from a culture of "doing it all at the same time" to focusing on priorities?

According to one observer, "Political stability and leadership continuity are the single most important factors in Jönköping's success." Sweden's general election in September 2006 brought a new majority into power and a new chair for Jönköping's council assembly. In this context, how will Jönköping be able to maintain its momentum? Will these changes alter the direction of Jönköping's journey and steer it away from its strategic focus on improvement? Or, as its leaders suggest, are staff members now committed "by their own will and conviction"? Is Jönköping so far along on its journey that improvement is deeply embedded in its system? Will national-level organizations, and particularly the SALAR, enhance their roles in supporting systemic improvement beyond the support of a few critical individuals?

Another county council in northern Sweden – Västerbotten – has recently gained recognition for its work on improvement. Västerbotten's approach mirrors Jönköping's to some extent, including an explicit link between the overall system strategy and daily improvement work, the use of improvement theory and methods, an emphasis on reflection and dialogue in improvement-focused meetings that bring together different levels of leadership, and high-performing microsystems (Andersson and Edström 2006). Little is known, however, about whether this work in Västerbotten is producing system-level performance improvements.

In a system that finds it difficult to accept and learn from "winners," will the lessons from Jönköping's journey and strategic investment, and the recent work in Västerbotten, accelerate large-scale improvement in other county councils?

References

Andersson, U. and A. Edström. 2006. *Towards a Healthier System: A Brief Description of the Process of Transformation in the County Council of Västerbotten.* Västerbotten: Västerbottens Läns Landsting.

Bergstrom, M. and K. Thorne. nd. *Putting Improvement at the Heart of Education: The University Collaboration on Improvement Knowledge in Sweden and Lessons from the University of Jönköping and the County Council of Jönköping.* Jönköping: Jönköping County Council, SALAR, School of Health Sciences (Jönköping University).

Berwick, D. 2006. *Full Scale: Improvement Takes Center Stage.* Presentation at the 11th European Forum on Quality Improvement in Health Care, Prague, Czech Republic. Retrieved December 13, 2006. <http://www.bmjpg.com/wed26/plenary1.ppt>

Bojestig, M., G. Henriks and S.-O. Karlsson. 2006. *Whole System Transformation.* Presentation at the 2006 Institute for Health Care Improvement Forum, Orlando, FL.

Bojestig, M., G. Henriks and T. Nolan. 2006. *Lessons Learned from Pursuing Perfection: Or, How to Solve Tomorrow's Problem Today.* Presentation at the 11th European Forum on Quality Improvement in Health Care, Prague, Czech Republic. Retrieved December 13, 2006. <http://www.bmjpg.com/wed26/m6.pdf>

Glenngård, A.H., F. Hjalte, M. Svensson, A. Anell and V. Bankauskaite. 2005. *Health Systems in Transition: Sweden.* Copenhagen: World Health Organization. Retrieved December 8, 2006. <http://www.euro.who.int?Document/E88669.pdf>

Institute for Healthcare Improvement. nd a. *Charting the Way to Greater Success: Pursuing Perfection in Sweden*. Cambridge, MA: Author. Retrieved December 14, 2006. <http://www.ihi.org/IHI/Topics/Improvement/ImprovementMethods/ImprovementStories/ChartingtheWaytoGreaterSuccessPursuingPerfectioninSweden.htm>

Institute for Healthcare Improvement. nd b. *Improving Patient Flow: The Esther Project in Sweden*. Cambridge, MA: Author. Retrieved December 14, 2006. <http://www.ihi.org/IHI/Topics/Flow/PatientFlow/ImprovementStories/ImprovingPatientFlowTheEstherProjectinSweden.htm>

Jönköping County Council. 2004. *Vaggeryd Primary Care Centre*. Presentation at the Clinical Microsystem Festival, Jönköping, Sweden. Retrieved November 9, 2007. <http://www.lj.se/info_files/infosida31595/Vaggeryd.pdf>

Jönköping County Council. 2005. *The Future Is Now: A Paper Written for the Swedish Quality Price Gota*. Jönköping: Author.

Jönköping County Council. 2007. *Budget 2007*. Jönköping: Author.

Langley, G.L., K.M. Nolan, T.W Nolan, C.L. Norman and L.P. Provost. 1996. *The Improvement Guide: A Practical Approach to Enhancing Organizational Performance*. San Francisco: Jossey-Bass Publishers.

Nelson, E.D., P.B. Batalden, T.P. Huber, J.J. Mohr, M.M. Godfrey, L.A. Headrick and J.H. Wasson. 2002. "Microsystems in Health Care: Part 1. Learning from High-Performing Front-Line Clinical Units." *The Joint Commission Journal on Quality Improvement* 28(9): 472–493.

Organisation for Economic Co-operation and Development. 2005. *OECD Health Data 2005: How Does Sweden Compare?* Paris: Author. Retrieved December 13, 2006. <http://www.oecd.org/dataoecd/15/25/34970222.pdf>

Stenberg, J. nd. *The Swedish Health Care System*. Presentation at a meeting of the Swedish Association of Local Authorities, Stockholm, Sweden.

Swedish Association of Local Authorities and Regions. 2005. *National Healthcare Quality Registries in Sweden*. Stockholm: Author.

The Swedish Institute. 2003. *Health Care System in Sweden*. Stockholm: Author. Retrieved December 13, 2006. <http://equip.ch/files/6/swedish_health_care1.pdf>

Appendix A. Priorities of the Swedish Association of Local Authorities and Regions (2005–2007) (Stenberg nd: 3)

1. Guarantee and financing of welfare
2. Efficiency and quality
3. The responsibility committee and self-government
4. A good collective agreement in 2005
5. Improved availability of human resources and competences
6. Strengthened co-operation in healthcare between municipalities, county councils and regions
7. Improved access to healthcare
8. A more flexible educational system
9. More people in jobs and more integration in working life
10. Improved health – reduced absence due to sick leave
11. Sustainable growth

Appendix B. Jönköping County Council's business strategy (Jönköping County Council 2005)

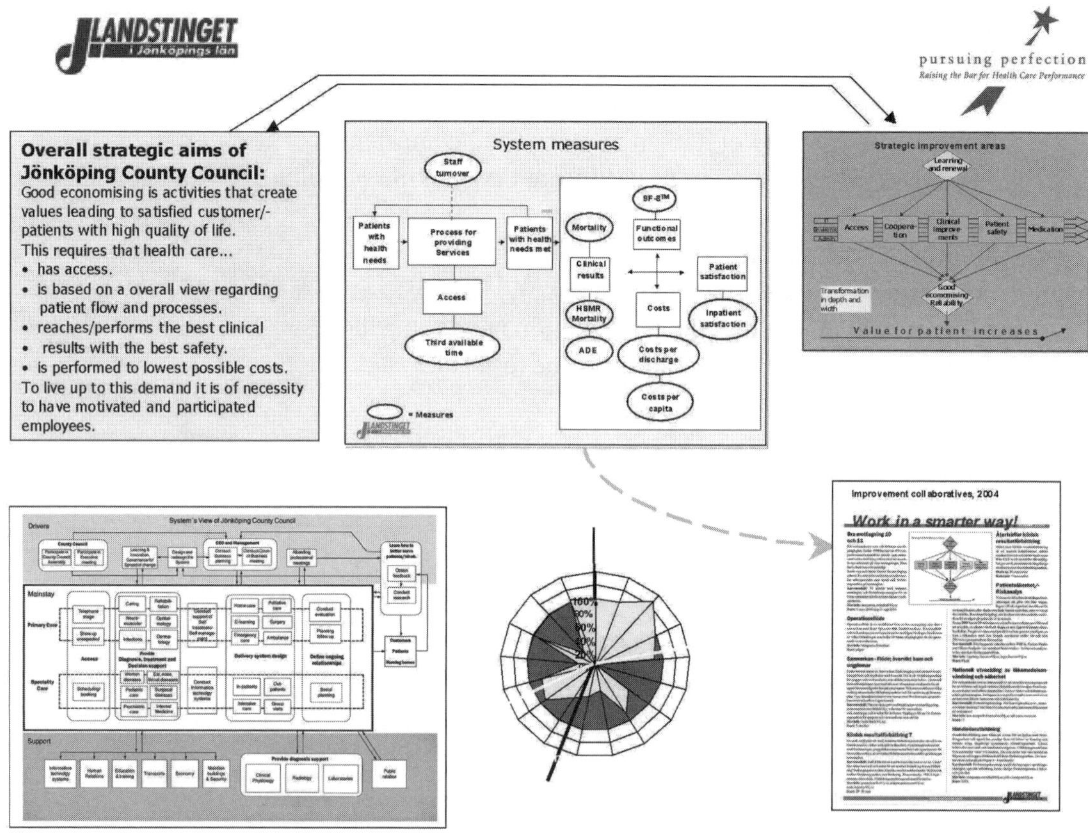

Used by permission.

Commentary: Jönköping County Council

Maura Davies, President and Chief Executive Officer
Saskatoon Health Region

Magic bullets. As senior leaders in the Canadian healthcare system, struggling with financial pressures, quality and patient safety issues, staff morale and staffing challenges, and the scrutiny of the public and government, we often wish there was a magic bullet – a single, foolproof solution. Chief executive officers (CEOs) tend to be voracious readers of journals and books that profile successful leaders and organizations, looking for findings we can apply to our organizations with similar results. We recognize, of course, that enacting positive change is not that simple. It takes our personal leadership to interpret these findings in the context of our own situations and to determine what, if anything, will fit. Without apology, all leaders should beg, borrow and steal good ideas that will improve quality of care, quality of work life, financial performance and public confidence in our health systems.

Over the past decade many strong organizations have surfaced as leaders that Canadian health system CEOs would love to emulate. Those of us familiar with the Institute for Healthcare Improvement (IHI) are extremely impressed with what we hear and see from organizations that have won the Malcolm Baldrige award and/or have been part of the

Pursuing Perfection project. At times, the CEOs of these largely American hospitals and health maintenance organizations (HMOs) appear to be a privileged inner circle that others can only admire from afar, hoping that a little wisdom will rub off to help us achieve some modest success.

In the midst of this esteemed group has surfaced Jönköping County Council. This organization has a name most North Americans struggle to pronounce and is situated in a part of Sweden most of us would not be able to locate on a map. Yet, as the case study authors point out, Jönköping has been cited as "a model of healthcare system transformation that ranks among the best in the world." Wow! Perhaps we have finally found it. Could Jönköping have the formula that will help us move from a series of quality improvement efforts, with variable results, to a high-performing system that demonstrates how care should be provided? Many people think so, as evidenced by the numerous articles that have been written about Jönköping and the throngs of disciples who travel to Sweden to see the system in action.

First, let's look at the results. These are truly impressive. Jönköping achieves the best overall ranking in Sweden for efficiency, timeliness, safety, patient centredness and effectiveness. With regard to efficiency, savings are approximately 2% of net costs. The ability of Jönköping's organizations and units to reinvest cost savings has created buy-in and momentum for change, while explicitly linking corporate strategy, quality improvement and fiscal responsibility. Timely access to services, including access to specialists, has been achieved through alignment of capacity and demand, open access scheduling, strategies to reduce demand for in-patient services (including a 20% reduction in department of medicine admissions) and redeployment of resources to the community. Patient-safety results include a dramatic reduction in sepsis, a 30% increase in influenza vaccination rates and reductions in both morbidity and mortality. A patient-centred approach, epitomized by the Esther initiative, has brought patients and clinicians together in a joint effort to improve the system. Further, Jönköping's focus on removing waste and improving quality as a means of cost reduction has demonstrated that quality improvement and improving care effectiveness are good business strategies.

Indisputably, the results from Jönköping are impressive and have been sustained over a significant period of time. This suggests that it is worth taking a much closer look at this Swedish model to see how these results were achieved.

Much has been written on this topic, and others more familiar with this system will offer their opinions. It has been suggested that political stability and leadership continuity over almost two decades have been important to Jönköping's outcomes. Visionary leadership has been credited for some of the success. Putting quality at the centre of strategic and business planning has also frequently been cited. Learning from others, engaging clinical leaders and building in-house capacity for large-scale staff education in quality improvement also appear to be critical. Alternative funding models for physicians and the willingness of health professionals to adopt expanded roles and new models of care likewise enabled many changes.

None of these concepts is new – change management literature, healthcare conferences and journals endlessly preach these ideas. In our own way, Canadian health system CEOs try to live them in our own organizations. We know that visible, passionate leadership from the top is essential for quality improvement. We know that true system transformation cannot be achieved by a series of disconnected quality improvement projects owned and led by the converted. We know that many effective quality improvement strategies have been tested elsewhere and can be adapted to our organizations and environments. We know that staff engagement, particularly among staff members and physicians directly involved in patient care, is more likely to produce results that are real and credible.

Why, then, is change so difficult to effect? Why do we struggle so hard to make the strategic investments needed for quality while maintaining operations and meeting the demands of our government accountability agreements and public expectations regarding access? Why are we so easily discouraged when short-term, often politically motivated agendas seem to run counter to our longer-term strategies? How do we provide leadership that is strategic, persistent and inspiring?

On the surface one could attribute much of Jönköping's success to IHI. Early in their journey, senior Jönköping leaders attended the annual IHI forum, during which they developed a deeper understanding of process and systems-level improvement, improvement methodology and the need to build workforce-wide capacity for improvement. Jönköping's leaders developed an informal relationship with IHI and tapped into that organization's expertise and training. They participated in IHI's Breakthrough Series and adopted IHI's focus on clinical microsystems as a focus for their own improvement work. And they self-funded their participation in Pursuing Perfection, achieving financial and clinical results that outperformed all other Pursuing Perfection sites.

There is no question that IHI contributed to Jönköping's success. In many cases, IHI served as inspiration. Jönköping's leaders leveraged IHI and the Pursuing Perfection collaborative to build capacity for improvement and adopt leading practices. Fortunately, IHI is now helping to spread the word about Jönköping's success and the learnings we can all take from its experience.

But for me, as a CEO, I need to view Jönköping's success through a leadership lens. To a large degree, Jönköping's success is a result of inspired, persistent, transformational leadership by CEO Sven-Olof Karlsson and other senior leaders whom he selected to lead this remarkable organization.

Let's look at this facet a little closer. The literature on transformational leadership often describes four characteristics of this leadership style: idealized influence, inspirational motivation, intellectual stimulation and individualized consideration. Embedded in the description of Jönköping are many examples of how transformational leadership succeeded.

It appears to me that Karlsson's leadership style was, at the very least, a critical success factor. By personally attending the IHI forum, he modelled idealized influence through his willingness to learn. Karlsson was open to new ideas that challenged the status quo, and he strategically invested in learning and the establishment of Qulturum as a building block for Jönköping's quality improvement. Through his lengthy, stable leadership, Karlsson also established strategic alliances with government to build trust and buy time for results to be realized. Karlsson and Jönköping's other leaders likewise built strategic partnerships with a medical school, other health professions' programs and physicians to help build learning and research capacity related to quality. By engaging clinical leaders and the public and by measuring and communicating results, Karlsson built trust and pride as improvements were achieved.

What lessons do I take away from these endeavours? Never forget the responsibilities senior leaders have as role models and the importance of building strategic alliances that build trust. Above all, brag shamelessly when things are improving because doing so will help instill pride in hard-earned achievements.

Transformational leadership also involves inspirational motivation: the ability to communicate a compelling vision clearly and confidently. Such communication inspires and supports individuals to excel, confident that extraordinary results can be achieved. For me, this aspect of transformational leadership is exemplified by Jönköping's continuous efforts to do better, even when it was exceeding the performance of other county councils.

The illustration depicting Jönköping's improvement journey as a development stair illustrates this effort. Leaders believed they could fundamentally redefine their system by demonstrating a constancy of purpose, investing in learning and realigning resources.

And what lesson do I take away from this? A leader's clarity of vision, willingness to set the bar high and confidence in the future can positively infect a whole organization. That is our job as leaders.

So, we health system leaders influence and inspire. Yet even that role is insufficient unless we also provide intellectual stimulation. Jönköping's leaders excelled at doing this. They tapped into the world's leading quality experts as coaches. They leveraged IHI teachings and programs. By reinvesting savings at the clinical microsystem level and requiring staff members to self-fund most improvement initiatives, Jönköping's leaders empowered people to make changes.

They supported this work by building capacity at a scale few of us have ventured: 4,000 of 9,000 staff members trained in quality improvement methodology. This investment in intellect acknowledged the talents and dedication of the people within the organization, with extraordinary results.

What lesson do I take away? Simply that good intentions are not enough if people do not have the knowledge and skills to make improvements. We need to make these strategic investments at a much larger scale in order to build capacity. We must then create cultures in which quality improvement initiatives become self-funded throughout our organizations. Quality as our primary business strategy needs to become our new mantra.

Influence, inspire, stimulate intellect – sounds like that list should be enough. But transformational leadership is also about individualized consideration, caring at a personal level for those with whom we work. I do not know enough about Jönköping to assess whether this aspect of transformational leadership characterized its leaders.

References in the case study to future uncertainties, however, serve as warning bells. Even when inspired and equipped to achieve, staff members are human and can feel overwhelmed. The fatal flaw of many leaders is to be overly ambitious, to be focused on so many results that their systems implode from the sheer weight of all the projects. This is where individualized consideration becomes so important. Leaders need to constantly check the pulse of their organizations and the people who work there. They must look at both high-level corporate results and the impact of those efforts on the morale, quality of life and well-being of staff members. In healthcare organizations we tend to do this poorly. For me, the Jönköping example is a powerful reminder that I need to strive unwaveringly for a balance between transformational change and supporting and caring about the people who help achieve that change.

There are many ways to analyze Jönköping County Council's success. And there are many critical success factors that warrant deeper understanding so we can apply these learnings to achieve success in other health systems. Transformational leadership is not the only answer. However, through the eyes of this leader, it is an important ingredient and one that inspires and motivates me in my own leadership journey.

5

Intermountain Healthcare

Salt Lake City, Utah, US

Highlights of recent achievements

In the 30th-anniversary Intermountain Healthcare (IHC) annual report, Chairman Merrill Gappmayer and Chief Executive Officer (CEO) Bill Nelson reflected on their organization's evolution and the constancy of its mission over the past three decades:

> We began as a multi-hospital system and today we are an integrated system combining doctors, hospitals and health plans. … Early in IHC's history, our trustees committed our organization to becoming better, not bigger. That is still our philosophy today. IHC's hospitals and clinics have grown to provide access to a growing population but still serve about the same proportion of inpatients they did in 1975 … due to the influx of competitors, IHC's share of outpatient surgeries has actually decreased. … We continually seek to improve our services and to become "ever better." (Intermountain Healthcare 2005a: 4–6)

IHC strives to be "an organization driven by excellence" (Intermountain Healthcare nd a). For years IHC and its organizations have been recognized for excellence in several areas, spanning integration, information systems, clinical care and financial performance (Intermountain Healthcare 2006a):

- Since 1999 IHC has been ranked the top integrated health system in the United States (US) by *Modern Healthcare Magazine* and Verispan research firm. Based on a survey and Verispan's Integrated Health Network (IHN) rating system, top regional, non-specialty healthcare systems are chosen for their ability to operate as a unified organization in each of eight categories: integration, integrated technology, contractual capabilities, out-patient utilization, financial stability, services and access, hospital utilization and physicians (Health First 2005).
- IHC's Latter-Day Saints (LDS) Hospital was selected four times as one of America's best hospitals by *US News & World Report* in four different medical specialties: respiratory disorders, pulmonary medicine, endocrinology and diabetes care. *US News & World Report* rates hospitals in 16 specialties and overall by surveying physicians on reputation and by collecting data on mortality and a mix of care-related factors such as nursing and patient services. The 50 hospitals in each specialty with the highest scores are listed (Intermountain Healthcare 2006b).
- The American Nursing Association designated LDS Hospital as Utah's first Magnet Hospital. Magnet status is a designation of nursing excellence based on an appraisal of quality indicators and standards of nursing practice as defined in the American Nurses Association's Scope and Standards for Nurse Administrators (American Nurses Credentialing Center 2007).
- For the seventh time in eight years, in 2006 Hospitals & Health Networks and the American Hospital Association named IHC one of the most technologically advanced and savvy hospital systems in the US in the 100 Most Wired Hospitals list. This recognition is based on a survey representing 1,255 hospitals nationwide that asks hospitals to report on their use of information technology to address five key areas: safety and quality, customer service, business processes, workforce and public health and safety (Hospitals and Health Networks 2006).
- In 2004 IHC's LDS Hospital and McKay Dee Hospital Center received a National Consumer Choice Award for Medical Excellence. This award is based on a nationwide consumer survey by the National Research Corporation representing more than 400,000 individuals in Utah and other areas throughout the US.
- IHC continues to have the highest bond rating for a US non-profit healthcare system. As a result of its adequate financial reserves and prudent management, IHC is able to borrow at lower rates and to pass savings on to consumers in the form of lower rates for services (Intermountain Healthcare nd b).

IHC's reputation for clinical excellence is based on a strong foundation of evidence-based medicine and clinical process management that has resulted in dramatic improvements in patient outcomes and costs. There are several examples of such improvement:

- In 1999 IHC standardized care processes for the prescription of appropriate medications for cardiac patients at discharge, including beta-blockers, statins, ACE/ARB inhibitors, antiplatelet medications and warfarin. Over a two-year period the proportion of cardiac patients receiving appropriate medications at discharge increased by 50% to proportions of more than 90%, far exceeding the US average. These process improvements at IHC have been associated with significant improvements in clinical outcomes for this group of patients, including significant reductions in mortality and readmission rates of congestive heart failure and ischemic heart disease patients (James 2005b; Lappé et al. 2004).
- In 2001 IHC standardized processes for initiating appropriate elective inductions for women waiting to deliver (<39 weeks' gestation). This resulted in a decrease in the rate of induction from 29% to 5% over two years, thereby exceeding the goal of reducing the rate of inappropriate inductions by 50%. This reduction led to substantial decreases in the rate of unplanned Caesarean sections and the average number of hours in labour and delivery (in electively induced patients). More appropriate elective inductions have resulted in a decrease in costs to the system of $400 per birth and $10 million per year (James 2005b).
- In 2002 IHC clinicians standardized bilirubin screening in babies. Screening for bilirubin increased by more than 80%, from 12% in 2002 to 99% in 2005. This has resulted in a significant decrease in the number of babies born at IHC that develop hyperbilirubinemia and associated complications (James 2005b).
- In 2003 clinicians adopted measures for maintaining tighter glucose control of patients in intensive care units (ICUs). These changes led to a statistically significant reduction in the rates of mortality in this patient group. This improvement is now being spread – with similar success – to patients undergoing cardiovascular surgery at IHC (Intermountain Healthcare 2005b).
- In 2004 clinicians at IHC standardized care for patients on ventilators, thereby reducing the average number of days for each patient on a ventilator by more than a day. These improvements were associated with a 10% reduction in the rate of ventilator-associated pneumonia over two years. More appropriate ventilator use at IHC is also associated with a shorter length of stay in ICU and a reduction in cost by more than $3,000 per ICU patient.

These examples of clinical improvements are underpinned by a rigorous review of evidence as well as by standardization and redesign carried out through data collection and analysis of protocols and complex care processes. A key champion at the centre of this evidence-directed, clinical quality improvement at IHC is Dr. Brent C. James, IHC's vice-president of medical research and continuing medical education and the executive director of the IHC Institute for Health Care Delivery Research. James is widely recognized in North America and internationally for his work on clinical process management and for encouraging a transformative shift from what he terms autonomous "craft-based medicine" to evidence-directed, team-based medicine focused on patients and clinical processes.

While evidence-based protocols, data collection and analysis of clinical processes have been used elsewhere as strategies for improvement, few healthcare systems have successfully translated these efforts into sustained system-wide improvements in healthcare. How have James and his IHC colleagues used such strategies to create a system capable of improvement?

Method: Exploring a system capable of improvement

To address this question, in October 2006 a team of researchers from the University of Toronto's Department of Health Policy, Management and Evaluation visited IHC. This site visit was part of an initiative called Quality by Design, which aims to identify and define elements of healthcare systems capable of improvement with a view to helping to inform strategic investments in improvement capability in Ontario. Quality by Design is funded primarily by the Ontario Ministry of Health and Long-Term Care in partnership with the University of Toronto's Department of Health Policy, Management and Evaluation.

IHC was one of five healthcare systems selected from a short list of high-performing systems nominated by a panel of international leaders and experts. In Salt Lake City the team met with and interviewed James, other administrative and clinical leaders and support staff working to make improvements. This case study highlights the findings of that site visit.

The System and its environment

IHC is a non-profit healthcare system and the largest provider of healthcare services in Utah, one of the fastest growing states in the US. With annual revenue of $3 billion, IHC employs over 26,000 people across more than 200 facilities throughout Utah and Idaho. IHC provides care across the continuum (except for long-term care) in 21 hospitals, over 80 out-patient clinics, counselling centres, home health agencies and over 100 medical group practices.

The central administrative offices for IHC and its flagship LDS Hospital are located in Salt Lake City. IHC's 2,200 hospital beds are clustered in nine main hospitals, which account for 95% of the beds and volume (see Table 1 for a summary of IHC's clinical statistics). Twelve of IHC's hospitals are located in urban areas (Salt Lake City-Ogden and

Provo-Orem), where they have a strong market presence; the nine remaining hospitals are in rural areas of Utah and southern Idaho. The construction of three new hospital sites is under way and will largely replace current sites (with 300 additional beds). Most notably, in late 2007 the Intermountain Medical Center – a $400 million facility – will replace LDS Hospital (Intermountain Healthcare 2006a).

IHC has over 3,200 affiliated physicians, who account for over 60% of all physicians working in the area. A third of these physicians are employed by the IHC system. Approximately 600 of IHC's employed physicians belong to the Intermountain Medical Group, a network of multi-disciplinary physicians working in IHC's physician, urgent care and occupational health clinics (Intermountain Healthcare nd c). It is estimated that 1,250 physicians of those affiliated provide 90% of the care in the system.

Table 1. IHC annual clinical statistics for 2005

Acute admissions: 123,011
Acute patient days: 497,151
Births: 29,732
In-patient surgeries: 37,700
Emergency department visits: 429,124
Home care visits: 170,720
Ambulatory surgeries: 96,435
Out-patient visits: 5,559,053

Source: Intermountain Healthcare (2006a). Used by permission.

Under the leadership of Dr. David Burton, IHC began to develop its own health plans in 1983. Today, IHC's health plans and its five provider networks have 460,000 members, making up 40% of Utah's commercial market. The development of IHC's health plans has been an important strategy for the health system, protecting it from the excesses and fluctuations experienced by other plans. IHC's primary competitor is Columbia Hospital Corporation of America (HCA). Overall, IHC has managed to keep costs affordable for patients, with competitive health plan premiums and in-patient charges that are 27% lower than the national average and out-patient surgical charges that are 35% lower than those in other Utah facilities. IHC continues to realize enough cost savings to give plan members a rebate (Intermountain Healthcare 2005a).

IHC was established on April 1, 1975, when the Latter-Day Saints Church donated 15 hospitals it owned and operated as a community partnership to this new organization. The Latter-Day Saints hospitals were among the first in the Intermountain area – IHC's flagship LDS Hospital was established in 1905. The donation was made on the condition that a non-profit organization would be formed to operate the hospitals on behalf of the communities they served. IHC was created as a charitable, non-profit, secular organization that owned and managed its hospitals on behalf of the people of Intermountain West. Community leaders governed the newly created organization as unpaid volunteer trustees and named Scott Parker as inaugural CEO. Within a few years several hospitals asked to join IHC and communities invited IHC to build facilities. By 1982 IHC had begun to provide non-hospital services (Intermountain Healthcare 2005a).

Although there is no formal relationship between the Latter-Day Saints Church and IHC, the Church maintains a strong presence in the organization's culture and values. James attributes the constancy of IHC's mission, its commitment to the community and its collaborative culture to the organization's historical roots. For example, he says, "Acting for one's own benefit, at the expense of the collective good, violates the principles on which IHC was founded and is still strongly frowned upon by leaders and staff at the organization." In addition, an important part of IHC's mission is to provide residents "with access to health services, regardless of ability to pay." IHC provides more than $85 million in uncompensated care annually (excluding bad debts, which amount to more than $75 million per year) (Intermountain Healthcare nd d).

IHC's journey to a system capable of quality improvement

Structural integration

In its early days leaders described IHC as a multi-hospital system – "a loose confederation of competing hospitals." By 1986, in the context of escalating healthcare needs and costs and declining reimbursements, Parker – IHC's CEO – saw the integration of hospital operations as a necessary step to improve efficiency. Eliminating a layer of management, the IHC hospital system was restructured into regions with a single parent board of trustees (and advisory boards for facilities), a centralized management structure with a shared general ledger and coordinated budget planning. In addition to realizing operational efficiencies, leaders hoped to improve quality of care while reducing costs and focusing on prevention. A major barrier to achieving this goal was the conflicting aspirations of different parts of the system, notably providers, hospitals and insurers. Parker articulated a vision emphasizing synergy, and physicians, hospitals and health plans began to communicate and work more closely together in order to align their efforts toward achieving higher quality, lower cost and prevention.

In 1993 leaders took further steps to more formally integrate physicians, hospitals and health plans in an effort to "improve the total process of care." A task force explored and recommended options for physician relationships with IHC. The system's leadership hoped to give physicians an organizational voice and to bring clinical sciences into prominence. The task force endorsed a new relationship for physicians that would enhance their integration into the IHC system, including a medical division for physicians who chose to be employed by IHC. As a result, the Intermountain Medical Group was created and physicians were invited to play a more significant role in IHC's management and operations (Intermountain Healthcare 2005a). The Intermountain Medical Group proved to be strategically important for engaging physicians in improvement by providing a laboratory for clinical innovation and holding physicians accountable for results. By the mid 1990s IHC had become a structurally integrated health system.

Developing a critical understanding of healthcare costs

As early as 1985 CEO Parker required that leaders and managers at IHC demonstrate a return on investment (ROI) for all new initiatives. In order to find more robust ways of calculating ROI, IHC's Department of Finance, led by Steven Busboom, began working on an idea that would separate a hospital's contribution from a physician's contribution to the care of a patient. This work led to the development of one of the first activity-based costing systems in US healthcare (James 1989). According to many observers IHC leadership's early understanding of costs and the information systems needed to track them was rare in the healthcare arena.

Linking the study of variation to leadership of improvement

With physicians becoming increasingly integrated into the system, IHC leaders needed to find ways to support their work and interests, especially for emerging clinical champions. In 1986 Dr. Steven Lewis, IHC's senior vice-president of medical affairs, recruited Dr. Brent C. James from the Harvard School of Public Health to "reach out to physicians in the system, and do research." James, who had initially completed his surgery residency at IHC in the late 1970s, was returning to the Utah-based system with strong statistical and clinical expertise. James began his new role by working on studies of variation in access to care. He quickly became intrigued by variation in clinical practice and quality of care, especially through his work on transurethral prostatectomies (TURP) that showed wide variations among physicians on the grams of tissue removed by surgical time (James 2001a). James noted that issues of practice variation had several causes, including complexity, poor judgment/uncertainty and human error. He felt that despite healthcare's rapidly improving science, these causes highlighted performance and execution problems (2001b). Expanding his work on variation, James began to lead a series of quality, utilization and efficiency (QUE) studies at IHC.

In 1987 James shared his work on variation with Dr. Paul Batalden, a physician peer and clinical leader then at Park Nicollet Clinic in Minneapolis, Minnesota. Batalden – who shared James' interests in clinical quality – introduced James to the work and principles of Dr. W. Edwards Deming, an American statistician and teacher who pioneered quality improvement and who is widely credited with having trained Japanese leaders on methods for improving manufacturing quality. In 1987 James participated in Deming's four-day seminar on quality improvement. Deming's teachings, and particularly his notion that "clinical and cost outcomes are two sides of the same coin," had a profound impact on James, especially given the growing emphasis on ROI among IHC leaders. James returned from the seminar with a deeper appreciation of the principles and methods that could improve variation and the "production" of healthcare: the knowledge that quality drives down cost and that both should be quantified simultaneously.

Given James' medical background, he recognized early on the importance of actively engaging physicians and other clinicians in systematically examining data and mapping clinical processes to identify causes of variation and to test improvement. James created clinical oversight teams composed of physicians and nurses to participate in this work. One of the most notable examples of James' early leadership was his work on reducing post-operative wound infections and tracking associated outcomes and costs at LDS Hospital. James involved clinicians in closely studying and testing all steps of the operative process to determine the point at which patients were at greatest risk of developing wound infections. This process led the team to identify variations in the practice of pre-operative delivery of prophylactic antibiotics as the critical opportunity for improvement (Classen et al. 1992). Eventually, the standardization of surgeons' ordering practices and timing of delivery dramatically reduced the risk of post-operative infection by 50%. Applying the knowledge he had gained from Deming and using the activity-based costing system, James estimated cost savings of $30,000 per (prevented) infection.

Building on the ideas and results that emerged from the QUE studies, in 1989 James published *Quality Management for Health Care Delivery*, which "presents evidence to support the proposition that an organized system to achieve high quality care can lead to lower health care costs. In the present national environment a highly structured approach to the pursuit of quality is essential" (James 1989: 1). In this book James articulated the ideas that were to inform the journey on which IHC was about to embark.

Developing a strategic focus on improvement

By 1989, as James and clinical teams began to improve clinical processes and demonstrate better clinical outcomes and costs using a structured approach, CEO Parker and his leadership team gave quality improvement a more prominent role in IHC's core strategy. Creating an infrastructure to support a strategic focus on improvement, the senior leaders created the Quality Mission Statement and formed and led IHC's Quality Council and, eventually, the Core Quality Committee. They also placed responsibility for organization and management of quality improvement with the vice-president of professional services (Intermountain Healthcare 2005a). To create more formalized scientific support for the improvement work that James was leading with clinical teams, IHC's leadership established the Institute for Health Care Delivery Research (hereafter referred to as the Institute) under James' leadership (Intermountain Healthcare nd e). Shifting from a focus on quality assurance, in 1990 IHC explicitly adopted the principles of total quality management (TQM) as an important part of its culture. In 1991 IHC received the Healthcare Forum/Witt Award: Commitment to Quality (Intermountain Healthcare 2005a).

Enabling the improvement of quality and cost with information systems

In addition to the leadership's commitment to quality improvement as a core strategy, a critical accelerator to improvement across the IHC system was the evolution of an integrated information system. As James notes, "An early start created the strongest medical informatics system globally ... and much of Intermountain's success in integrating patient care is attributed to this strong clinical informatics system."[1]

The use of electronic data has a long history at IHC. In 1964 physician Homer Warner initiated research into clinical information systems and decision support tools for cardiology at LDS Hospital. Warner and his colleagues eventually created HELP, one of the first hospital clinical information systems based on the episodic medical record (HCT Project 2005; Warner et al. 1968). As a result IHC became the first hospital system in the US with an electronic medical record (EMR) system. HELP is still the backbone of IHC's clinical informatics system and is considered by James and others as "one of the finest and most complete electronic medical management systems." Important add-on components of the HELP system include the use of a single, unique identifier for each patient, which makes it possible to link data and for providers to access comprehensive information from any location, as well as built-in case-mix risk adjustment (Narus and Clayton 2002).

Building components of HELP internally created significant advantages for IHC: most critically, it afforded the freedom and flexibility to test new approaches and to customize a system that was congruent with the organization's core strategy. For example, in the late 1980s HELP provided appropriately detailed data for James' studies on variation and tests of process improvement with clinical teams and the ability to link these hospital data to enable activity-based costing. Today IHC's leadership anticipates future system-level priorities and goals by providing resources for the planning and integration of new data elements and analyses into their system one to two years in advance.

After several years of building the initial components of HELP internally as a hospital clinical information system, IHC altered its information architecture to develop HELP2 – a longitudinal electronic patient record linked to a clinical data repository, health data dictionary and decision-support applications called the Enterprise Data Warehouse (see Figure 1). After eight years of development this repository now integrates clinical data with other information, including existing administrative data (hospital, clinic, health plan, clinical laboratory); state birth reports; tumour, cardiovascular and neonatal registries from external sources; and even manually entered discharge documents (Narus

[1] All unattributed quotations by James and others were gathered by the Quality by Design team in conversations with James undertaken during our preparation of this case study.

and Clayton 2002). The Enterprise Data Warehouse contains 25 years' worth of medical records and provides IHC staff with an extraordinary knowledge base about their patients, the care that they and others provide and its clinical outcomes and costs – all at various levels of aggregation and analysis. Using this infrastructure IHC developed an ambulatory medical care record system used by nearly all its employed physicians (HCT Project 2005). The in-patient system is still largely the old HELP system (attempts to develop applications using the new infrastructure were not fully successful). To complete the in-patient portion of its EMR system, IHC is now partnering with General Electric (GE). The system, which is called Centricity, will be built in Salt Lake City in partnership with GE (HCT Project 2005).

Figure 1. Integration profile of IHC's clinical information system

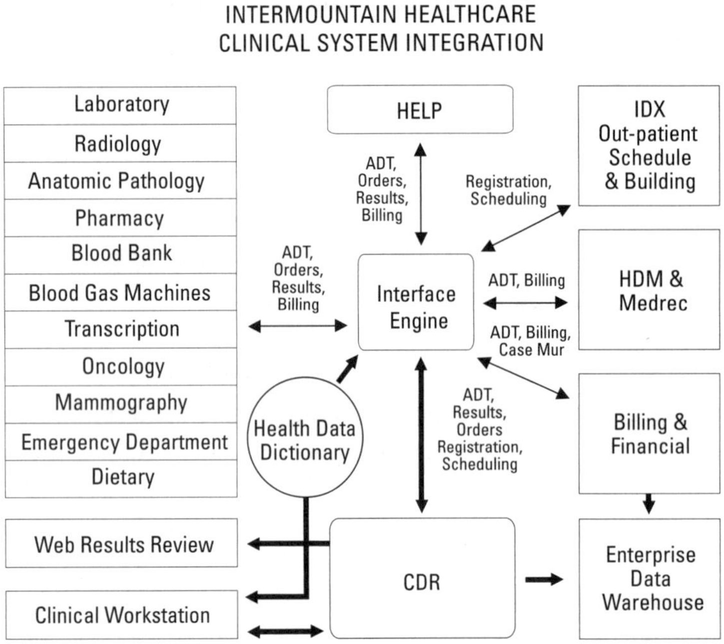

Source: Adapted from Narus and Clayton (2002).

Overall, the ability to build on and link key clinical process, outcome and finance measures enables the information system to develop and track a balanced and relevant set of measures for accountability and system performance as well as day-to-day clinical process improvement. Systems elsewhere are often limited by the availability of data in administrative databases; as a result they frequently maintain a disproportionate focus on accountability for finances and facilities management.

In addition to developing its first-class information system, IHC has invested in the use of its information for clinical decision-making and inter-professional collaboration. The interface between the EMR and care providers is at the point of care; in some of IHC's facilities, providers can enter and view data using clinical workstations in patient rooms (Narus and Clayton 2002). For decades clinicians working in LDS Hospital's ICU and other areas have conducted patient rounds at computer terminals where they can view all patient information, including laboratory and diagnostic imaging reports. In addition, an outcomes tracking system is available to staff on IHC's intranet, displaying standard reports customized for clinical programs that include control charts, comparative benchmarks and other tools for monitoring and flagging significant changes over time. Although a few clinical programs operate completely electronically, an IHC analyst estimates that still only 10%–15% of data is exclusively electronic at the point of care across the IHC system: "There is still a lot of paper to data entry going on." The GE partnership is intended to help expedite a more complete shift to electronic documentation.

Although physicians and other clinicians at IHC were initially reluctant to use the EMR system, increased productivity and quality helped convince many of them of its benefit. In the spirit of IHC's evidence-based approach to care and quality improvement and James' Institute, a number of empirical studies were conducted to illustrate for clinicians that using the EMR system would decrease waste, improve reimbursement and aid in decision-making (Narus and Clayton 2002). A recent report suggests this evolution of business intelligence tools at IHC now enables analysts to spend 90% of their time – which they used to devote to data collection – working with clinicians and managers to improve processes (Sanders 2002). The integrated data systems are also helping to demonstrate that quality and cost can be jointly pursued as two important imperatives for the system, rather than be seen as competing goals.

Developing improvement knowledge and skills – the Advanced Training Program

In order to facilitate the study and improvement of clinical processes using data from IHC's information systems to achieve better performance for the system, clinicians and leaders had to develop their own knowledge and skills in the use of improvement methods and tools. According to James, "You have to have training in quality improvement to change the culture."

Having furthered his own learning at Deming's seminar, James developed educational programs for IHC clinical staff and leaders and offered them through the Institute. By 1990 this education had evolved into the Advanced Training Program (ATP), which addresses quality improvement theory, measurement and tools, healthcare policy and systems and leadership. Since its inception the ATP has gained recognition from sector leaders such as Donald M. Berwick, president and CEO of the Institute for Healthcare Improvement (IHI), who has said, "The ATP is the finest training program we know of for bringing front-line clinicians, health care leaders, and internal change agents to a deeper understanding of what it means to make quality the core strategy for an organization" (Intermountain Healthcare nd f).

The ATP does not endorse one specific approach or method for improvement (e.g., Plan-Do-Study-Act, Model for Improvement, Lean, Six Sigma); instead, it teaches a core set of improvement principles and introduces tools from a variety of approaches. A key principle of the ATP is that it is action-based and participants are required to apply their learning to an improvement project. Participants are paired with Institute staff members who provide mentorship and coaching support as they work on their projects between sessions. Participants in turn share their project results at the conclusion of their training. In addition to teaching more than half of the ATP, James brings in some well-recognized external quality improvement experts as faculty, including Ken Kizer, David Eddy and James Reinertsen. The Institute offers two versions of the program: an 11-day mini-ATP course largely geared to clinicians and a full 20-day ATP course (Intermountain Healthcare nd g).

In the early 1990s ATP participants were predominantly drawn from within the IHC system. Bringing seasoned clinicians, managers and administrators together to learn the same core theory, methods and tools was a revolutionary concept at the time. According to James,

> The course has helped to create a palpable cultural change at Intermountain. ... The group learning and mentored project work fostered an environment of interdisciplinary collaboration ... and it created more widespread support for quality improvement ... so that it wasn't just me. Participants could bear personal testimony to successful quality improvement.

Since 1991, graduation from the full ATP course has been a requirement for all IHC senior managers and leaders. James notes that over 30 to 40 of IHC's physician leaders have become champions of quality improvement following ATP participation.

To date 2,000 people have graduated from the ATP (including external participants), generating more than 1,000 quality improvement projects. Quantifying results of the ATP projects from IHC participants, James estimates that the program has yielded a 4-to-1 ROI for the IHC system. Today only 20% of participants are from within IHC. Because the Institute is required to break even in order to pay staff and not to generate profit, James has been able to continue to offer the ATP to external participants at an affordable rate. Participants' backgrounds are varied: 40% physician executives, 20% nurse/other clinician executives, 15% administrative staff, 10% senior executives and 10% academic researchers. Participants come from a broad range of international and national jurisdictions, and an explicit goal of the program is the continued networking of students and alumni. According to James there are more than 15 ATP-type programs around the world and he hopes to expand this number.

Clinical integration strategy

Background

Under Parker's continued leadership, by the mid 1990s IHC had made important strategic investments in improvement capabilities. These included giving physicians and clinical scientists more prominence in managing the system, developing leadership-level quality oversight infrastructure, creating an integrated data repository and launching a training program for improvement knowledge and skills. After 20 years under Parker, its inaugural CEO, IHC named a new CEO, Bill Nelson.

Shortly after his arrival in 1995 Nelson noted some key challenges facing IHC's improvement strategy. Most notably, clinical quality improvements and parallel cost improvements were largely focused on only one area of the system. Furthermore, managers and clinical leaders were still successfully using advocacy (rather than evidence) to dictate priorities for improvement. Nelson asked James and Dr. David Burton, a senior clinical leader and IHC's senior strategic planner, to lead the development of a new strategic quality plan that would transform improvement at IHC from an emphasis on projects in parts of the system to a core business strategy that could add value across the system. Nelson envisioned a strategy focused on designing an improvement system that would systematize and deploy better-quality outcomes and costs throughout IHC and that could "cut through the advocacy to create a sense of discipline and purposeful focus at IHC." The system's new leader hoped to build on the investments already made to make improvement a system imperative rather than an organizational or individual responsibility.

Responding to Nelson's strategic vision, Burton and James developed a strategy they called "clinical integration." Based in part on the Baldrige model and Deming's work, this strategy focuses on a data-driven analysis and prioritization of key value-added processes and on the reorganization and realignment of the system around a set of high-priority clinical areas. Using data on service delivery, priority clinical areas were identified. Within these priority clinical areas clinicians and other leaders were to map and develop evidence-based care models for vital processes and then build them into workflows. This approach to process management also involves aligning management structures and systems (e.g., information systems, management infrastructure, accountability mechanisms, incentives) to the redesign and standardization of care. According to James (2001c: 34), "Clinical integration shifts the management paradigm further from a financial/administrative model to a clinical process model – the core way we actually accomplish work and add value."

Selection of priority clinical programs

In the first phase of the strategy development Burton and James used a set of criteria and data to redesign and focus the system around specific programs across IHC regions. The prioritization criteria included patient volumes, cost per case (in-patient and out-patient), variation in clinical quality, team-based (or microsystem) processes of care and social equity (see Table 2 for a sample of the data used in this exercise). As a result of this process nine clinical programs were identified as priorities: Cardiovascular, Neuromusculoskeletal, Surgical, Women and Newborn, Intensive Medicine, Pediatrics, Behavioral Health, Oncology and Primary Care. Across these clinical programs, the Cardiovascular and Women and Newborn programs were ranked as the top two priorities and further development of the strategy began in these two areas.

Table 2. Sample of cost data used to prioritize IHC's clinical programs

Clinical Program	Hospital In-Patient and Out-Patient Cost ($US)	% of Total Cost
Cardiovascular	$129,442,947	18.5%
Neuromusculoskeletal	$128,675,965	18.4%
Surgical Specialties	$116,646,327	16.7%
Women and Newborn	$114,984,231	16.4%
Medical Specialties	$94,773,645	13.5%
Pediatric Specialties	$44,552,204	6.4%
Behavioral Health	$17,185,283	2.5%
Total: Clinical Programs	$646,260,602	92.4%
ICU & Trauma	$31,079,870	4.4%
Unassigned	$22,759,375	3.3%
Total: All Hospital Cases	$646,260,602	100%

Source: James (2001c).
Used by permission.

Development of evidence-based clinical process models

In the second phase of the strategy development, clinicians in each priority clinical area worked in collaborative groups called "development teams" to map key processes. Development teams include a team leader who is a specialist and expert in the clinical field and clinicians who represent regions across the IHC system. Team members work together to create and adapt care process models, including evidence-based practice guidelines and clinical protocols using conceptual flow diagrams and other methods and tools (James 2001c). The goal of each team's work is to "reflect the inherent hierarchical process/outcomes structure of every clinical process." As shown in Figure 2, teams start with a high-level clinical process model (e.g., labour and delivery), and use that as a starting point for developing increasingly more detailed models of evidence-based care for each process.

Figure 2. High-level clinical process model – labour and delivery

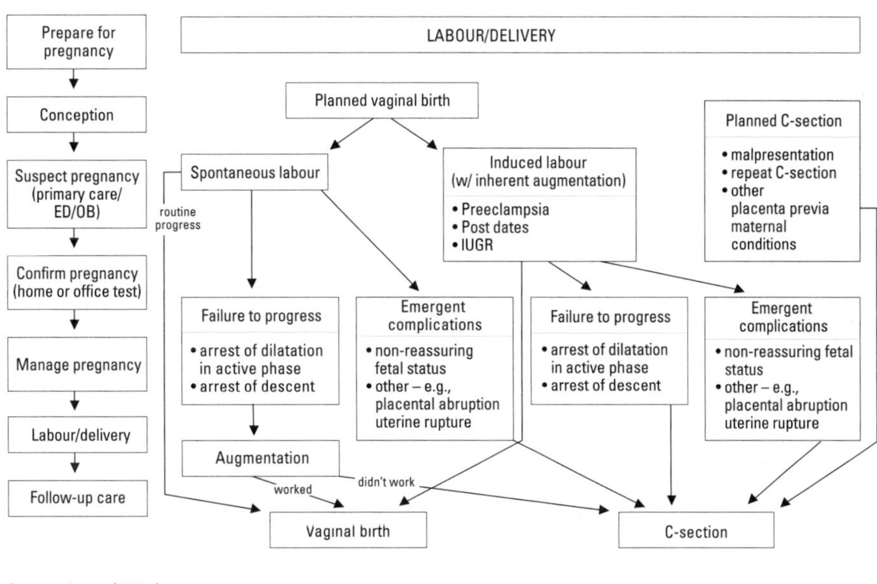

Source: James (2001c).
Used by permission.

There is one development team for each major clinical process. Within each team core, work groups are assigned to specific processes. Development teams are charged with working on four types of care processes: clinical conditions, non-condition specific clinical processes, service quality and administrative processes. A member of each team also has the task of staying current with the best available evidence and IHC's current performance in order to identify ongoing opportunities to adapt current process models and to develop new process models. The teams hold regional clinical learning days to engage clinicians in defining strategic improvement goals, and they share the clinical process models more broadly within their clinical priority areas, seeking feedback prior to proceeding with further phases of the strategy.

For each priority area development teams identify a family of processes that account for a large proportion of volume and cost. Burton and James note that 10% of clinical processes accounted for 90% of volumes. As shown in Table 3, the Women and Newborn team determined that labour and delivery had a family of eight key processes.

Table 3. Sample of data on women and newborn family of processes

Women and Newborn Family of Processes				
Processes	**DRGs**	**In-patient and Out-patient Costs ($US)**	**%**	**Cumulative %**
Pregnancy and Delivery				
Vaginal delivery	372–375	$29,657,385	27.6%	27.6%
Prematurity	382–388	$25,222,166	23.5%	51.1%
Complicated term newborn	385, 389–390	$11,037,703	10.3%	61.4%
C-section	370–371	$10,929,007	10.2%	71.6%
Normal newborn	343,391	$8,415,758	7.8%	79.4%
Non-continuing pregnancies	378–381	$2,169,248	2.0%	81.4%
Fertility/infertility	361–362	$1,656,029	1.5%	82.9%
Post-partum and other	376–377, 384	$1,343,002	1.3%	84.2%
Total: Pregnancy and Delivery		$90,430,298	84.2%	
Benign gyn conditions	356, 358–360, 364–365, 368-369	$14,973,415	14.0%	98.2%
Malignant gyn conditions	353–357, 363, 366–367	$1,922,540	1.8%	100.0%
Total: Women and Newborn		$107,326,253	100%	

Source: James (2001c).
Used by permission.

James estimates that the clinical process models continue to be adapted every six months. Based on IHC's evaluation of the implementation of this strategy, clinical teams work on a maximum of four clinical process models in a clinical setting at one time. According to James, "Any more than four and the paper shuffling overwhelms us."

Integration of process models into information systems

In addition to leading the creation of clinical models for improvement through process management, the development teams are instrumental in subsequent phases of the strategy. To help build the clinical process models into workflow, the teams generate a list of desired outcomes for tracking reports using flow diagrams to identify key measures for monthly reporting and the desired level of aggregation of those measures. For labour and delivery, for example, teams identified a series of outcome measures for tracking, including Caesarean delivery/Vaginal birth after Caesarean (VBAC) rates, measures of clinical process failure, satisfaction and cost (see Table 4). The teams work with support staff to develop reports using existing computerized data, standardized manual systems or newly created data systems.

Table 4. Outcomes for tracking – labour and delivery

Caesarean and VBAC delivery rates
• Overall Caesarean delivery rate • Primary Caesarean delivery rate • "Planned" Caesarean delivery rate • VBAC delivery rate • Caesarean delivery rate among planned vaginal births • Caesarean delivery rate for dystocia • Caesarean delivery rate for fetal distress • Summary Caesarean rates across all sections • Overall unplanned Caesarean delivery rate by physician • Caesarean delivery rate for dystocia by physician • Caesarean delivery rate for fetal distress by physician
Clinical process failures • Proportion of vaginal deliveries with stage-4 complications • Average number of stage-2/3 complications per vaginal delivery • Proportion of Caesarean deliveries with stage-4 complications • Average number of stage-2/3 complications per Caesarean delivery • Proportion of NICU admissions
Satisfaction outcomes • Proportion of patients rating practitioner excellent • Proportion of patients rating practitioner poor/fair • Proportion of patients rating labour and delivery nurses excellent • Proportion of patients rating labour and delivery nurses poor/fair • Proportion of patients rating floor nurses excellent • Proportion of patients rating floor nurses poor/fair • Proportion of patients rating overall care excellent • Proportion of patients rating overall care poor/fair
Cost outcomes – relative resource utilization (RRU) • Average RRUs per normal vaginal deliveries without VBAC or secondary surgical outcomes • Average RRUs per VBAC delivery • Average RRUs per vaginal delivery • Average RRUs per vaginal delivery with secondary surgical procedure • Average RRUs per Caesarean delivery

Source: James (2001c).
Used by permission.

James reports that when comparing the availability of data in IHC's system in the mid 1990s to the requirements generated throughout the development of the clinical integration strategy, IHC's information system had only 50%–70% of the data needed. The clinical integration strategy was a key driver for the development of the clinical repository described earlier in this report. According to James (2001c), "In the long term … the primary purpose of an electronic medical record is protocol support. … We were not able to show a return on investment for our electronic medical record systems until we combined them with our clinical improvement. … Informatics builds the tools; clinical quality improvement builds the content."

To facilitate use of data for decision-making, worksheets were developed that automatically retrieve all the necessary clinical information, including standing order sets customized to patients, automated advisories and alerts and monthly reports posted on the intranet. As an example, the clinical integration strategy supports general practitioners (GPs) and their practices in key high-volume, high-cost conditions such as diabetes, chronic heart failure and asthma. GPs receive ongoing electronic updates with specific indicators for their patients' management in the form of patient worksheets. These include patients' general status as well as disease-specific information. Patients' problems and chronic conditions are detailed, and the worksheets include medication profiles, preventive care summaries, pertinent laboratory results and pertinent exams as well as passive reminders to physicians, organized by illness (e.g., regular eye checks for diabetes patients).

Clinicians develop and test prototypes of these tools prior to integrating them formally into the system. James describes the integration of clinical process models into decision support systems as "codifying knowledge through expert system support." Although this strategy enhances the standardization of clinical care based on evidence, it is meant to "provide a shared baseline" that allows physicians to vary decisions based on individual patient needs. The strategy supports evidence-based decision-making by building it into workflow, but does not dictate it.

Development of educational materials

Following the integration of data elements from the clinical process models into IHC's information systems, assigned members of the development teams participate in the design of educational materials both for clinical teams in the priority areas and for patients. IHC has a department of eight staff members who develop educational materials as part of the clinical integration strategy. These materials are aimed at helping guide clinicians as they put evidence into practice.

The ATP and other educational and training programs offered at the Institute include a focus on clinical integration. The patient-oriented materials assist patients to understand what they should expect and how they can participate in their care. James estimates that it takes nine months to develop and integrate a clinical process model into workflow.

Integration into management and support structure

IHC's senior leadership redesigned its management and accountability structure (see Figure 3) to support its clinical integration strategy (James 2001c). The theory behind this redesign is that each clinical priority program, such as Women and Newborn, will become a "centre of excellence" with resources to support ongoing improvements in care.

Figure 3. Clinical integration management and accountability structure

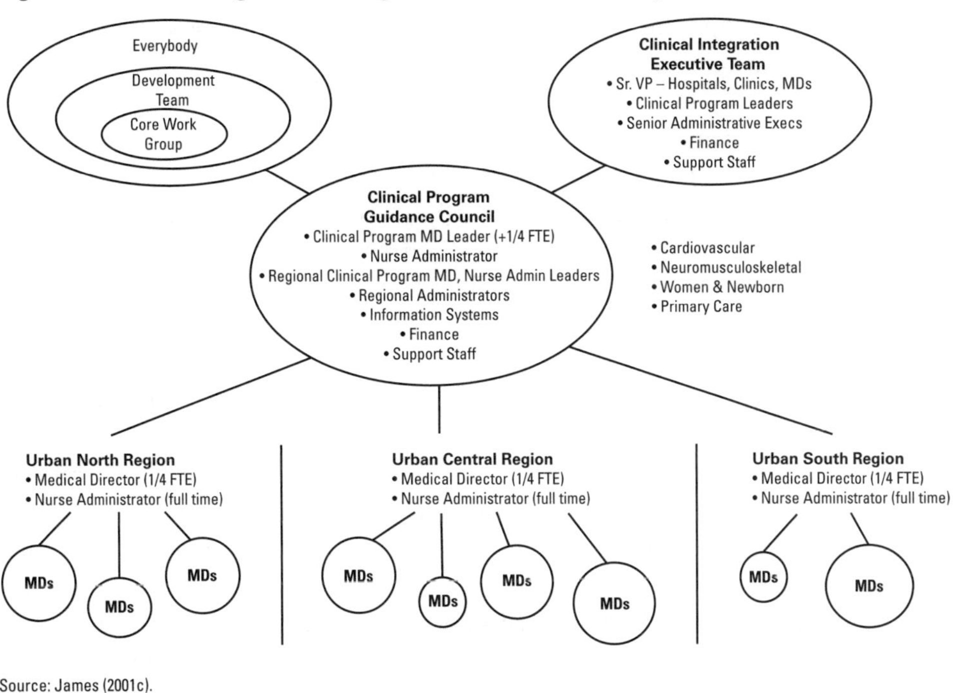

Source: James (2001c).
Used by permission.

In each clinical program, regional management teams comprising a medical director (0.25 full-time equivalent [FTE]) and a nurse administrator (1 FTE) provide leadership within IHC's Urban North, Urban Central and Urban South regions. Medical directors are carefully selected based on credibility with their peers in the specific clinical area, demonstrated management and leadership skills and ongoing clinical practice and improvement knowledge. A medical director's role is to work with front-line clinical staff; he or she identifies issues in the implementation of clinical process management, sets clinical goals and holds clinical teams accountable for performance. Nurse administrators oversee each clinical program's operations and support the use of rapid cycle improvement in the implementation of clinical process models.

In addition to the regional structure, each priority clinical program is led at the system level by a central program management team that is also made up of a medical director (0.25 FTE) and a nurse administrator (1 FTE), as well as a statistician, a data manager and a support team (e.g., finance, human resources). The central program management teams oversee priority- and goal-setting for the system, budget-planning for the program area, coordination for process management and support across regions. The statisticians and data managers play a critical role in managing the data flow within the clinical programs, supporting teams as they implement new clinical process models and reviewing system outcomes.

Regional and central clinical program management teams as well as development teams meet regularly as a guidance council to review clinical and financial outcomes, set improvement goals, identify resource and support needs, pinpoint opportunities for improvement and share ideas and practices. Each priority clinical program's guidance council reports to a clinical integration executive team that provides system-level leadership for the deployment of the strategy and that ultimately reports to IHC's board.

Every year IHC's board members – half of whom have a medical or nursing background – work with the executive team to set between two and four board goals for each clinical program. These goals typically include at least one each of clinical, financial and service-quality goals, and they drive budget and planning for the clinical programs. In addition to these board goals the guidance council and program management teams select and monitor a series of additional goals in order to gauge implementation of the evidence-based clinical process models. Statisticians draw on the data repository to create registries for the clinical programs and to prepare customized regional, system-level and board performance reports showing progress on goals; this work is in addition to the outcomes tracking available to staff on the intranet. The data in the performance reports and on the intranet are as timely as one month from patient care and, in some cases, one week. The resulting organizational structure focuses on care delivery and links information systems designed to provide data on key organizational processes with a structure that manages and continually seeks to improve core clinical processes.

Aligning incentives for clinical integration

In addition to the redesigned management structure, IHC's leadership has used information and incentives to support the clinical integration strategy. Within each clinical program physicians are given a set of core indicators that measure their own results against peer, regional and system-level results and goals. According to James, these reports encourage a form of "healthy competition that pushes people ahead and has been one strategic lever used to shift physicians towards acceptance of quality as a standard business process and operation." Regional-level medical directors use physician-level data as evidence of contributions to system-level improvement and to guide performance evaluations of employed physicians. Practice groups may be financially rewarded for improvement. Recently, some groups have received up to $25,000 in recognition of their contributions to achieving system-level goals. Senior leaders at regional and system levels have 25% of their salary contingent on the achievement of board goals.

Value for investment in clinical integration

After more than a decade of implementing this strategy across several priority programs, has the clinical integration strategy accomplished the vision Nelson set out in 1995?

As evidence of the spread of improvement across IHC, James estimates that the system is now regularly achieving 80% of its goals (higher targets are set every year). Several program-specific improvements in clinical and financial outcomes that have emerged as a result of this strategy are described in the introductory section of this case study and demonstrate measurable clinical and financial value. The centre-of-excellence concept has created an infrastructure and discipline for focused, evidence-based improvement that moves beyond projects to create system responsibilities and everyday work processes. The clinical integration strategy and its structured, phased approach of selecting key processes, mapping evidence-based models, automating information systems and workflow, developing competencies and integrating itself into management structure and incentives are now being applied to patient safety and the prevention of adverse drug events (James 2005a). James estimates that the variable cost savings resulting from the clinical integration strategy is $15 million US, on a $4 million US investment.

James notes that harvesting quality savings can be accomplished using three strategies:

- Targeting specific improvement projects to achieve internal savings
- Using evidence of improved results in contract negotiations with payers
- Partnering with purchasers in "shared risk"

IHC leaders pay careful attention to all three of these strategies. Because clinical process redesign can reduce hospital and other service utilization revenues, it is important to take a broad system view and to use these improvements to negotiate with payers. According to James (2001c), "You must align contracting strategies to harvest savings back to your organizations; otherwise, clinical quality improvement is a fast way to destroy your organization financially." In the past, several external factors affected IHC's return on investment. In particular, costs at IHC were decreasing as a result of improvement (e.g., community-acquired pneumonia); however, there was no parallel improvement in revenue because the Diagnosis-Related Group (DRG) coding system "was cheating" them. Improvements in the system over time have changed this.

Overall (and inclusive of the effects of clinical integration), James estimates IHC has saved approximately $100 million US through clinical quality improvement. Although IHC does not have a formal reinvestment savings plan, the savings are evident through excess system capacity and are directed toward capital investment. Purchasers are also beginning to benefit from quality improvement. Drawing on a recent surplus, IHC refunded 6% of annual insurance premiums to the 460,000 members of its health plans.

Internal and external supports for quality improvement at IHC

IHC has additional internal support resources beyond the management and infrastructure developed to support clinical integration as the core strategy. Nine statisticians working in the priority clinical programs are employed at James' Institute. In addition to supporting these programs, these statisticians support the development of the data repository, mentor ATP participants and help individual teams and clinicians with research. At a corporate level IHC employs analysts dedicated to the management of the clinical repository, a hospital analytics team responsible for reporting standards and providing support to clinical programs and a tactical team focused on specific business intelligence tools. Furthermore, IHC has a corporate quality management department and a team of nurses responsible for managing the external reporting and regulatory requirements of national and accreditation bodies (e.g., Centers for Medicare and Medicaid Services [CMS], The Joint Commission on Accreditation of Healthcare Organizations [JCAHO], Healthcare Effectiveness Data and Information Set [HEDIS]), thereby insulating the priority clinical programs from these demands. Although some of IHC's core goals and measures align with externally driven measures, many do not. James notes that many of these externally driven measures are "not designed for front-line use and their definitions are not functional." Individual organizations across IHC also have their own quality management departments.

To external observers the linkage and interaction between these support resources and the clinical integration strategy is not always clear, and there appears to be some overlap among these roles as well as potential redundancies. The extent to which clinical programs use specific types of support seems dependent on factors such as relationships and preferences. In addition, although a vital resource for most in the execution of the clinical integration strategy, the Institute has recently been perceived by some as an entity that is increasingly external to IHC.

Unlike some other high-performing systems, IHC appears to have developed and executed its improvement strategy by focusing and building its improvement capability internally. In addition to its information system, the development of training and skills has been homegrown. Unlike the case with several other US organizations, IHI is not a critical support resource for IHC. IHC participated in earlier collaboratives, and James and other IHC clinicians provide expertise and advisory support for IHI. However, IHC's priorities and targets differ from IHI's. According to James, "We didn't participate in 100,000 lives because we had been working on the same interventions and achieving targets for years … and we had moved on."

Challenges and future directions

IHC's strategy for improvement is based on evidence-directed clinical process management in carefully selected priority areas as well as on the alignment and integration of decision support, training and education, management and accountability. It also depends on incentives for this work. This strategy is widely recognized as having been successful in creating system-level transformation and is being implemented at the Mayo Clinic and a number of other health systems elsewhere. As one group of researchers has observed, "One of the best examples of an acute care provider that has used outcome information for strategic advantage is IHC" (Thompson et al. 2000: 579).

Like all strategies, however, IHC's has its challenges, and these raise several questions about future directions at the organization. IHC leaders note that although it was initially intended to have a broader focus, the strategy has not yet been used to improve administrative processes; rather, some separate support resources appear to be emerging for this work. In addition, certain non-clinical processes (e.g., patient flow) now require a more nimble organizational strategy. To date, focused work within priority clinical programs has had limited cross-program collaboration on such critical issues and, according to a senior-level staff member, "There is a need to shake up the silos."

Furthermore, at a corporate level IHC has recently developed a new set of extraordinary goals for clinical excellence, service excellence, operational effectiveness, physician engagement and community engagement. Will a new management structure and model be required for cross-program work and the achievement of new corporate goals, or can these be built on top of what has already been developed? What will these innovations do to the momentum created so far as leaders engaged in the clinical integration strategy continue to spread the concept to other priority program areas?

Led by clinicians, the IHC strategy has been extraordinarily successful at initiating a major cultural shift throughout the system by engaging front-line clinicians in defining excellence in clinical care and by working actively in teams on improvement. However, despite some of the innovations mentioned earlier in this report, creating automated tools that physicians and other clinicians feel comfortable using is an ongoing challenge for IHC. How will the new in-patient EMR that will be developed in partnership with GE help, or will it potentially pose further challenges?

The extent to which non-employed physicians have engaged in strategy deployment also varies. Despite the flexibility built into the system and its bottom-up development, an ongoing challenge is the perception of physicians outside the IHC medical group that the clinical integration strategy comes at the cost of local and professional autonomy and micromanagement from high-level decision-makers. IHC has assumed that achieving improvements among those physicians closely aligned with the system will help to win over the rest. But will IHC again need to change its relationship options to attract more physicians as employees or articulate strategies to develop more clinical champions among the non-employed group? Will it require an enhanced relationship between IHC and medical schools so that the principles of clinical integration and improvement are introduced to physicians earlier in their education?

A critical success factor for IHC has been its investment in the development of improvement capability through decision support and training in improvement skills and knowledge. The tension and potential overlap between the various sources of support at corporate and regional levels and within the Institute is an ongoing challenge. Will IHC's leaders streamline these resources and initiate clearer mandates and expectations for their use? Current support for clinical programs implementing the clinical integration strategy appears to emphasize analytical support more than support in the use of improvement methods, tools and change management. Clinical leaders are expected to have this knowledge and these skills as a result of their participation in the ATP, and this is also part of the nurse administrators' role. Is this a reasonable strategy and do clinical leaders actually have the time needed to actively support teams in improvement and change management? Will the Institute continue to grow to support external organizations and participants, and how will this affect its identity as a critical resource for internal support at IHC? What more will be needed?

After more than a decade as CEO, Nelson and his team – including James – continue to lead IHC. But beyond the Institute's ATP, how is IHC developing its leaders? Leadership continuity and mission constancy have been critical to the success of IHC's plan. Will eventual changes in leadership change the current direction from evidence-based clinical improvement to one of operations and growth? How much of IHC's success is supported by its social and cultural environment? And that begs the question, would IHC have been as successful using this strategy in vastly different healthcare environments such as California or New York?

Finally, how will IHC continue in its quest to be "ever better"?

References

American Nurses Credentialing Center. 2007. "ANCC Magnet Recognition Program® – Recognizing Excellence in Nursing Services." Silver Spring, MD: Author. Retrieved January 21, 2007. <http://nursecredentialing.org/magnet/>

Classen, D.C., R.S. Evans, S.L. Pestotnik, S.D. Horn, R.L. Menlove and J.P. Burke. 1992. "The Timing of Prophylactic Administration of Antibiotics and the Risk of Surgical-Wound Infection." *New England Journal of Medicine* 326(5): 281–286.

HCT Project. 2005. *Local Health Information Infrastructure Initiatives.* Q&A with CIO Marc Probst. San Francisco: Montgomery Research. Retrieved January 21, 2007. <http://www.HCTProject.com>

Health First. 2005. "Health First Ranked One of the Top 100 Integrated Healthcare Networks in the US." Rockledge, FL: Author. Retrieved January 10, 2007. <http://www.health-first.org/news_and_events/hf_verispan_top_100_2005.cfm>

Hospitals and Health Networks. 2006. "The 100 Most Wired Hospitals." Chicago: Health Forum Inc. Retrieved January 21, 2007. <http://www.hhnmag.com>

Intermountain Healthcare. nd a. *Mission, Vision and Values.* Salt Lake City: Author. Retrieved January 4, 2007. <http://intermountainhealthcare.org/xp/public/aboutihc/mission.xml>

Intermountain Healthcare. nd b. *Intermountain – Affordability Reducing Costs.* Salt Lake City: Author. Retrieved January 21, 2007. <http://intermountainhealthcare.org/xp/public/about-intermountain/affordability/reducingcosts.xml>

Intermountain Healthcare. nd c. *Intermountain Medical Group.* Salt Lake City: Author. Retrieved January 11, 2007. <http://www.intermountainhealthcare.org/xp/public/doctors/medical-group/>

Intermountain Healthcare. nd d. *Intermountain Healthcare – Our Nonprofit Mission.* Salt Lake City: Author. Retrieved January 4, 2007. <http://www.intermountainhealthcare.org/xp/public.aboutihc/nonprofit/>

Intermountain Healthcare. nd e. *Institute History.* Salt Lake City: Author. Retrieved January 11, 2007. <http://intermountainhealthcare.org/xp/public/institute/about/history.xml>

Intermountain Healthcare. nd f. *Advanced Training Program.* Salt Lake City: Author. Retrieved January 11, 2007. <http://www.ihi.org/IHI/Programs/ConferencesAndTraining/AdvancedTrainingProgram.htm>

Intermountain Healthcare. nd g. *Institute of Healthcare Delivery Research – Education Programs.* Salt Lake City: Author. Retrieved January 11, 2007. <http://intermountainhealthcare.org/xp/public/institute/education/>

Intermountain Healthcare. nd h. *IHC Primary Care Clinical Programs: Adult Diabetes Patients in Your Practice*. Salt Lake City: Author.

Intermountain Healthcare. 2005a. *Annual Report 2004.* Salt Lake City: Author.

Intermountain Healthcare. 2005b. *Healing for Life – Annual Nursing Update.* Salt Lake City: Author. Retrieved January 21, 2007. <http://www.intermountainhealthcare.org/xp/public/documents/corp/nursingupdate.pdf>

Intermountain Healthcare. 2006a. *Annual Report 2005.* Salt Lake City: Author. Retrieved January 4, 2007. <http://intermountainhealthcare.org/xp/public/documents/corp/annualreport.pdf>

Intermountain Healthcare. 2006b. "LDS Hospital Again Ranked One of America's Best Hospitals in *U.S. News & World Report* Magazine's 2006 Rankings of Nation's Top Health Care Centers." Salt Lake City: Author. Retrieved January 10, 2007. <http://intermountainhealthcare.org/xp/public/lds/aboutus/news/article21.xml>

James, B.C. 1989. *Quality Management for Health Care Delivery.* Chicago: The Hospital Research and Education Trust of the American Hospital Association. Retrieved January 4, 2007. <http://intermountainhealthcare.org/xp/public/documents/institute/articles_qmmp.pdf>

James, B.C. 2001a. *Applying Research to Affect Clinicians and Clinical Governance.* Presentation at the 4th International Conference on the Scientific Basis of Health Services, Sydney, Australia. Retrieved January 11, 2007. <http://cme.ihc.com/xp/ihc/documents/institute/conferencepresentations.pdf>

James, B.C. 2001b. *The Scientific Basis of Quality Improvement*. Presentation at the 4th International Conference on the Scientific Basis of Health Sciences, Sydney, Australia. Retrieved January 4, 2007. <http://cme.ihc.com/xp/ihc/documents/institute/conferencepresentations.pdf>

James, B.C. 2001c. *You Manage What You Measure: Tracking Clinical Outcomes*. Presentation at the Sharp HealthCare Quality Leadership Conference, San Diego. Retrieved January 21, 2007. <http://intermountainhealthcare.org/xp/public/documents/institute/sharp530.pdf>

James, B.C. 2005a. *Creating an Integrated, High Quality Health Care Delivery System that Supports Medication Safety.* Presentation to the Institute of Medicine Committee on Identifying and Preventing Medication Injuries, Washington DC.

James, B.C. 2005b. *Quality and Cost – What You Can't Afford to Ignore.* Presentation at the Introduction to State Health Policy – A Seminar for New State Legislators (Agency for Healthcare Research and Quality), Rockville, MD. Retrieved January 21, 2007. <http://www.ahrq.gov/news/ulp/statepolicy/james.ppt>

Lappé, J.M., J.B. Muhlestein, D.L. Lappé, R.S. Badger, T.L. Bair, R. Brockman, T.K. French, L.C. Hofmann, B.D Horne, S. Kralick-Goldberg, N. Nicponski, J.A. Orton, R.R. Pearson, D.G. Renlund, H. Rimmasch, C. Roberts and J.L. Anderson. 2004. "Improvements in 1-Year Cardiovascular Clinical Outcomes Associated with a Hospital-Based Discharge Medication Program." *Annals of Internal Medicine* 141: 446–453.

Narus, S.D. and P.D. Clayton. 2002. "Clinical Information Systems at Intermountain Healthcare." *Imaging Economics* (February). Retrieved January 4, 2007. <http://www.imagingeconomics.com/issues/articles/2002-02_12.asp>

Sanders, D. 2002. "Intermountain Healthcare: Designing, Developing and Supporting an Enterprise Data Warehouse (EDW) in Healthcare." In Protti, D.J., ed., *How Business Intelligence Is Making Healthcare Smarter: World View Report 10.* 2005. London: NHS Connecting for Health. Retrieved January 4, 2007. <http://www.connectingforhealth.nhs.uk/newsroom/worldview/protti10/>

Thompson, D.I., C. Sirio and P. Holt. 2000. "The Strategic Use of Outcome Information." *Joint Commission Journal on Quality Improvement* 26(10): 576–586.

Warner, H.R., R.M. Gardner, T.A. Pryor and W.M. Stauffer. 1968. *Computer Automated Heart Catheterization Laboratory. UCLA Forum in Medical Science #10.* Berkeley: University of California.

Commentary: Intermountain Healthcare

Rick Roger, Senior Editor, *Healthcare Policy*
Former CEO, Vancouver Island Health Authority

It is the energy generated by my first exposure to Brent James that sticks with me. The acknowledged champion, architect and major builder behind the Intermountain Healthcare (IHC) success story was presenting at an early 1990s gathering of the Quality Management Network, an extension of the American National Demonstration Project on Quality Improvement in Healthcare. Attendees were treated to a substantial treatise on the measurement and management of quality. Inspired and brimful with new learning to share, I carried a dog-eared version of *Quality Management for Health Care Delivery* (James 1989) for years thereafter, drawing on it with each opportunity to discuss quality with medical or managerial colleagues.

James is IHC's vice-president of medical research and continuing education and executive director of IHC's Institute for Health Care Delivery. For two decades we have listened to his provocative voice and, during that time, James has become a compelling influence rooted in statistical quality control. At that meeting in Boston so many years ago, I thought I witnessed a true force for systems understanding and change – not an economist or an accountant, but a research- and quality-oriented physician moving far beyond the traditional healthcare finance textbooks of the time.

James' work, outlined in the quality, utilization and efficiency (QUE) studies mentioned in the case, featured division of measured costs and observation of input variation and possible waste into physician-related and generic organizational components. Back on the ground in Victoria, we started to augment our own experimentation with *patient*-specific resource consumption profiles with *physician*-specific utilization patterns. These were expressed in numbers or units of nursing workload, commissioned treatments and diagnostic tests. Introducing what we knew of outcome-based analysis, we briefly enjoyed improved relationships with an engaged medical staff leadership. As this portrayal of extended reach illustrates, James had significant influence beyond Utah and IHC, a classic "power of one" situation. This was a case of solid, cause-driven effort combined with the will to make good, witnessed long before Jim Collins popularized the phrase "level 5 leadership" (Collins 2001) to describe exceptional dedication and accomplishment.

Fast forward and we still find Dr. James on healthcare blogs demystifying the connections between quality and cost. Sadly, the thrill of learning for many of us is often coupled with disappointing grades. As Canadian health service providers, do we not find ourselves all too often stuck in a performance management rut, quite unable to achieve the results expected of us? Why, we ask ourselves, have we been unable to connect "will" with "way"? Where and how did we lose traction while IHC and a select few other organizations motored ahead? What are the vital few things we must do better? How can we apply lessons learned? Surely these are among the questions that motivated the University of Toronto researchers to investigate strategy deployment and sustainable improvement.

What mysterious ingredients are necessary for a breakthrough in achievement? Arguably, strong organizational leadership, clear goals, constancy of purpose, good governance, sound organizational tactics, aligned incentives and committed staff members are the most important constituent elements. The IHC case study identifies most of these elements in play, leaving us to wonder: Is it a baseline level of synergy among these factors that sustains progress, or is there more to appreciate in the picture?

As the case study authors acknowledge, it is a daunting prospect to disentangle interwoven tactics, situate observed strategies in context and clarify connections between and among adopted strategies, sanctioned targets, primary tactics and supporting resources. And this might be the most important consequential challenge for us: that is to say, finding ways to draw on the time, intellectual honesty and emotional energy needed to look deeply into our own organizations and the managerial interventions of recent years in order to assess our performance objectively and to view ourselves as others see us. Unfortunately, "we suck" is not quite the engaging mantra sought for our annual reports, or that all-so-important conversation starter with our board chairs.

Spurred by advances in evidence-informed medical practice, a concurrent movement to strengthen the evidence base of managerial decision-making has developed. Although there are formalized approaches available, our immediate purpose here may be better served by the work of Sir Douglas Black. Clinician, statesman and author of a renowned report on inequities in health 35 years after the establishment of the United Kingdom's National Health Service (NHS), Black was known for his sense of humour (one obituary quotes him professing, "My secret is never to retire; I enjoy committees") and respected for his ability to grasp and communicate the material essentials of highly complex undertakings (Tucker 2002). I have adapted Sir Douglas' "daft laddie" questions, initially addressed to advocates of new medical interventions as well as defenders of established practice (White 1992), as a frame of reference:

What is the aim of managerial intervention or set of interventions in question?

The case study authors note several interventions, including structural realignment, the integration of physicians in management, the identification and nurturing of sustaining organizational champions, the development of tools and measures, the formalization of incisive strategy, clear messaging, coalition building, incentive alignment and targeted educational programs. These constructive measures were implemented at IHC in parallel with information system advances focusing on clinical outcomes, procedure management, quality charting, point-of-care communication, patient involvement and cost assignment. Evidence-based clinical process modelling was enabled, in part, by information system technology that was, in turn, improved by the process model prototypes. Fundamental to the observed success, all of this activity was seemingly directed with unwavering purpose at the consistent further improvement of patient care, becoming "ever better" (not necessarily bigger) in response to the vision adopted by trustees early in IHC's history.

Does the intervention do any good? Does it make a discernible difference to anyone?

Coupled with validated results, the awards and distinctions received by IHC clearly indicate that the measures introduced did make a discernible difference. The problem for those looking on is to establish with some degree of rigour what in particular worked, which interventions are best combined with others and what sequencing would be most appropriate in other organizational contexts. More than once during my years as an adherent, I have heard James answer the question "What should our organization do first to gain traction and establish a pattern of positive results?" James' response most often involves developing knowledge and skills using a variant of his advanced training program, which brings in improvement projects and new clinical champions as inevitable by-products. In essence, engage, start the journey and reap the benefits. So, yes, Dr. Black, a set of interventions worked at IHC, but we are not all that certain which of the ingredients flavoured the stew, and which stimulated and then satisfied the appetite for sustained effective practice.

How many people are potentially able to benefit? What portions of these people actually get help? What system determines who gets this help?

This grouping of Black's questions starts to bring the subject matter home to a Canadian audience. We know from the case study that IHC's market share has stabilized at a level where it provides a substantial – but not a universal – base of coverage, hardly a surprise given that the United States regulatory environment discourages continual growth in regulated markets. IHC does offer financial assistance to qualifying patients and no doubt works to not threaten competitors while responding to community needs. Might it be, though, that what we are observing is a system capable of delivering superior results, but only for a subset of the population? This is not a comfortable possibility for those schooled in the Tommy Douglas tradition. A pragmatic consideration also emerges: How do we start to understand the generalizability of observed results to broader populations? Factors other than care quality enter the equation, but the thinking behind Black's insightful questioning challenges us to address the population scale impact as a primary consideration. No one knew better than Black that the NHS, hardly alone among national health schemes, failed to meet the initial expectation of delivering the greatest health benefits to the least-favoured members of society.

What does the intervention or set of interventions cost? Are there potential substitute interventions at different cost levels? Who pays?

IHC contends that "because of cost-cutting and quality-control efforts, Intermountain's average in-patient charges are 19% lower than the Utah average, according to 2003 Utah Department of Health data, and 27% below the national average" (Intermountain Healthcare 2007). The case study documents efforts to drive out unwarranted cost and to increase affordability, but we are left uncertain as to the cost of the enabling interventions. For instance, although efforts to develop a first-class information system for the enterprise are well described, missing is any attempt to quantify what must be a substantial cost, or to express this as a percentage of the cost per case. The new electronic record under development with General Electric will add to both cost and value, but the hard facts necessary for cost–benefit analysis are not available to us. Conversely, the clinical program regional management team structure is well detailed, and imputable costs appear quite reasonable for this component. Finally, there can be little doubt that the Advanced Training Program has paid for itself several times over with realized savings and cost recovery. Surely Dr. Black would be highly impressed with Dr. James' constructive efforts in this regard.

What impact might the intervention make on the demand or effectiveness of other activities, procedures or services?

Comprehensive analysis of any clinical intervention will document unintended as well as intended consequences as referrals flow from instigating and enabling tests, screenings and treatments. Migrating from the clinical to the managerial world, the answer to the "impact question" emerging at IHC is intriguing to a Canadian audience. The case study provides evidence that IHC's set of managerial interventions is not only working now, but also positioning the organization well for future effectiveness and ongoing accomplishment. The impact elsewhere in the IHC system is readily contemplated: international recognition, more subscriber interest in IHC's associated insurance plans and contracts, easier access to capital, a sustainable critical mass of activity, a shot at improved staff retention and sound medical staff relationships. Outside the organization we should suspect ongoing reactive behaviour from competitors in both the care delivery and insurance markets. All good for IHC, but all very market driven and aimed more at competition than collaboration. Could Dr. Black, were he still with us, conclude anything else?

Upon considering the case study's findings we are left to ponder what they all mean for Canada. What might we learn and what can we adopt? What might we best avoid and where is the roadmap needed to move the agenda forward?

Puzzled by the intricacies of the issues, and with vision clouded by past experience, I am drawn again to James and Black, mapping mind-only dinner conversations with the passionate twosome, one sadly departed for some five years this past September. Unusual guest choices perhaps (ancient philosophers and contemporary entertainers are the predominantly cited candidates in magazine interviews), but the potential understanding gained from the mythical meeting of minds is of great intrigue. It would be such an enriching opportunity to examine the quality implications of contemporary Canadian approaches to primary health, demand management, supply management, incentives and sanctions, technology appraisal, workforce sustainability, end-of-life care, service integration, coordination and patient/client involvement. Although the list of discussion topics is endless, nothing would be more important than to consider the impact of alternative models of medical staff engagement and compensation.

And as my fictional dinner conversation draws to a close, I fancy myself distributing recent press clippings from just about any province, and attempting to steer the conversation to the environment in which we hapless Canadians attempt to engender quality improvement. What must we do to avoid further movement toward what Jim Collins (2001) describes as a "doom loop" with ever- changing executives, destabilized middle management, a shifting array of overlaid strategies, dissatisfied staff members and questionable results? James would be well positioned to respond with a discourse on the benefits of dedicated effort focused within an overriding and well-understood sense of mission. From Black, I would hope to hear a reminder that, upon honest reflection, well-organized systems based on principles of essential justice and fairness are strong enough to survive any threat. James would no doubt reiterate the importance of education and shared learning. I would be disappointed not to be the recipient of some very straight talk from Black on aboriginal health, housing the homeless and the importance of targeting services to disadvantaged populations within a comprehensive system dedicated to universal accessibility. And somewhere over the evening of conversation, I would seek an assurance from both distinguished guests that we do indeed have enough time remaining still to start doing more of the right things the right way more often than not.

References

Collins, J. 2001. *Good to Great: Why Some Companies Make the Leap ... and Others Don't.* New York: Harper Collins.

Intermountain Healthcare. 2007. *Affordability: Reducing Costs.* Salt Lake City, UT: Author. Retrieved October 30, 2007. <http://intermountainhealthcare.org/xp/public/about-intermountain/affordability/reducingcosts.xml>

James, B.C. 1989. *Quality Management for Health Care Delivery.* Chicago: The Hospital Research and Education Trust of the American Hospital Association. Retrieved January 4, 2007. <http://intermountainhealthcare.org/xp/public/documents/institute/articles_qmmp.pdf>

Tucker, A. 2002, September 12. "Obituary: Sir Douglas Black." Retrieved November 1, 2007. <http://www.guardian.co.uk/obituaries/story/0,3604,791819,00.html>

White, K.L. 1992, September 24. "Health Care Research: Old Wine in New Bottles." Paper presented at the University of Virginia's History of the Health Sciences Lecture Series. Retrieved October 9, 2007. <http://historical.hsl.virginia.edu/kerr/documents/OldWine.pdf>

6

Henry Ford Health System

Detroit, Michigan, US

Highlights of recent achievements

"2005 was a very successful year." (Henry Ford Health System 2006)

– Nancy Schlichting, CEO of the Henry Ford Health System

Nancy Schlichting had good reason to claim success for the Henry Ford Health System (HFHS). For example, the Henry Ford Hospital was included in Solucient's 2005 list of 100 Top Hospitals: Performance Improvement Leaders (Center for Healthcare Improvement 2005) and it "earned $46.5 million on net patient revenue of $728.7 million in 2005, compared with a loss of $27.5 million on net revenue of $461 million in 2001" (Wilson 2006: 24). "Henry Ford's leap onto the list of most improved hospitals for the first time occurred as a result of a comprehensive strategy involving cuts, growth strategies, and improvements in clinical quality" (Wilson 2006: 25).

HFHS' website contains multiple examples of other national and state recognition (Henry Ford Health System nd a):

HFHS

- Ranked as the top integrated healthcare system in Michigan and sixth in the nation in a 2004 national survey

- Received the 2004 Governor's Award of Excellence for enhancing patient care at Henry Ford Hospital (HFH) and in its emergency department

Henry Ford Hospital

- Ranked sixth nationally for safety and quality in the 50 Exceptional US Hospitals listing in the April 2005 issue of *Consumers Digest*
- Ranked among the top 50 hospitals in America by the American Association of Retired Persons (AARP), which reviews more than 4,500 hospitals nationwide based on factors such as mortality, physician ratings, accreditation scores and training programs
- Named one of the nation's top 100 hospitals for the treatment of stroke, according to a study released by HCIA-Sachs Institute
- One of the top performers in the country for reducing surgical infections during a single year, as part of a national collaborative sponsored by Medicare

Henry Ford Medical Group

- Received the 2004 American Medical Group Association's Acclaim Honoree Award that recognized its Department of Psychiatry for setting a national benchmark for depression care and suicide prevention

Henry Ford Wyandotte Hospital

- Recognized for its sustained decrease in ventilator-acquired pneumonia and bloodstream infection by the Keystone ICU Project

Clinical improvement initiatives

HFHS has undertaken major improvement initiatives and has achieved significant results in a variety of key clinical areas. Here are a few examples:

100k Lives

HFHS signed up for all six interventions in the 100k Lives campaign sponsored by the Institute for Healthcare Improvement (IHI). These included reduction of surgical infections, implementation of rapid response teams, improved care for acute myocardial infarction, prevention of adverse drug events, prevention of central line–associated bloodstream infections and prevention of ventilator-associated pneumonia. Some initiatives, such as reducing surgical infections, were already under way prior to the campaign but gained momentum from these focused efforts. There is multi-department, multidisciplinary support for all the projects, which include all the system's clinical leaders (e.g., 30 people sit on the bloodstream infections committee). The large committees meet every other week and then each member goes back to his/her area to try a change (e.g., a physician with his/her residents). There was no template or common approach followed for the projects, and the six were "wildly different from each other," commented quality office support staff. The results, however, are significant, as illustrated by Henry Ford Hospital's accomplishments (see Appendix A):

- 50% reduction in surgical site infection rates, including a 19-month period with no vascular surgery infections
- An average reduction of 0.9 days on a ventilator and an overall reduction of intensive care unit (ICU) length of stay by 0.65 days; vent bundle compliance over 90%
- Bloodstream infections in the ICUs over 11 months at 0.68 per 1,000 line days compared with a National Nosocomial Infections Surveillance System (NNIS) 10th percentile of 1.7 per 1,000 line days for major teaching hospital ICUs; 97% compliance in line placement audit
- 33% reduction in time from patient-arrival-at-facility to catheterization at HFH, with a median of 93 minutes in third quarter of 2005; 82% compliance with care bundle; 22% reduction in all acute myocardial infarction (AMI) mortality at HFH since 2002
- Response to over 1,200 calls in first eight months by rapid response teams; reduced blue alert rate by 30%; reduced hospital length of stay by 0.2 days
- 15.9% reduction in mortality rate at HFH since the start of the initiatives
- Estimated 190 lives saved in 2005 and estimated 134 surgical infections avoided since June 2002 at HFH

Pursuing Perfection in depression management (behavioural health)

HFHS won an initial planning grant from the IHI–Robert Wood Johnson Foundation Pursuing Perfection project in 2001. Despite not receiving funding in the second phase of applications, HFHS went ahead with seven HFHS Pursuing Perfection projects, including a depression management project. This team (the Blues Busters) started with meetings every Saturday morning (held around the medical director's kitchen table) and in the evenings; much of the work was done on team members' own time. The team has achieved significant success in meeting their goal of "no suicides" in the HFHS (see Figure 1).

Each team member was assigned to a project area that matched their skills, and they formed their own teams to map processes and identify barriers. Team members made significant changes to all processes: they looked at depression as a chronic illness; developed care guidelines with detailed tools, checklists and protocols; and trained all therapists in cognitive behavioural therapy. The culture shifted such that now their goal for any project they undertake is 100%; as described by the director of quality for behavioural health: "We don't make it every time, but that is our ultimate goal."

Figure 1. Perfect Depression Care initiative results

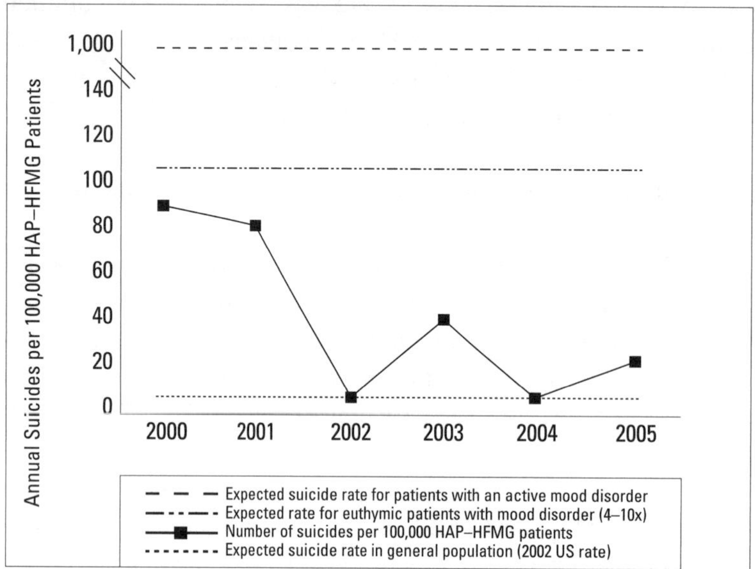

This run chart shows the running 12-month rate of suicide for each year since inception of our Perfect Depression Care Initiative. For reference, the figure also shows the annual rate of suicide in the general population (~11 per 100,000 population, based upon the 2002 US Census), as well as the reported rate in patients with a history of a mood disorder who are currently in remission (~4-10X the rate in the general population). Of note, the rate of suicide in patients with an active mood disorder is estimated at 80–90X the rate in the general population, and the suicide rate in patients with a history of suicide attempts is 100X the rate in the general population.

The observed suicide rates ranged from 89 per 100,000 for the baseline year (2000), 77 per 100,000 for the start-up year (2001), and 22 per 100,000 for the follow-up interval (the average rate for 2002–2005). The overall Poisson regression model two degree of freedom chi square test for a period effect was statistically significant, $x^2= 9.8$, $p=0.007$. The difference in suicide rate for the follow-up period was significantly lower than that for both the baseline year ($p=0.004$) and the start-up year ($p=0.014$).

This dramatic and sustained reduction in suicide rate is unprecedented in both the clinical and quality improvement literature. The improvement is even more impressive given that at baseline the rate of suicide in our patients was at the lower end of the expected range for a sample of patients with mental disorders.

Source: HFHS' director of quality for behavioural health.
Used by permission.

Chronic Care Excellence initiative

In 2004 HFHS and the Big Three automobile companies launched a major initiative to improve management of heart failure, coronary artery disease, diabetes and depression. Led by an experienced physician, the demonstration project emphasizes clinical microsystem redesign (Mohr and Batalden 2002) and the implementation of electronic prescribing in clinics. The focus is on at-risk patients whose disease conditions are not under control because of risk factors such as blood pressure, glucose, obesity, smoking and medication use. The project's goals are to facilitate patient self-management and avoid in-patient readmissions through better-integrated care paths. Care design teams, each with a project manager, prepare and implement changes that will be rolled out through the system. The e-prescribing project demonstrates decreased paper costs, reduced adverse drug events and errors and increased prescription of generics.

HFHS and its environment

HFHS' most recent successes were achieved by a health system operating in a very constrained context. However, HFHS' senior leaders have an emphatic message for staff members: "We are not, and never will be, a victim of our circumstances and the conditions around us" (Chief Operating Officer [COO] Bob Riney) (Henry Ford Health System 2006).

HFHS is a non-profit healthcare enterprise based in Detroit, Michigan. It provides care to more than one million residents in the southeast part of the state. Founded by Henry Ford in 1915, HFHS was modelled after the Mayo Clinic as a healing environment with a focus on innovation. It includes seven hospitals – ranging from a 100-bed mental health facility to the 903-bed Henry Ford tertiary care teaching hospital – as part of a comprehensive integrated system providing primary, preventive, acute and specialty services. The diverse community-based services comprise 24 ambulatory care centres that include four free-standing emergency departments, ambulatory pharmacies, cancer centres, multiple eye care centres, nursing homes, hospice services and home care. A 16-member board of trustees governs the system, assisted by over 220 volunteer community representatives on advisory and affiliate boards.

HFHS statistics (Henry Ford Health System nd b):

- 17,000 full-time equivalent employees, including 3,000 nurses and 4,000 allied health professionals; 17,000 total HFHS employees
- 2.2 million patient visits annually and more than 51,000 out-patient surgical procedures performed annually
- 69,000 patients admitted to hospitals annually
- Revenue: $3.05 billion; net income, $112 million; uncompensated care, $142 million (2005 data)
- More than 1 million residents in southeast Michigan receive care from HFHS
- More than 28% of HFHS patient visits are by persons aged 65 and over
- 20% of ambulatory care and 10% of acute care services in southeast Michigan are provided by HFHS
- Payer distribution: Health Alliance Plan, 32%; Medicare, 34%; Medicaid, 11%; Blue Cross, 14%; other, 9%, including Alliance Health and Life Insurance, Aetna Health Plans, United Healthcare, PPOM and Preferred Health Plan's Health Choice

Over 900 physicians and researchers in the Henry Ford Medical Group staff the Henry Ford Hospital and 24 medical centres. It is one of the largest medical group practices in the United States (US). In addition, several member hospitals and medical centres are staffed by over 1,000 community-based private physicians associated with HFHS.

HFHS is affiliated with Wayne State University's medical school. HFHS' research arm, originally started with a Ford Foundation grant of $50 million, is now self-sustaining and brought in $55 million in grants from outside sources in 2005.

The Health Alliance Plan (HAP) covers 3,000 employer groups and 550,000 members in managed care and health insurance programs. HAP members receive care both within the HFHS and from external providers. In 2004 and 2005 it earned the National Committee for Quality Assurance's Excellent Accreditation status (Health Alliance Plan nd).

HFHS operates in a very competitive environment in southeast Michigan, marked by a struggling economy and flat population growth. The local economy is driven by the Big Three automobile manufacturing companies, leaving HFHS vulnerable to fluctuations in their financial situations. As the companies lose market share and cut jobs, employees lose their benefits, including HAP membership. As a consequence HFHS loses income from HAP premiums and is called upon to provide unreimbursed care to a growing number of uninsured patients. Medicare and Medicaid payment cuts and flat third-party payments also contribute to the fiscal challenges.

Both Henry Ford Hospital and the system's corporate headquarters are located in downtown Detroit, a city that has suffered from the automobile companies' economic woes. This is a difficult location to which to attract patients from the better-off suburban populations. However, the geographic spread and diversity of HFHS locations in the region help to counter this challenge. The decision to locate the system's corporate headquarters in downtown Detroit is seen as an investment – and vote of confidence – in the downtown community.

In the face of so many challenges, how is HFHS realizing its goals and making such outstanding achievements?

Method: Exploring a system capable of improvement

In May 2006 a team of researchers from the University of Toronto's Department of Health Policy, Management and Evaluation visited HFHS. This site visit was part of an initiative called Quality by Design, which aims to identify and define elements of healthcare systems capable of improvement with a view to helping to inform strategic investments in improvement capability in Ontario. Quality by Design is funded primarily by the Ontario Ministry of Health and Long-Term Care in partnership with the University of Toronto's Department of Health Policy, Management and Evaluation.

HFHS was one of five healthcare systems selected from a short list of high-performing systems nominated by a panel of international leaders and experts. In Detroit the team met with and interviewed administrative and clinical leaders and improvement team leaders and members, as well as support staff working to make improvements. This case study highlights the findings of that site visit.

The strategy: Integration, alignment and performance improvement

Nancy Schlichting became chief executive officer (CEO) in 2003 (from 1998 to 2003 she was executive vice-president and COO). Under her leadership HFHS has adopted a strategy of integrating and aligning the system's various component organizations and activities. Examples of the integration efforts include streamlining the system's governance structure and work under way to extend the electronic health record across the whole system. HFHS is also building another significant structure – the HFHS Strategic Framework – as part of its drive to align individual and organizational efforts across the system.

HFHS' Strategic Framework

HFHS is setting high performance goals combined with accountability mechanisms and measures in seven areas of key importance to the organization:

- People
- Service
- Quality and safety
- Growth
- Research and education
- Community
- Finance

These areas are visually represented in a diagram as seven pillars supporting HFHS' mission and vision (see Figure 2). The system was restructured with cross-functional teams accountable for each of the seven pillars and HFHS executive leaders both acting as chairs and participating as members of the teams. For example, the CEO chairs the Growth and Service Excellence committees while the COO and chief quality officer co-chair the Quality Forum. The annual strategic plan and performance reporting systems are explicitly tied to the seven pillars. A monthly Dashboard Report reviewed by 100 executives and managers and their leadership teams includes graphs of measures and targets for financial performance, growth, nurse and physician turnover (people) and patient satisfaction (service). Key quality and safety performance measures and targets are derived from the six Institute of Medicine aims (safe, timely, efficient, effective, equitable and patient-centred care) (see Table 1). The performance-awards incentive structure (bonuses) for both unit-level groups of employees and individual physician employees is based on achieving the financial and patient satisfaction goals across the system.

Figure 2. HFHS' Strategic Framework

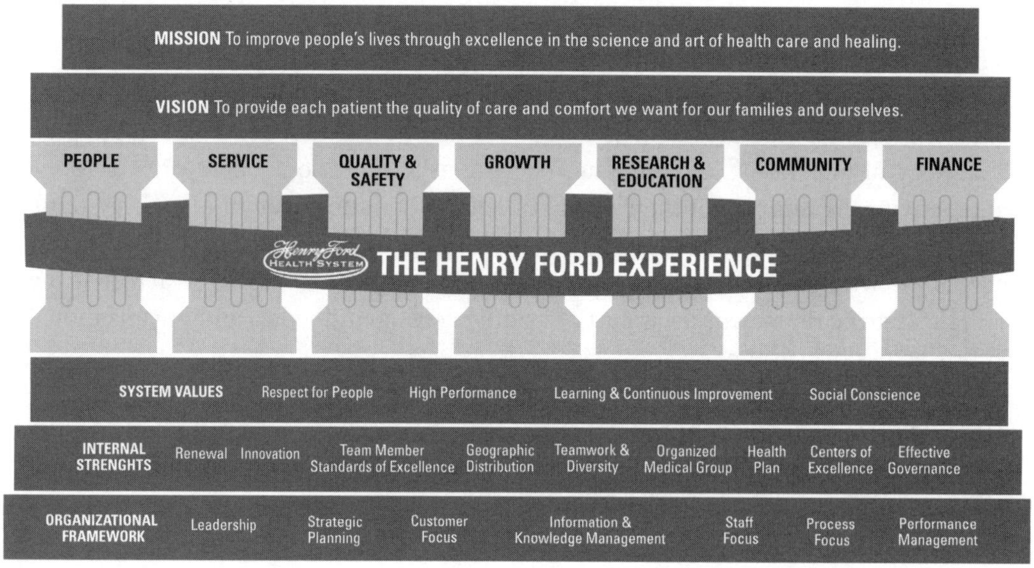

Source: Adapted from figure provided by HFHS.
Used by permission.

In the Strategic Framework diagram the foundation on which the seven pillars stand includes HFHS' values and internal strengths as well as the seven elements of the organizational framework (the Baldrige Award's criteria categories) (Baldrige National Quality Program 2007):

- Leadership
- Strategic planning
- Customer focus
- Information and knowledge management
- Staff focus
- Process focus
- Performance management

Table 1. Key quality performance measures – 2006

Institute of Medicine Aim	Performance Measure
Safe	# of patient falls, % of falls with injury
	% of reported medication errors with severity 1 or 2
	Infection rates • surgical site infections/1,000 cases • central line infections, ICU and Dialysis • vent-associated pneumonia
	Pressure ulcers – % with Stage 1–4 PU not present on admission (quarterly prevalence study, NDNQI comparison)
	Employee injuries at work • total injury claims/quarter • % resulting in 8 or more days lost
	Culture of safety: % favorable ratings on two specific questions within the Employee Opinion Survey: 1) Senior management shows patient safety is a top priority, and 2) Employees are encouraged to speak up about patient safety concerns.
	Use of fistulas for dialysis
Timely	Access to non-stat CT/MRI/GI/Mamm – in-patient/out-patient
	OR delay days affecting LOS – patient days/1,000 discharges
	Access to routine physician appointments (3rd avail) • primary care: % of docs w/ 3rd in 14 days • specialties: % of docs w/ 3rd in 14 days
Efficient	Readmissions w/in 30 days (same DRG)
	Emergency Dept – left without being seen (LWBS)
Effective	Mortality • raw mortality; also reporting mortality for medicine patients, surgical patients, CABG, and valve replacements • MHA normalized mortality
	Core measures – % at/above Michigan 75th %ile
	HEDIS scores • Women's health (Cervical Ca screen, mammography, chlamydia) • Pediatrics (childhood & adolescent immuns, asthma meds) • OB (prenatal and postpartum care) • % of measures at/above nat'l 75th %ile
Equitable	Health status • difference in hemoglobin A1C control by race, gender • difference in mammography completion by race
Patient-centred	Press Ganey "overall quality of care" (GPA target)
	ACAHPS member satisfaction w/ customer service • satisfaction w/ customer service • satisfaction w/ plan approval of healthcare

Source: Provided by HFHS. Used by permission.

HFHS has undertaken a self-assessment against the Baldrige criteria and is working toward applying for the award. Teams led by senior executives were struck to carry out the self-assessment for each category. In the words of one senior administrator: "What this has done is validate that we're doing all the right things, that quality improvement is part and parcel with every other thing we do and it's not this separate activity. ... Nobody believed it ever was, but there are still some behaviors that suggest that some people might think it's a parallel path, but it all goes together." This strategic framework includes a focus on system growth. As they construct new buildings and add services, and as volumes increase, system leaders evaluate the impact these innovations will have on quality and safety as well as on the other performance pillars. A focus on quality and safety improvement is integrated into HFHS' strategic plan, with an emphasis on performance improvement and measurement across all seven pillars. "The focus on quality," one senior administrator noted, "has re-engaged the workforce."

HFHS' Strategic Framework has become the focus of cascading communication about the strategic goals throughout the entire organization, featuring huge kick-off events attended by all managers and followed by discussion of a video outlining the key goals in every unit and department. The importance of customer service and excellence across HFHS is represented in the diagram by the "Lance Armstrong–like band" labelled The Henry Ford Experience that wraps around all seven pillars. As Chief Medical Officer Dr. Mark Kelley put it, "The Henry Ford Experience is about excellence in all that we do. ... Patients want a totally positive experience from start to finish." Internal system alignment is required to accomplish this goal in order to coordinate, in Kelley's words, "services and product lines so quality and service are the same system-wide." Kelley also noted the need to find "innovative ways to share information" and best practices across HFHS so staff and units can learn from each other (Henry Ford Health System 2006).

Organizational development, service excellence and culture change

> *"We are investing in culture and the people, namely, how you select, orient and develop people. There are programs about service and quality, not just clinical quality, but quality principles more broadly."*
>
> – An HFHS senior administrator

Renewal

All HFHS employees participate in an organizational development initiative called Renewal, which is a two-day, off-site experience. The program emphasizes the influence of role models by using a concept known as "the shadow of a leader," a phrase mentioned by both managers and staff members. Three quarters of HFHS employees have completed Renewal, and two-hour refresher modules are in development. According to one project manager, "It was a powerful opportunity to reflect on your own values and the organization's values, personalities, your strengths and weaknesses as a person, and how your contribution fits with the greater organization/system. ... It helps you recognize what your filters are, that filter what you hear."

Service excellence and Wyandotte Hospital

The importance of service excellence is a recurring theme at HFHS. At Wyandotte Hospital (350 beds), for example, the CEO takes a hands-on approach to leading the service excellence process. He speaks of the need to align accountability with the seven pillars using "major metrics of service excellence to tie back to remuneration" in order to "hardwire this in." He also participates in new employee orientation and personally does rounds, thereby maintaining a visible presence throughout the hospital. And he advocates an approach developed by the Studer Group (executive coaching and organizational development consultants; see http://www.studergroup.com) and uses their terminology, including the "nine principles" and "six must-haves." The "key drivers," he emphasizes, are culture, commitment, consistency, communication, reinforcement and acceptance. The Wyandotte CEO commented, however, that the HFHS CEO "did not altogether buy in to the Studer model" at the beginning and "it was not a slam-dunk getting others to buy in and be interested." With the increased emphasis on service excellence, each business unit appointed a service excellence administrator to help spearhead the efforts.

The service excellence work at Wyandotte began a few years ago during a merger and cost-cutting (and employees' resulting anger about both), yet it has raised employee and patient satisfaction scores (the former, dramatically). However, when asked where the CEO thought the hospital was on its development trajectory, "about halfway" was the reply.

All Wyandotte management meetings begin with discussion of service excellence issues. In the context of attracting community physicians (who are independent contractors and not part of the HFHS practice group), they talk about "treating physicians as our customers" and "improving processes that make it easier for them to practice here." Service excellence teams, overseen by a steering committee, are working on behavioural excellence, leadership development, reward and recognition, physician satisfaction and employee satisfaction. The Satisfaction, Measurement, and Resource Team (SMaRT), for example, acts as a resource for departments to help them interpret patient satisfaction survey results, to identify successes and opportunities for improvement and to implement a tool for measuring internal customer satisfaction. They call their quality improvement process ICAST (identify, collect data, analyze, study, test), an acronym that links to "the shadow of a leader" Renewal concept.

Patient satisfaction and Fairlane emergency department

HFHS uses Press Ganey for patient satisfaction surveying and Gantz Wiley for annual employee surveys. Both patient and staff satisfaction have become key metrics for individual departments, business units and the system as a whole. As an example, Fairlane Medical Center's emergency department in Dearborn had the system's poorest patient satisfaction scores (28th percentile), the longest length of stay and "a reputation as a place where you should not send patients," recalled the emergency department's medical director. After consulting with staff, Fairlane began in 2003 to redesign the department's triage and registration processes. This redesign process began with setting up a team of staff volunteers who worked to "sell the changes to their colleagues." Senior management also made all staff members aware of the patient satisfaction scores, held quarterly reviews, discussed specific questions and scores with staff, sought ideas about how to fix the problems and helped to implement them. Wait times dropped from 120 to 40 minutes and overall satisfaction ratings rose from 77.9 to 88.3 over two years. When scores improved Fairlane staff celebrated: All the nurses were given "really good stethoscopes" and the registration staff received cardigans.

Fairlane emergency department's medical director referred to the HFHS Renewal program and "the shadow of a leader" concept when talking about the powerful influence of role models. He reported that his door is always open to any staff member and Fairlane's organizational structure is very flat, allowing the director to spend time discussing with staff members how they fit in with the "greater scheme of things and the HFHS strategy." He emphasized the way improved patient satisfaction increases volumes, which improves hospital finances, which in turn means Fairlane will have the means to do what is needed to make it easier to improve care. Fairlane also developed an emergency department performance guarantee, which documents the department's values and how staff members put patient expectations into action (see Figure 3). All new staff members participate in a ceremony of signing a poster-sized copy of the guarantee, which displayed in a case in the lobby where patients can see it.

Resources and structures to support quality

Office of Clinical Quality and Safety

HFHS has a corporate Office of Clinical Quality and Safety (OCQS), which has sections covering regulatory issues, infection control, risk management, patient satisfaction, medical informatics and quality and safety initiatives. The office has approximately 35 staff with a budget of about $3.5 million (including the quality staff for HFH as well as system-level coordination of quality improvement initiatives and infection control at the various sites).

Figure 3. Fairlane Medical Center emergency department performance guarantee

As an employee of the Fairlane Emergency Department,

I understand that...	So I will...
Our reputation is the most valuable thing we own.	Dedicate myself to Clinical Excellence and Exceptional Patient Service.
I am here to help people feel and get better.	Treat you with kindness.
Patients are scared and vulnerable.	Be gentle. Tell you what to expect. Provide physical comfort. Smile appropriately and provide eye contact. Be respectful and courteous at all times. Keep your family informed.
Patients put their trust in me.	Treat your problems seriously and efficiently. Satisfy your personal needs.
Patients must know that I care about them as individuals.	Ignore no one. Listen attentively. Show respect for all cultures and backgrounds.
Patients' time must be respected.	Work quickly and efficiently to do my best.
I am part of a team.	Promote patient satisfaction by working as a team member with other Fairlane employees and medical staff. Assume responsibility for what another is unable to accomplish. Do what I say I will and do it well every time. Never make excuses.
I represent the Fairlane Emergency Department and I am responsible for solving problems.	Take the initiative to solve problems, not point fingers. Seek an appropriate time and place for discussing sensitive issues/frustrations.
Great things happen when we listen to our patients and to each other.	Always make time to listen.
I may someday be a patient.	Treat patients and their families as I would like to be treated.

Source: Medical Director, Emergency Department, Fairlane Medical Center.
Used by permission.

OCQS is co-led by long-time HFHS staff members: the chief quality officer (CQO) and a vice-president of planning and performance improvement. The CQO, a respected and experienced clinician who also serves as Henry Ford Hospital's chief medical officer, and the vice-president, who has an industrial engineering background, make an effective leadership team; with this pairing, noted the CEO, "We now have the right leadership for quality initiatives." Likewise, the OCQS department directors each have at least 10-plus years' experience at HFHS and are very knowledgeable about clinical improvement methods. The office also includes an infectious disease physician, a physician involved in internal medicine residency education and quality improvement, and a statistician who supports quality initiatives such as 100k Lives.

In addition, a separate Management Services group includes a dozen industrial engineering, operations (clinicians with management experience) and management consulting staff members whose focus is process design. The vice-president of planning and performance improvement described the group's role as providing "the science side of improvement" and "implementation support." The Management Services group earlier charged users for its services, although this bill-back practice was discontinued around 2004. OCQS and Management Services used to be two separate silos but were brought together under the vice-president, who commented, "We have not yet been asked to cost-justify the quality work. Again, I think it is recognized that this is necessary work." So much so that in the midst of other cuts during an earlier financial crisis, HFHS kept its OCQS staff to support quality initiative projects and work as well as increased the bedside nursing complement and staffing ratios.

OCQS staff members also respond to numerous regulatory and external reporting requirements. Internal practices must be audited against standards produced by multiple agencies, and compliance must be documented. For example, the National Quality Forum (NQF) has published *Safe Practices for Better Healthcare* (2003). Preparation for accreditation processes, including the Joint Commission on Accreditation of Healthcare Organizations (JCAHO), is no longer a once-in-three-years effort; JCAHO surveyors can drop by unannounced, as they did recently at HFHS. Although such visits create a lot of work, they can provide an impetus for positive change. "We get a lot of work that crosses boundaries, like the system policy work," noted one of the OCQS directors.

System Quality Forum

The System Quality Forum comprises HFHS' senior leadership team related to quality and is responsible for the quality and safety pillar in the HFHS Strategic Framework. It is co-chaired by the COO and CQO, includes HFHS' CEO, all chiefs (e.g., medical, nursing), all quality directors from across HFHS, the CEO of every business unit (e.g., hospitals and ambulatory sites), the chief medical officer (who acts as CEO of the Henry Ford Medical Group) and the vice-president of planning and performance improvement. The forum had been meeting quarterly but, as one member put it, "The CEO said we should meet monthly; if we are meeting monthly to discuss growth and service, we should meet monthly to discuss quality. ... It is our way of getting very systemic in our approach, and reporting the right things to our board." OCQS directors noted that the forum has been transformed; people leave with to-do lists and a sense of ownership, taking responsibility for doing something about problems.

Annual Quality Expo

The annual Quality Expo has been held for 15 years at HFHS. Staff members apply to present their improvement projects in a storyboard format, categorized by the six Institute of Medicine aims mentioned earlier in connection with HFHS' New Strategic Framework (safe, timely, efficient, effective, equitable and patient-centred care). Books of project descriptions are published each year (approximately 80 initiatives). External judges review the storyboards, and prizes are awarded and ribbons placed on posters that demonstrate good examples of teamwork and flow diagrams as well as on ones that follow quality management principles. Quality Expo is an opportunity for staff to learn about and celebrate successful changes. In addition, it helps reinforce the need to practise process improvement techniques such as the IHI's Plan-Do-Study-Act (PDSA), because submissions must describe the various cycles of improvement that teams went through to achieve improvements.

Quality improvement models and methods

Early history of quality improvement at HFHS

Efforts to formally structure improvement at HFHS began in 1988 with the introduction of a total quality management (TQM) approach under then-CEO Gail Warden and Senior Vice-President Vinod Sahney. Sahney and Warden have written extensively about this experience, chronicling the decision to pursue TQM, how they learned about the concepts from industry, how they adapted them to healthcare and the intensity of efforts made to educate senior leaders and train staff (Sahney and Warden 1991). They developed a Henry Ford Quality Management Process as well as an HFHS Quality Framework, which were merged into the strategic planning process at that time (Sahney and Warden 1993). A team of Hospital Corporation of America (HCA) consultants led by Dr. Paul Batalden designed and delivered the education programs for senior leaders and trained in-house staff to continue the education rollout throughout the organization. A Managed Care College was set up in 1992 to teach clinical staff about evidence-based medicine and improvement methods; this was disbanded, however, when HFHS suffered financial cutbacks (Sahney 2003).

Warden and Sahney were high-profile contributors to national quality improvement efforts in the US beginning in the late 1980s. They supported the foundation of the IHI, establishing early connections between HFHS and IHI and involvement in IHI initiatives that have continued to this day. Under their tenure HFHS participated in

IHI's Pursuing Perfection program, undertaking seven projects (which went forward internally even though they did not secure external funding as formal members in phase two of the program).

More than a decade of investment in improvement education and planning under the previous executive leaders preceded the current era of improvement efforts at HFHS. However, since around 2002 there has been a sharper focus and increased constancy of purpose driven by "immense pressure from external regulatory and accrediting bodies, and the emergence of both pay for performance and public reporting" (OCQS staff member). The CQO estimates that 60% of the current staff was part of HFHS during those earlier initiatives. When we asked the CEO and COO how the Warden–Sahney quality strategy differed from the current strategy, they replied that the former was "the view from 30,000 feet," whereas "now it's all about execution – the how-to."

Quality improvement at HFHS today

HFHS teams presently use a variety of improvement models and methods, in some cases explicit (such as Lean or rapid cycle) and in others more generic problem-solving approaches. For example, the cardiac catheterization lab director and his AMI Care team (participating in the 100k Lives campaign) used Lean process analysis to reduce the door-to-balloon time from an average of 218 minutes in 2002 to less than 90 minutes system-wide in 2005. They dissected complex activities into quantifiable steps and worked to reduce the time each step took by avoiding duplication, minimizing steps, defining roles and organizing activities in parallel.

In other cases teams have selected tools from among different approaches. The physician who leads the Chronic Care Excellence initiative said that staff engaged in that initiative did not explicitly use Lean process analysis; they did, however, identify gaps, and develop work plans and revise them. He commented that certain processes are more amenable to Lean process analysis than others, and they did have some people trained in Lean methods: "Lean is more aligned with our culture than Six Sigma but the vice-president of planning and performance improvement likes some of the [measurement-oriented] tools in Six Sigma." The initiative director also said that Lean thinking works well with clinicians; however, a cultural change is needed to spread Lean system-wide. One of the project managers commented that Lean is "Six Sigma lite" and easier to adapt than Six Sigma, which needs too much fine-grained data.

Members of teams participating in 100k Lives projects debated the merits of PDSA cycles as a method. Some felt it was a useful framework for learning how to internalize making changes: "When I was doing changes less frequently I thought about PDSA more; but when doing changes daily, I think less about it" (physician). In the surgical site infection prevention initiative the physician leader said they used the PDSA language and methods when discussing the changes and results: "Physicians are comfortable with it; it's like a study." Others thought it was less important; one physician said, "PDSA is not that necessary or important. You need to be curious and want to try different things. ... Frontline staff had lots of input. They would not recognize PDSA but they can tell you the changes they've made to care. ... We wouldn't have called it PDSA unless we had to fill out a report!"

Many HFHS staff participated in Quality 101 training designed by Dr. Paul Batalden in the 1990s. Yet that training does not seem to be applied explicitly in most current projects. When describing the depression care initiative, the behavioural health quality director commented,

> Over time, HFHS has trained people in five different quality models, but I'd be hard-pressed to identify the one we use. It's eclectic; we [in behavioural health] have pulled the best of all of them. I started with Deming and then CQI. We do a lot of rapid cycle and process mapping. We use Tap Root, root causes analysis, for things that we don't want to see happen, like elopements.

Additional improvement-methods training was offered at HFHS after that initial round of courses. For example, a Q201 course on measurement was developed by the quality initiatives administrator, who has a background in statistics and experience in the automotive industry. During their self-assessment against the Baldrige criteria, the Process Focus team debated the benefits of having one system-wide quality model and methodology for promoting consistent language and training for staff. Team members agreed it could be advantageous and are considering adopting a uniform approach that is a hybrid of different methods.

Physician involvement

Physicians are leading many of the improvement initiatives at HFHS and physician leaders interviewed emphasized such involvement as a requirement for success: "There has to be institutional support but it cannot be administration-led; it has to be about patient care."

Physician champions and leaders are very important. However, as one physician leader pointed out, "It can be tricky to find the right champions, as not all physicians see the big picture and understand improvement and systems. ... Even some of the local champions who are good in the initial phase can't spread the change, and you may even need a new champion for sustaining change." In the Chronic Care Excellence initiative, each care design team has a provider champion and project manager and most have physician leaders.

There is, however, danger inherent in person-dependent change initiatives. For example, strong physicians led the Pursuing Perfection orthopaedics and prostate cancer projects. Those individuals then left HFHS with, as one staff member said, "that knowledge in their heads."

There are several innovative initiatives under way at HFHS aimed at involving residents in quality improvement. An internal medicine physician runs a program for over 100 residents adapted from the American Board of Internal Medicine's Practice Improvement Module. Residents work in teams to collect data and design improvement plans. They vote for the project they will undertake collectively, based on selection criteria (i.e., easy and low cost, generalizable, doable within a reasonable time, measurable, innovative, producing results that will matter). In 2006 residents chose blood pressure control for diabetic patients.

Physicians as employees

Because Henry Ford Hospital physicians are employees, that facility's department chiefs and heads may have more leverage than would be the case if the physicians were independent contractors. At Henry Ford Hospital, for example, changes are incorporated as part of physicians' performance expectations and reviews. The Wyandotte Hospital, in contrast, has community physicians with privileges, and its CEO said they are considered to be "customers."

The importance of local data and the role of information systems

Another key message from HFHS' experience is the importance of local data in addition to credible external data from published studies and collaboratives. When asked what it took to improve the clinical initiatives, many staff members replied "leadership"; when probed further, they said that leadership translated into resources necessary for gathering local data. For example, a full-time OCQS staff member was assigned to do chart and record-based abstraction from the surgical site infection reduction project.

Even without such resources there is a feeling at HFHS that local data are so important that the cardiac catheterization lab director and the nurse practitioner themselves go through all the ambulance run sheets, manually abstracting needed times for the door-to-balloon process for all AMI patients from all sites. The director then holds monthly meetings with all those involved, including ambulance services, to review the results and look for learning opportunities. Reflecting on past accomplishments, the director reported that he gave comparative time data back to the physicians (without identifiers), and "the competition among the type-A personalities got the numbers down." (With good humour he referred to this as "channelling constructive energy.") This physician also commented that he has clear accountability as a leader to the CQO for achieving targets on indicators such as door-to-balloon times, noting that when expectations are not met the CQO comes "knocking at my door."

HFHS has been implementing electronic patient records via a system called Care Plus. To date, this has taken place largely on the ambulatory side. HFHS is now designing the system for use on the in-patient side, an innovation that will include computerized physician order entry. In addition, there is already an electronic radiology records system in place. The chief of anesthesiology said his department does not yet have electronic anesthetic records because none of the current systems are good enough and "they will have only one chance to get it right." He also noted that such a system does not provide all the answers for all problems, nor would it have helped with all the detailed data they needed for the surgical wound infection reduction project.

The director of the anticoagulation clinic initiative said his team "began with paper records but that would have made the changed processes unaffordable. The computerized results software helped move things along." Likewise, the e-prescription initiative in the Chronic Care Excellence project has been a successful information technology-related undertaking. The electronic records system facilitates integration and coordination of patient care across HFHS. OCQS staff reported the electronic records help with reminders, provide better data and enable more efficient data collection and reporting.

Challenges

Competing demands

HFHS staff members are involved in a large number of improvement projects; as one team member noted, "There is *a lot* going on." At HFHS there is a strong impetus to participate in external initiatives such as the IHI's 100k Lives campaign: "You could not *not* do it," said one staff member. This drive exerts additional pressure over and above the regulatory compliance demands outlined earlier. One physician described her frustration with this situation: "JCAHO [accreditation body] makes us go through hoops but hasn't made us improve. If you really want to change, it has to come from within. JCAHO just makes us document stuff."

Not all front-line staff members are adapting quickly to the changes. OCQS staff reported "some push-back and resistance from some of the staff about the amount of stuff we are throwing at them." A few project team members expressed some frustration about the sometimes conflicting demands placed on them by the large number of projects (described as a "hodgepodge"), which often involve competing standards or protocols that need to be reconciled. "We have to package it for staff so that they don't see it as random acts of change," a team leader pointed out. One physician noted that although the 100k Lives initiatives had positive impacts on patient outcomes, staff members had not seen any of the changes decreasing the nursing or pharmacy workloads.

People in supporting roles talked about the challenges of trying to work with all the project teams, on one hand, encouraging engagement of as many staff members as possible in improvement work ("lighting a thousand candles") but on the other, trying to manage the logistics of the resulting "thousand points of light." Many clinical leaders of initiatives emphasized the need for dedicated human resources to do the work, such as project managers, data collectors, quality support personnel and, in some instances, clinical positions.

Corporate quality support resources are spread a bit unevenly among HFHS' projects, and the improvement skill and knowledge levels at the sites are somewhat variable. Given the number of improvement projects, improvement support staff commented that it was not yet clear how all the grass roots–level efforts aligned with the corporate strategy: "There are too many [projects]; we need to focus. They don't all line up in the same direction but they line up better than they have ever lined up [before]."

In the present competitive healthcare environment – characterized by external report cards and pay-for-performance exerting pressure on organizations – a number of people felt that HFHS had little choice about participating in a large volume of quality initiatives. In that regard the system's patient satisfaction and service excellence work is, to some extent, market-driven.

HFHS' motto is "We're Henry Ford. We can." (See http://www.henryfordhealth.org/.) In accord with that motto the organization has a reputation for excellence and a can-do improvement culture, which is illustrated by one team member's observation, "We don't ask, 'Why should we?' anymore. We ask, 'How can we?' ... Leadership sets the expectation – by setting goals and putting their money where their mouth is – that we will do it." But this reputation comes at a cost; it requires the intense, sustained efforts of many staff members. The internal drive to apply for all the external awards possible is such that OCQS staff would like to have a professional writer's help to prepare the application documentation.

Sustainability and hurricane-proofing

Members of many of HFHS' project teams expressed concern about the sustainability of the improvements they were implementing. The Chronic Care Excellence team members were not sure how the redesigned care processes would be embedded. When asked what it was like working on their different projects, one member of a 100k Lives team said, "It was gruelling." He was promptly corrected by a chorus of colleagues exclaiming, "It *is* gruelling!"

Team members are struggling with how to engrain changes while helping staff members cope with information overload. The groups emphasized the importance of ongoing monitoring and feedback to staff: "You have to do it each day, each shift. ... We have to keep reinforcing, because it's not habit yet." One physician project leader spoke of the need for "hurricane-proofing" the change initiatives against the inevitable next cycle of budget reductions and staff cuts by seeking firmer financial support to protect human and other resources.

Conclusion

Almost 20 years ago the previous HFHS administration launched the initial TQM efforts by making investments in resources and training. These investments generated numerous improvement initiatives that met with varied degrees of success. This experience may have contributed to the system's current performance improvement capabilities.

HFHS' current leaders (who took over in 2003) are pursuing a top-down strategy of aligning and integrating the diverse activities and structures that constitute the system. Service excellence in all aspects of operations is the focus of wide-ranging organizational development efforts that involve staff and are aimed at promoting consistent cultural change. Improvement is monitored through balanced scorecard-like reports with performance measures for each of the strategic plan's seven key foci. Cascading communications are used extensively to engage staff members in discussion of service excellence and how their individual and unit activities link with corporate goals.

Physicians lead HFHS' many clinical improvement initiatives. The system's improvement and project management staff provides support while also responding to external regulatory and reporting requirements. Clinical project leaders emphasize the importance of locally gathered data and the development of information systems capable of providing outcomes data.

This wide array of clinical improvement projects is achieving positive results. At the same time, however, it presents several major challenges. Chief among those hurdles are finding ways to adequately support all the efforts and ensure that all the individual projects align with HFHS' goals. Project leaders also expressed concern about the sustainability of improvement efforts and the need to protect resources in the event of future financial constraints.

References

Baldrige National Quality Program. 2007. *Health Care Criteria for Performance Excellence.* Gaithersburg, MD: Author. Retrieved December 18, 2006. <http://www.quality.nist.gov/PDF_files/2007_HealthCare_Criteria.pdf>

Center for Healthcare Improvement. 2005. *The 100 Top Hospitals Performance Improvement Leaders – 2005.* Stamford, CT: Thomson Healthcare. Retrieved December 8, 2006. <http://www.100tophospitals.com/winners/pilwinners.aspx>

Health Alliance Plan. nd. *Considering HAP?* Detroit: Author. Retrieved December 8, 2006. <http://www.hap.org/info/enroll.php>

Henry Ford Health System. nd a. *Henry Ford Facts and Statistics.* Detroit: Author. Retrieved December 8, 2006. <http://www.henryford.com/body.cfm?id=38768#national>

Henry Ford Health System. nd b. *Henry Ford Facts and Statistics.* Detroit: Author. Retrieved November 12, 2007. <http://www.henryfordhealth.org/body.cfm?id=38768>

Henry Ford Health System. 2006. *Continuing the Winning Streak: The Henry Ford Experience 2006* [Video presentation and guided discussion]. Detroit: Author.

Mohr, J.J. and P.B. Batalden. 2002. "Improving Safety on the Front Lines: The Role of Clinical Microsystems." *Quality and Safety in Health Care* 11: 45–50.

National Quality Forum. 2003. *Safe Practices for Better Healthcare.* Washington, DC: Author. Retrieved December 19, 2006. <http://www.qualityforum.org/projects/completed/safe_practices/>

Sahney, V.K. 2003. "Generating Management Research on Improving Quality." *Health Care Management Review* 28(4): 335–347.

Sahney, V.K. and G.L. Warden. 1991. "The Quest for Quality and Productivity in Health Services." *Frontiers of Health Services Management* 7(4): 2–38.

Sahney, V.K. and G.L. Warden. 1993. "The Role of CQI in the Strategic Planning Process." *Quality Management in Health Care* 1(4): 1–11.

Wilson, L. 2006. "High-Octane Hospitals." *Modern Healthcare* 36(18): 24.

Appendix A. Progress report on 100k Lives campaign – January 2006
(Provided by Henry Ford Health System quality management staff, May 5, 2006. Used by permission.)

Surgical infection reduction

Efforts to improve surgical infection rates at Henry Ford Hospital were launched in 2002 with a surgical infection prevention collaborative sponsored by CMS. A 10-member team (physicians, pharmacists, nurses, etc.) was assembled to review the CMS proposals. Over the next three months a number of changes were initiated:

- Assigning responsibility for antibiotic administration to the anesthesiologist.
- Changing policies around antibiotic discontinuation.
- Removing all razors from the preoperative areas.
- Converting all skin preparation to chlorhexidine.
- Improving glucose control in the surgical ICU and the OR.

The effort led to a more than 50% reduction in surgical site infection rates including a 19-month period with no vascular surgery infections.

Today, each surgery at Henry Ford Hospital that is monitored shows marked improvement.

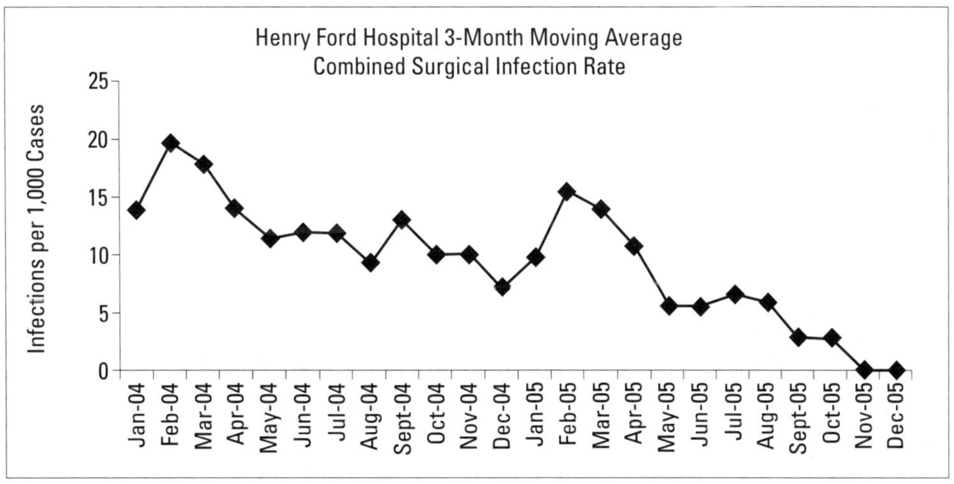

One outgrowth of the surgical infection reduction program was the launch of a hospital-wide program to improve glucose control. As a result:

- A steady improvement in glucose control for all patients resulting in a significant improvement in overall infection rates.
- The rate of glucose readings above 250 has been reduced by 85% in the ICUs.
- The rate of hypoglycemia continues to be the same as when the program began.

The highly successful tight glucose control program at Henry Ford Hospital was recognized as a finalist for the Codman award from JCAHO in 2005.

Ventilator bundle

As part of the IHI critical care collaborative, Henry Ford Hospital began an effort to improve ICU care including the implementation of the vent bundle in 2003. Teams were assembled in all four adult ICUs.

Some of the issues that we uncovered while implementing the IHI recommendations included:

- Patients transferred from floors on weekends were not always placed on protocols.
- Heads of beds, lowered for procedures, were not immediately returned to 30 degrees.
- Reminders didn't exist to place sequential compression devices on patients for DVT prophylaxis when heparin was discontinued.
- Daily weaning trials were often conducted after rounds.

After the above issues were identified and corrected, daily "quick rounds" were instituted to verify that ventilator bundle and glucose protocols were followed. When the rate for the ventilator bundle improved to above 90% other results became evident:

- An average reduction of 0.9 days on a ventilator.
- An overall reduction of ICU length of stay by 0.65 days.

For the last eight months, ventilator bundle performance at Henry Ford Hospital has been nearly 90%. Despite successful implementation of the ventilator bundle, the ventilator-associated pneumonia rate remains near national average rates. In recent months, the hospital has focused on aggressive oral care and a pilot program of using mouthwash containing chlorhexidine.

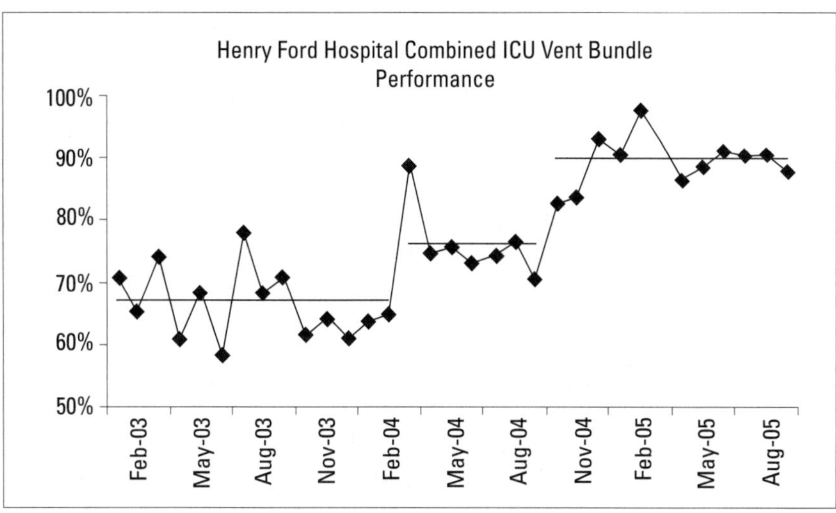

Bloodstream infection reductions

Initial efforts to reduce bloodstream infection rates by switching to chlorhexidine skin prep and developing a line kit with all required materials were offset by the introduction of a valve-based, needle-less system.

After a year, the system was replaced with a traditional needle-less line system. This resulted in a total turnaround in bloodstream infections. In addition, reductions in bloodstream infections have continued based on education reinforced by tracking of compliance with line placement bundle. The results include:

- Bloodstream infections in the ICUs over the last 11 months at 0.68 per 1000 line days compared with an NNIS 10th percentile of 1.7 per 1000 line days for major teaching hospital ICUs.
- Line placement audits show compliance of 97% in our latest audit.

Our aim at Henry Ford Hospital is to eliminate bloodstream infections. In order to accomplish that goal, efforts are under way with a number of key innovations:

- An interactive CD ROM to improve medical education related to central lines.
- A simulation-based training program for all medical staff.
- Development of a line placement team to ensure a high level of experience.
- Focused education on line maintenance with audits of nursing practice.

In September 2005 Henry Ford Hospital ICUs had no bloodstream infections. While we celebrate this special achievement, we are working hard to make it the norm.

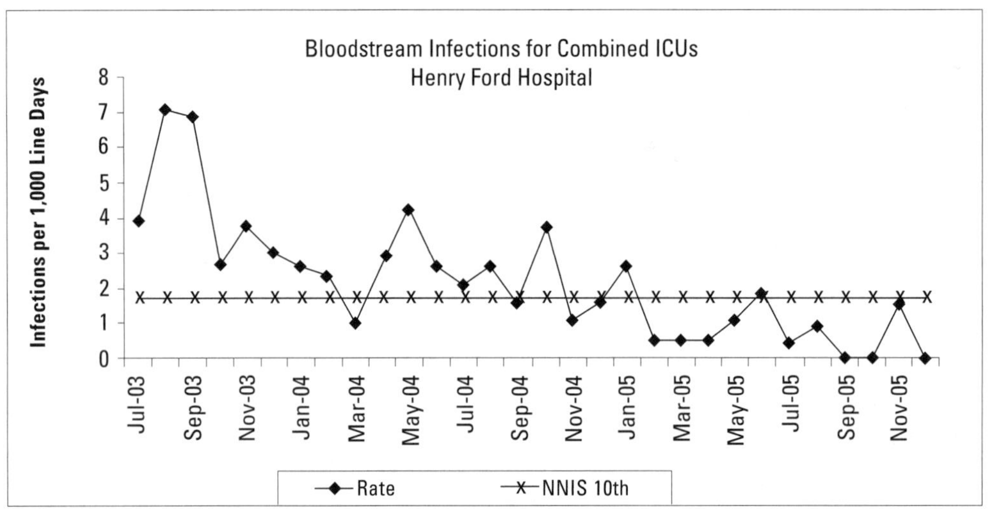

Care for heart attack patients

Improvements with AMI care have focused on the care bundle as well as reducing the time between when a patient enters a Henry Ford facility in metro Detroit until the patient undergoes cardiac catheterization at Henry Ford Hospital.

As a tertiary facility, Henry Ford Hospital is the primary referral site of all AMI patients for three emergency departments within ambulatory centers and several community hospitals.

As a pilot program, a system-wide improvement to improve response time was launched between Henry Ford Bi-County Hospital in Warren and Henry Ford Hospital in Detroit. Over a period of months a team worked with the emergency departments and ambulance agencies to streamline processes. Later, the program was spread to other Henry Ford locations and other community facilities. The improvements have resulted in:

- 33% reduction in patient arrival at a facility to catheterization time at HFH with a median of 93 minutes in 3rd Quarter 2005.
- Improved care bundle performance. (82% in 3rd Quarter 2005)
- 22% reduction in all AMI mortality at HFH since 2002.

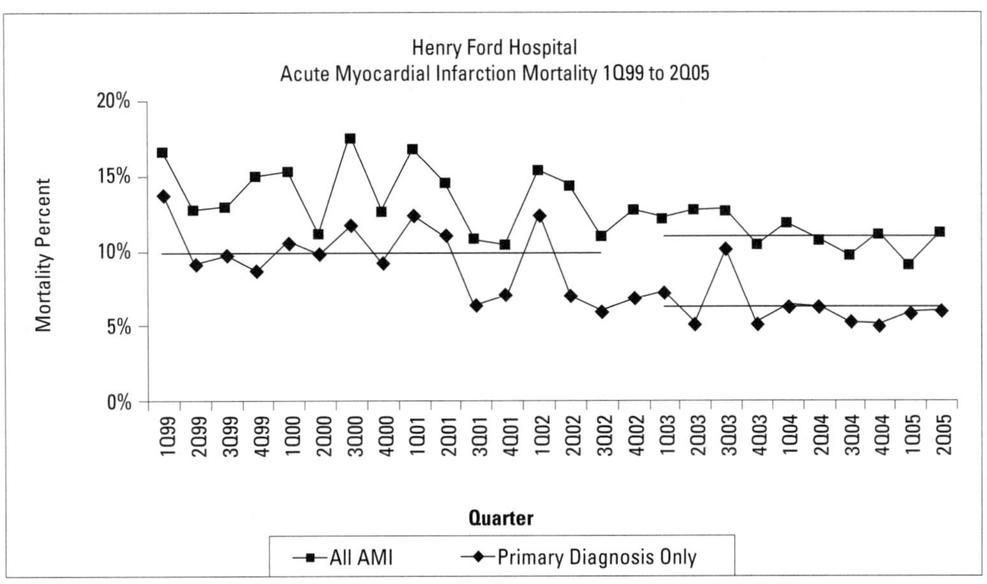

Rapid Response Team

Rapid response teams have been one of the most successful improvements to Henry Ford Hospital.

In December of 2004, rapid response teams were launched. Today two rapid response nurses are in the hospital 24/7. All nurses on general practice units have been trained on how, when and why to alert the rapid response team. In addition, all the residents have also been trained. In the first eight months the rapid response team has:

- Responded to over 1,200 calls.
- Reduced the blue alert rate by 30%.
- Reduced hospital length of stay by 0.2 days.

The rapid response team has been a huge success and has been equally well-received by residents and nurses. Henry Ford Hospital uses a single nurse responder combined with a concurrent page to the resident assigned to the patient. If the care needs to be escalated, the ICU fellow will be contacted.

This model appears well-suited to a teaching hospital environment. Initial concerns about the team interfering with the medical education process have all but disappeared. Residents have found that having extra resources available to watch over the highest acuity patients allows them to take more aggressive action without over-burdening the responsible nurse. The rapid response team can help allow a nurse to keep up with his/her other patients.

The success of the rapid response team has been a support to nurses as well as means to observe nursing practices. A report from the rapid response team on nursing practice issues is an agenda item at every Nursing Practice Council. This input has been used to focus efforts on skills validation.

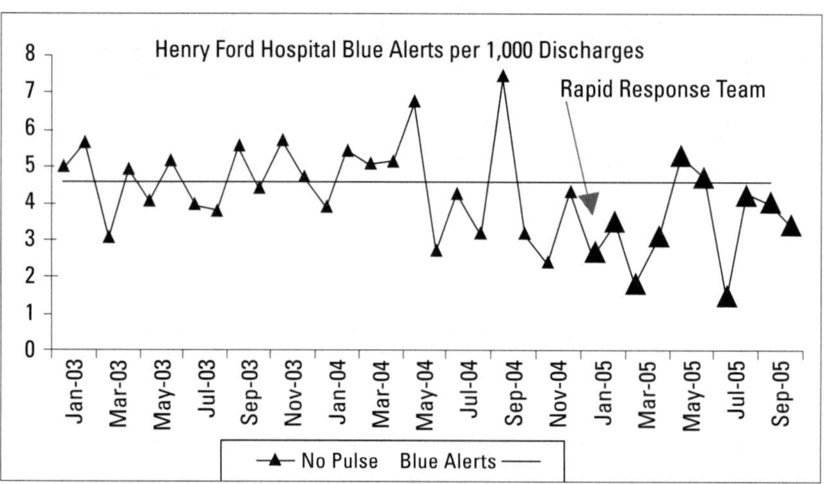

Overall results

The ultimate success is determined by mortality.

- Mortality at Henry Ford Hospital in the last year is down 15.9% since the start of the initiatives. (In September 2005 alone, mortality was down 32% from the baseline.)
- In 2005, Henry Ford Hospital has saved an estimated 190 lives.
- Improvements in surgical infection prevention avoided an estimated 134 surgical infections since June 2002.

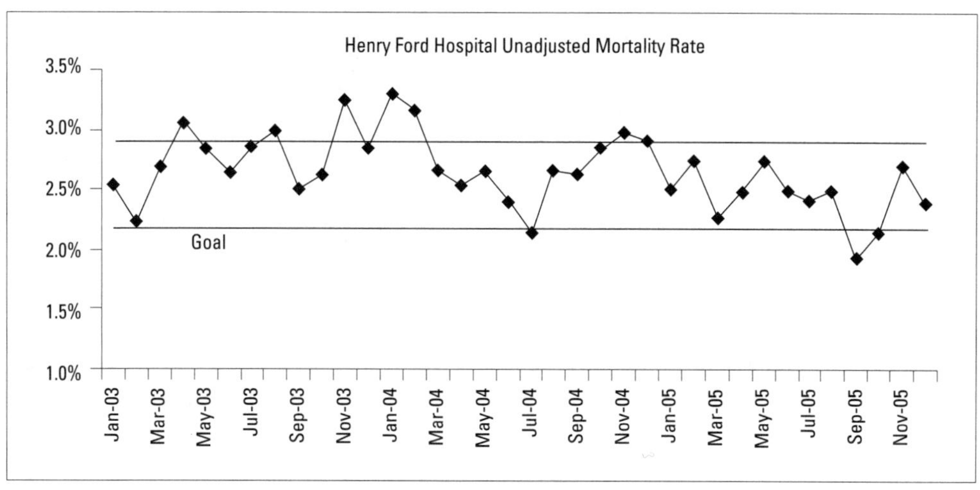

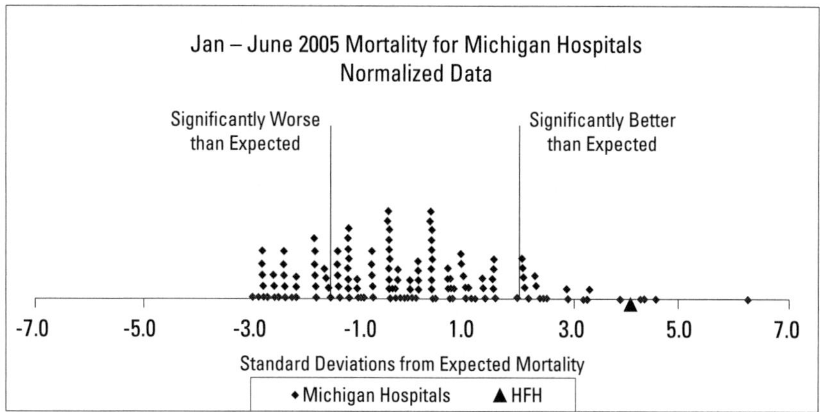

Mortality at Henry Ford Hospital in the last year is down 15.9% since the start of the initiatives. In September 2005 alone, mortality was down 32% from the baseline.

Commentary: Henry Ford Health System

Jack Kitts, President and Chief Executive Officer
The Ottawa Hospital

"2005 was a very successful year," reported the chief executive officer (CEO) of the Henry Ford Health System (HFHS). That year, Henry Ford Hospital was identified as a performance improvement leader in Solucient's 2005 list of 100 Top Hospitals: Performance Improvement Leaders. Although a similar national ranking system does not exist for Canadian hospitals, it is advisable for boards and senior administrators in Canadian hospitals and regional health authorities to learn from performance improvement leaders in the United States. In the accompanying case study of HFHS, much can be learned and emulated in the Canadian context.

Case study

In 2003 the new CEO of HFHS adopted a strategy of integration, alignment and performance improvement. The organization's strategic framework was restructured to support clear performance goals focused in seven key areas (people, service, quality and safety, growth, research and education, community and finance). The framework included clear lines of accountability for reaching those goals. A cascading communication exercise ensured that the strategic goals were understood throughout the entire organization. Investments in the corporate Office of Clinical Quality and Safety (OCQS) supported the process transformation and the creation of key quality and safety performance measures and targets. Further investments in clinical information systems ensured that local data were available for measuring and improving performance.

Canadian context

Over the past few years there have been several reports, both federal (Romanow 2002; Kirby 2002) and provincial (Mazankowski 2001) calling for the transformation of Canada's health system. In response, the federal government created an arms-length Health Quality Council and a Canadian Patient Safety Institute to report annually on the status of healthcare quality and safety in Canada. Increasing attention has also been directed at both reducing wait times and creating clarity around accountability for healthcare providers.

The sustainability of Canada's health system is in doubt, as critics of medicare predict that we will not be able to meet the demands of an expanding aging population. Some of the significant challenges facing the Canadian government, the provincial ministries of health and health service providers include the following:

- Growing wait lists
- A call for wait time guarantees
- Shortage of health human resources
- Inadequate health information systems
- Increasing costs of new drugs and technologies
- Insufficient physical capacity

In the context of so many challenges, it is essential for health service providers, hospitals and regional health authorities to focus on becoming performance improvement leaders. HFHS recognized the need for such massive transformation. While its administrators looked at every aspect of the organization, they succeeded by focusing significant effort and investment in four key areas: leadership, accountability, performance measures and a culture of quality and safety. Given the challenges facing the Canadian health system, healthcare administrators as well as government policy- and decision-makers may be well advised to adopt a similar approach to help transform Canadian hospitals and regional health authorities.

Leadership

HFHS redesigned both governance and management structures to ensure integration and alignment at all levels. Once the organizational goals had been defined and communicated throughout the organization, leaders and managers at all levels understood where the organization was going and, most importantly, what they needed to focus on to help HFHS get there.

The importance of demonstrable commitment from the board of governors, the CEO and senior administration is clear. It is apparent that physician involvement was equally important. The case study authors tell us that "physician champions and leaders are very important" at HFHS; however, most of the organization's physicians are employees. Clearly, this relationship provides HFHS administrators and department heads with significant leverage in gaining compliance with organizational directions.

In the Canadian system, meanwhile, physicians are not employees. Rather, they are given appointments and privileges. However, this difference need not be prohibitive in engaging physicians as leaders. Administrators should ensure that all department and division heads truly understand organizational goals. This is particularly true for academic centres where patient care, education and research are all part of their mandate. Once an organization's goals are understood, physician leaders' roles and responsibilities must be clearly stated. Finally, a process for measuring, monitoring and managing performance must be implemented. In this way, physician leaders and champions can and will help transform Canada's health system.

Accountability

At HFHS the annual strategic plan and performance reporting systems are explicitly tied to the organization's "seven pillars." Once HFHS had established clear organizational goals, it then created a structure to ensure that individuals in the organization could be held accountable for reaching those goals. The organization was restructured into cross-functional teams that corresponded to each of the seven pillars. HFHS executive leaders were assigned as both chairs and participating members of those teams. In this way, clear lines of accountability were established for each pillar. Once executives and teams were identified for the pillars, HFHS ensured that key performance indicators and targets were created for each team. A Dashboard Report – including graphs of indicators and targets for finances, growth, people (nurse and physician turnover) and service (patient satisfaction) – was reviewed monthly and necessary actions were taken, as required.

Performance measurement

Healthcare organizations have been slower than most to embrace the adage, "You can't manage what you can't measure." Clearly, HFHS' decision to underscore the importance of information systems and local data in making the organization a performance improvement leader was key to its success.

Historically, health organizations have not invested sufficiently in information systems. This has led to widespread collection of diverse sets of data that, for the most part, may be inaccurate, outdated and not comparable to data produced by other health organizations. Lack of confidence in health system data has hindered efforts at measuring and comparing peer healthcare organizations for benchmarking exercises and other performance improvement initiatives.

Certain more progressive organizations have, however, adopted the principle that measuring performance is an essential work in progress. Increasingly, governments and health service providers are working to improve both the accuracy and timeliness of performance data. By continuing to use and improve data, HFHS was able to create performance indicators to reflect performance in key areas of the organization. HFHS understood that becoming a performance leader requires significant investments and attention to collecting local data. Its administrators also understood the importance of using external data from a variety of sources, including published studies and collaboratives. Standardized patient satisfaction and employee satisfaction surveys, participation in the Institute for Healthcare Improvement's 100k Lives campaign and participation in the JCAHO accreditation are some of the ways that HFHS uses credible external indicators to help drive performance improvement.

In Canada, more and more credible initiatives (e.g., the Required Organizational Practices of the Canadian Council on Health Services Accreditation; the Safer Healthcare Now initiative of the Canadian Patient Safety Institute) are helping senior health system leaders focus on improving quality and safety. Today's senior health system decision-makers must understand the importance of both credible external performance measures and local data. They must also continue to invest in information systems that will support their organizations' quests to become performance leaders.

Culture of quality and safety

Great leaders articulate clear visions for their organizations. Equally important, they ensure that everyone in their organizations understands their own value in helping achieve those visions.

The HFHS leadership recognized this truth and created a compelling vision statement: "To provide each patient the quality of care and comfort we want for ourselves and our families." They demonstrated their commitment to this vision through tangible investments in organizational development, service excellence and culture change. These investments included a significant increase in resources to support the newly formed OCQS. A number of initiatives aimed at creating a quality culture were implemented, the most compelling of which were the key quality performance measures. Reporting on these clearly defined what HFHS meant by quality and stated objective measures of the quality of care that was being provided. Each of the six categories of quality (safe, timely, efficient, effective, equitable and patient-centred) was assigned a number of performance indicators, and progress improvement in these areas was measured objectively. Through clear lines of accountability, the loop was closed and HFHS moved forward toward its vision.

Summary

In a few short years HFHS successfully transformed itself from being an average to below-average healthcare provider into a leading organization. The organization focused on leadership (including physicians), alignment and integration through clear lines of accountability for performance improvement, performance measurement through designing local performance indicators and the creation of a culture of quality and safety. Although the health system in the United States differs from Canada's, the strategies and tactics HFHS used are highly relevant to Canadian health service organizations seeking to be leading performers in the health system.

References

Romanow, R.J. 2002. *Building on Values. The Future of Healthcare in Canada.* Final Report. November 2002. Retrieved May 10, 2007. <http://www.hc-sc.gc.ca/english/pdf/romanow/pdfs/HCC_Final_Report.pdf>

Kirby, M.J.L. 2002. *The Health of Canadians – The Federal Role. Volume Six: Recommendations for Reform. The Standing Senate Committee on Social Affairs, Science and Technology.* Retrieved May 10, 2007. <http://www.parl.gc.ca/37/2/parlbus/commbus/senate/Com-e/soci-e/rep-e/repoct02vol6-e.htm>

Mazankowski, D.F. Premier's Advisory Council on Health. 2001. "A Framework for Reform: Report of the Premier's Advisory Council on Health." *Alberta Health.* Retrieved May 10, 2007. <http://www.health.gov.ab.ca/resources/publications/PACH_report_final>

7

Calgary Health Region

Calgary, Alberta

Background

Calgary Health Region (CHR) is one of nine health regions in the province of Alberta. Regionalization in Alberta began in 1993, motivated by financial and quality goals. Provincial leaders believed that regional governance could generate cost savings and improved healthcare services through economies of scale and coordination of services (Watson Wyatt Worldwide 1999). Initially Alberta created 17 regional health authorities (RHAs) responsible for the planning and delivery of hospital-based, continuing, community-based and public healthcare services. In 2003 the 17 RHAs were consolidated into nine.

In 1994, when the Calgary Regional Health Authority (CRHA) assumed responsibility for planning and delivering services, the system's components were not well coordinated or integrated (CRHA was renamed the Calgary Health Region in April 2003, and that name will be used for the remainder of this case). Despite regional governance, individual organizations were distinct and independent, each having different structures, policies, procedures and practices. There were few formal linkages between organizations, information systems were outdated and incompatible and planning and monitoring of services were limited. A variety of system changes were undertaken to address these issues (Watson Wyatt Worldwide 1999). (Appendix A outlines CHR's journey.)

Today, CHR is one of Canada's largest integrated, publicly funded healthcare systems. Serving a population of 1.2 million people, the region is home to some of the fastest growing communities in the country. It serves the city of Calgary and numerous rural communities stretching from the Rocky Mountains to the prairies. More than 25,000 staff members and 2,200 physicians provide services in over 100 locations, including 12 hospitals, three comprehensive health centres, 40 care centres and a variety of community and continuing care sites (Calgary Health Region 2007).

CHR has achieved numerous successes. For example, it has integrated care for patients across different organizations, improved access and flow to a number of clinical services and created an effective information infrastructure closely linked to efforts to improve the quality and safety of its services.

Selected achievements

CHR has undertaken a number of clinical improvement initiatives aimed at improving the quality of the patient experience and outcomes. Examples include:

- The Foothills Interventional Cardiology Service redesigned its processes for the management of acute myocardial infarction (AMI) patients and has reduced the time from symptom onset to reperfusion via percutaneous coronary intervention in patients presenting with ST-segment elevation myocardial infarction. This project, called Strategic Evaluation and Management of ST Elevation Myocardial Infarctions (STEMI), aims to reduce morbidity and mortality by reducing the door-to-balloon time. The redesigned process refines pre-hospital diagnosis, emergency room assessment and timely transfer to reperfusion suites and includes paramedic, emergency and cardiology services. Phase 2 of the project focuses on improvements in discharge planning and education in the transition from acute care to the community. Key achievements include improving reperfusion of 90% of patients at 120 minutes, in-patient and 30-day mortality rates of 3.1% and decreasing length of stay from 7 to 5 days (de Villiers et al. 2007).
- The Prostate Cancer Rapid Access Clinic, which opened in September 2005, has significantly reduced the time to confirm a diagnosis from 15 to 5 weeks. The clinic provides coordinated and accelerated access to urologists for examination, assessment and follow-up investigations of patients determined to be at risk for prostate cancer. In 2006 the average wait time was 2.9 days from booking to clinic appointment, and the average wait time from clinic to biopsy was 4.8 days. Prior to opening

the clinic, patients could wait up to 95 days for all diagnostic testing to be completed (Prostate Cancer Institute 2006).

- Several strategies have been implemented to optimize patient flow and increase capacity within CHR. These include the implementation of the Southern Alberta Coordination and Referral Centre, a call centre providing a single point of access for rural physicians to specialists within CHR; daily bed-planning meetings with patient-care units at each adult acute care site; increasing numbers of program-based patient flow coordinators; increased utilization of program-specific urgent assessment clinics to avoid acute care admission; and repatriation of appropriate patients to rural acute care sites (Calgary Health Region 2007).
- CHR has implemented the six interventions in the Safer Healthcare Now! campaign, along with an increased focus on the reporting of close calls and adverse events through a Safety Learning Reporting System (Calgary Health Region 2007).
- CHR has reduced wait times and improved patient outcomes for assessment and treatment of hip and knee replacement. The service redesign from referral through assessment, pre-surgical optimization of health, surgery, in-patient care, rehabilitation and ongoing monitoring has decreased wait times from referral to clinic visit from 145 to 21 days, decreased time from clinic visit to surgery from 58 to 7.5 weeks and decreased hospital and overall costs by 15% and 2% respectively (Alberta Bone and Joint Health Institute 2007) (see Appendix B).

Method: Exploring a system capable of improvement

What changes and strategic investments did CHR undertake in order to transform it into a higher performing system? How has CHR developed into a healthcare system capable of improvement? To answer these questions, a team from the University of Toronto Department of Health Policy, Management and Evaluation prepared this case study. One member of the team spent three months in a practicum with CHR's leaders. She held interviews with administrative and clinical leaders, front-line staff members and members of support staff at local, organizational and regional levels. She also collected and analyzed documents pertaining to CHR's development and services. These data provided insight into CHR's investments in building improvement capability and the challenges faced in sustaining improvements.

A system capable of improvement

In 1995 CHR began restructuring in order to emphasize regional activities and accountabilities. It integrated elements from individual organizations into a network of seven operational portfolios organized primarily by geography. Dr. Chris Eagle, CHR's president and chief operating officer, was the head of the anesthesia department at Foothills Medical Centre during this time. He recalls that early in the restructuring process, each portfolio

> provided a variety of programs to meet the needs of the community it served and was led by an executive director; [but] there was limited collaboration between portfolios and few incentives and mechanisms to encourage and enable collaboration and shared responsibility for healthcare services throughout the region.

In 1996 a regional medical system was created to support physicians and clinical leaders in working collaboratively to improve healthcare delivery. Still, Alberta in the mid 1990s was a very stressful and challenging environment for healthcare. Eagle recalled that, as "a consequence of a persistent provincial culture which depicted physicians as 'cost generators' and 'only supportive of self-interests,' a deep fracture existed between physicians and the health region."

In 1999 the Canadian Council on Health Services Accreditation recommended that CHR develop a more focused approach to regional quality improvement (QI) and performance measurement (Calgary Regional Health Authority 2000a). CHR responded by consolidating improvement staff from the different organizations to form the Quality Improvement and Health Information (QIHI) portfolio in 2000. QIHI's mandate focused on building improvement capability and supporting information management across the region. QIHI integrated corporate functions for performance and data management, QI and health system analysis; it also provided a clinical and administrative decision support service to the region (see Table 1 for a list of QIHI service units). QIHI's structure provided new learning opportunities for staff members and developed consistent definitions of quality and approaches to improvement.

By 2000 the leadership structure at CHR was reorganized around clinical programs jointly led by a vice-president and executive medical director who shared responsibility for service delivery. Regional services and program planning were managed through a matrix structure while specific site issues were the responsibility of the dual leadership at each site. For example, CHR had three intensive care units (ICUs) and each resided in a different portfolio. Operational functions and issues relating to intensive care at a specific hospital were the responsibility of the site's operational and medical leaders; regional executive medical and operational directors shared responsibility for issues relating to the intensive care program across CHR. Structuring the region in this manner facilitated the implementation and spread of clinical practice guidelines and initiatives. Table 2 lists the major milestones in CHR's development between 1993 and 2008 (see also Appendix A).

Table 1. Comparison of the former Quality Safety and Health Information portfolio and new Health Outcomes portfolio

Service Units of former Quality, Safety and Health Information portfolio	Service Units of New Health Outcomes portfolio
Leadership Team • Vice President • Executive Director • Director, Quality and Safety • Director, Health Information and System Management Quality Improvement/Quality Management • Quality and Safety Education • Quality Improvement • Clinical Integration • GRIDLOCC • Patient Concerns • Accreditation Patient Safety • Clinical Safety Evaluation • Patient Safety Framework • Patient Safety Education • Human Factors • Patient/Family Safety Council Health Information and System Management • Health System Analysis • Performance Measuring and Reporting • Survey and Evaluation	Leadership Team • Vice President • Executive Director • Director, Quality and Safety, Accreditation • Director, Clinical Outcomes • Director, Population Health Observatory • Director, Information Analysis and Evaluation • Medical Directors Divisions • Quality, Safety and Accreditation • Clinical Outcomes • Population Health Observatory • Information Analysis and Evaluation • Clinical Integration

This information is based on data gathered by the case study author during interviews with CHR's directors and from observations made during site visits. As of March 3, 2008, CHR had not yet finalized or published its portfolio divisions.
Used by permission.

Establishing direction for CHR's delivery of health services

CHR's board and executive leadership published a vision for the future entitled *Our Community Working Together for Excellence in Health. Report to the Community* (Calgary Health Region 2004). Extensive staff and physician input contributed to the development of seven strategic directions (Calgary Regional Health Authority 1999; Watson Wyatt Worldwide 1999):

- Responsive to public expectations – people should expect to transition from one service provider to another and know how and where to access appropriate care
- Support for healthcare and service providers
- Service delivery in the community – hospital-based services will effectively coordinate with community-based services and agencies

- Leadership and innovation – create a culture of creativity and harvest intellectual capital of all staff
- Balance the needs of individuals, communities and populations
- Build relationships with all stakeholders, especially patients
- Education and research – create a culture of continuous learning and the acquisition of new knowledge

Table 2. CHR regionalization and restructuring

1993	Alberta begins restructuring its healthcare system into nine regional health authorities, each with centralized regional governance.
1994	CRHA assumes responsibility for planning and delivery of services
1995	CRHA restructures from a collection of organizations into a network of portfolios segmented primarily by geography. Each portfolio is led by an administrative executive.
1996	Regional medical system created to enable collaboration between clinical and administrative leaders to improve healthcare service delivery.
2000	Clinical and administrative executives begin sharing responsibility for service delivery within each portfolio as well as regional programs (e.g., ICU).
2000	QIHI portfolio created to enable a more focused approach to improvement, consolidate initiatives and build regional capability.
2004	QIHI becomes Quality, Safety and Health Information (QSHI) to formally embed patient safety into regional framework, structures and accountability.
2008	CHR restructures its portfolio, leadership and data warehouse structures to support results-based improvement of outcomes in core clinical areas.

Implementing these strategic directions required effective leadership to address key issues and set priorities. A dominant concern with finances at all levels of management had to be refocused on setting appropriate and evidence-based targets and priorities. Information systems capable of supplying valid and timely data to decision-makers were also needed to support a regional performance measurement system.

In 2005 CHR extended these strategic directions and established a new five-year strategic service plan to help guide providers through unprecedented levels of growth and demand for healthcare services (Calgary Health Region 2005). The plan establishes the principles that underpin its promise to be "Leaders in Health – A Partner in Care," including the following:

- Focus on patient experience
- Emphasize wellness and community care
- Add capacity throughout the system
- Integrate all aspects of care
- Develop community-specific care
- Introduce innovation
- Embrace technology
- Build partnerships

Physician engagement

Engaging physicians in service improvements was an important ingredient in achieving these strategic directions. By 1999, recognition that only modest levels of physician engagement had been realized led to a new strategy. A Physician Partnership Steering Committee (PPSC) was formed in 2000 to identify opportunities to engage physicians in CHR planning and operations, reported Eagle. This committee solicited and prioritized physician-generated projects, managed a new physician partnership fund and advised the executive committee and CHR board on various business cases and recommendations (Calgary Regional Health Authority 2000b). The physician partnership fund – a three-year, $10 million commitment – provided "time-limited" funding to support the planning and development of physician-led pilot projects aimed at demonstrating innovative ways to improve service delivery. Proposals were accepted twice a year and $3 million was allocated each year to support between 10 and 15 projects (Calgary Regional Health Authority 2000b).

Other mechanisms were created to improve physician participation and communications. A medical task force was created to bring the voice of physicians to the regional executive leaders and board of directors. According to Eagle,

> There is plenty of "face time" between senior executives and physicians; a definite leadership presence and awareness of critical issues. ... The CEO, Chief Clinical Officer and Chief Medical Officer attend all meetings of the Medical Advisory Board. The Chief Medical Officer attends all medical staff meetings with the Medical Director at each [hospital] site.

CHR has sought extensive physician input in the design, implementation and use of the Patient Care Information System (PCIS). Similarly, physician input has been a critical component in the development of standardized order sets, medication safety and performance data, among other initiatives. Physicians receive financial subsidies and dedicated time to support their QI training and participation in improvement projects.

Building capacity for QI

In 2001 QIHI established clinical enhancement teams to provide dedicated support to clinical departments and portfolios. Each team is comprised of a part-time QI physician leader, QI consultant, data coordinator and dedicated health information analysis support. These teams support improvement projects across operational portfolios, working to improve services and integrate patient and family feedback.

Quality councils and committees were also established at all levels of the organization. The councils helped to facilitate the improvement of healthcare delivery processes, while the committees provided ongoing support and prioritization of QI initiatives. Initially, the committee structure, composition and scope of responsibility were variable and depended on the culture, resources and structures of each program or portfolio. Moreover, most proposals were accepted, which led to a large number of projects. This result left QI consultants, physicians, managers and providers struggling with their workloads and the need to find appropriate resources.

CHR invested in Institute for Healthcare Improvement (IHI) QI training for about 50 executive leaders, QI consultants and physicians. The training provided a better understanding of the philosophy, methods and tools required to expand QI into region-wide initiatives and shift from quality assurance to quality management. QIHI also developed a series of educational initiatives to provide a common frame of reference and toolkit. Education and coaching programs were developed to build competencies in QI, project management, change management and knowledge sharing for managers and front-line staff. The education curriculum includes courses (largely facilitated by QI consultants and physicians) such as Executive Leadership for Quality Improvement, Introduction to Quality and Safety, Fundamentals of Quality Management, QI Methods, Disclosure of Adverse Events, Health System Safety Analysis and Failure Mode and Effects Analysis.

Participation in improvement collaboratives

Armed with new knowledge, skills and energy, leaders and local teams participated in two major, IHI-sponsored collaborative learning projects focusing on process redesign: Waits and Delays and Surgical Patient Flow. These projects were CHR's first real opportunities to set challenging aims and to use improvement methods to do things very differently. One senior executive noted that these collaboratives "gave us the permission, ability and expectation to think differently about the way healthcare is delivered and refocus our attention on meeting patient needs. This was incredibly challenging. It took incredible courage to redesign medical services – for executives and physicians." Relationship building was critical in engaging all stakeholders in service redesign and heightening awareness of the far-reaching impact of changes.

Building on the lessons learned from these initiatives, a larger project was developed to address the need to improve access for patients requiring hip and knee-joint replacement. The Alberta Hip and Knee Replacement Pilot Project was one of Alberta's first QI initiatives, involving 3,400 patients in three health regions (Alberta Bone and Joint Health Institute 2007). Focusing on system redesign for hip and knee-joint surgery patients in primary care, specialist care, acute care and community care, the project aimed to reshape demand and capacity to improve access to specific orthopaedic services. Results were impressive, including a decrease in wait times from 145 to 21 days for patients receiving their first orthopaedic consult, from 58 to 7.5 weeks for patients from the first orthopaedic consult to surgery and a decrease in hospital length of stay from 6.0 to 4.7 days (Calgary Regional Health Authority 1999) (see Appendix B).

Challenges that limited coordination and spread of improvement efforts

CHR's collaborative projects involved numerous teams and hundreds of people from a broad spectrum of healthcare professions. But with 25,000 staff members and 2,200 physicians in CHR, senior leaders recognized the need to find other ways to spread the required knowledge and change. QI needed to move beyond acute care. Moreover, most learning involved just-in-time, project-by-project learning. The region's initial QI efforts did not incorporate system-wide or regional projects. Instead, QI was carried out locally by departments and programs. QIHI supported QI work in clinical programs and QI consultants, and physicians led these improvement initiatives. However, because there were no formal mechanisms for sharing common ideas, QI initiatives were limited in depth and scope. Although individual improvement teams became very good at doing program-based QI projects, there were few mechanisms to link these pockets of excellence with the rest of the organization. Also, this approach also did not include a measurement system that monitored ongoing projects. Consequently, programs would often achieve a certain level of change and then revert to their old ways within a short period of time.

In addition to these issues, the growing variety of new QI tools and methodologies – rapid cycle change, IHI Breakthrough Collaboratives, statistical process control, root cause analysis, healthcare failure mode and effects analysis (HFMEA) and the region's customized Health System Safety Analysis (HSSA) tool – caused confusion in some clinical programs. These new efforts met with resistance from some managers, staff members and physicians who were upset that QI was presented as a new idea. They believed they had always been striving to provide quality care despite resource constraints and changing expectations.

The underlying issue in these discussions revolved around local teams' roles and engagement. Looking back, senior leaders commented that they had relied on what they term a centralized "spider" model of decision-making, with decisions made by regional leaders. This approach proved to be ineffective for QI. Instead they believe they should have invested earlier in a "starfish" model of formal change management, in which front-line staff members and providers exert as much influence on project success as does central management and leadership. This model encourages local engagement and ownership, establishes an appetite for change and mitigates the risk of project death resulting from a shift in leadership priorities. Senior executives and leaders began using the starfish model to engage front-line staff and teams, leveraging the expertise of middle managers. They worked with physician leaders to ensure a shared understanding of key system drivers (i.e., access, quality and cost) and critical processes, to set clinical and process targets and to determine trade-offs necessary to achieve targets.

QIHI also established a quality management framework that incorporates performance measurement data relevant to QI (Figure 1). Developed and revised over five years, the framework links the principles of QI and patient safety to measurable improvements in processes and outcomes. The framework uses the Alberta Quality Matrix for Health (Figure 2), which maps the six dimensions of quality against areas of need (i.e., being healthy, getting better, living with disease or illness and end of life). This identification of the different quality dimensions of effectiveness, acceptability, safety and efficiency provided the scaffolding to support the region's vision, mission and values statements; to develop QI competencies; and to integrate QI into every aspect of care delivery (Quality, Safety and Health Information 2006). Ward Flemons, now responsible for this portfolio, noted that operationalizing this framework as a core business strategy across the region is still a "work in progress."

Performance monitoring and information management

In 2002 CHR adopted a Balanced Scorecard approach to monitor performance on established targets and corporate goals. Balanced scorecards were implemented at both the portfolio and individual (management and staff) levels as performance development tools. That year an information management strategic planning exercise identified three major priorities for information management:

- An Enterprise Master Person Index (with a unique patient identifier)
- A regional PCIS (e-health record)

- An information clearing house for corporate data

Together, these initiatives were needed to accelerate the analysis, monitoring and reporting of performance more broadly (Calgary Regional Health Authority 2000a).

Figure 1. Quality and safety framework

Source: Quality, Safety and Health Information (2006).
Used by permission.

The PCIS is a region-wide information system that relates data from diagnostic tests, assessments, treatments and other components of care for acute care patients. PCIS includes evidence-based order sets, discharge information, real-time order entry and clinical alert tools. This system has been implemented incrementally over five years and became fully functional in 2006. Data on clinical outcomes, care processes (e.g., missed appointments, wait times, compliance with standards) and other pertinent outcome, performance and service utilization data are used to create performance indicators and highlight opportunities for improvement (Scott and Gall 2006).

Figure 2. Alberta Quality Matrix for Health

ALBERTA QUALITY MATRIX FOR HEALTH

DIMENSIONS OF QUALITY / AREAS OF NEED	ACCEPTABILITY Health services are respectful and responsive to user needs, preferences and expectations.	ACCESSIBILITY Health services are obtained in the most suitable setting in a reasonable time and distance.	APPROPRIATENESS Health services are relevant to user needs and are based on accepted or evidence-based practice.	EFFECTIVENESS Health services are provided based on scientific knowledge to achieve desired outcomes.	EFFICIENCY Resources are optimally used in achieving desired outcomes.	SAFETY Mitigate risks to avid unintended or harmful results.
BEING HEALTHY Achieving health and preventing occurrence of injuries, illness, chronic conditions and resulting disabilities.						
GETTING BETTER Care related to acute illness or injury.						
LIVING WITH ILLNESS OR DISABILITY Care and support related to chronic or recurrent illness or disability.						
END OF LIFE Care and support that aims to relieve suffering and improve quality of living with or dying from advanced illness or bereavement.						

HQCA Health Quality Council of Alberta

Adopted June 2005 by the Health Quality Network, an HQCA collaborative consisting of: Alberta Cancer Board, Alberta College of Pharmacists, Alberta Health and Wellness, Alberta Medical Association, Alberta Mental Health Board, Aspen Regional Health, Calgary Health Region, Capital Health, Chinook Health Region, College of Association of Registered Nurses of Alberta, College of Physicians & Surgeons of Alberta, David Thompson Health Region, East Central Health, Federation of Regulated Health Professions, Health Quality Council of Alberta, Northern Lights Health Region, Palliser Health Region and Peace County Health.

www.hqca.ca Adapted from the Agency for Healthcare Research and Quality, U.S. Department of Health and Human Services under contract to the Institute of Medicine.

Source: Health Quality Council of Alberta (2005).
Reproduced with the permission of the Health Quality Council of Alberta.

A separate system called the Community Care Information System captures client-specific information across numerous programs, services and locations throughout CHR (including hospitals). It provides an integrated view of client information, which is used by healthcare professionals and service providers to create shared care plans. Together with PCIS, these two systems aim to link data on primary, secondary, tertiary and community care services (Scott and Gall 2006).

QIHI's performance reporting unit monitors performance in improving the quality of patient care; it also designs, develops and manages reporting protocols. In 2007 the performance reporting unit implemented an interactive electronic resource that enables staff members to access, monitor, analyze and compare key clinical outcome and quality indicators. Data can be presented in many different formats (e.g., dashboards and scorecards), which allow for regional or site-specific comparisons. Over 1,000 indicators are reported on a weekly basis; this enables managers to set specific improvement and performance targets and monitor ongoing performance (Quality, Safety and Health Information 2007).

These information systems and measures have accelerated the use of data for quality and performance improvement. For example, the Calgary Stroke Program uses performance data to monitor its ongoing performance and movement toward its goals of treating more patients in less time and improving outcomes for all stroke patients. QIHI's performance reporting unit works closely with the Calgary Stroke Program to create data sets linked to the specific goals of the program and region. Since 2004, emergency readmission rates for stroke patients in the CHR have decreased from 9% to 5% as a direct result of improvements to care delivery. Data are also used to monitor service utilization and changes in demand for services. The length of stay for stroke patients has decreased by four days since 2002, while mortality rates have decreased from 19% to 15% during the same period. This translates into annual savings of $4 million for CHR. Data also facilitate collaboration between programs and professionals, for example, to improve discharge processes (Quality, Safety and Health Information 2007).

CHR continues to seek new ways to use performance measures to assess current activities and guide improvements. Despite the growing use of data, some senior leaders have worried that there have been varying definitions of key metrics and insufficient emphasis on outcomes measurement, factors that have limited the potential impact of this information. In order to improve accountability, analysis and reporting, a decision was made in January 2008 to remove data collection and reporting from the purview of Health Outcomes (formerly QIHI). Data collection and information system development were included in an Advanced Technologies and Enterprise Reporting portfolio.

Adverse events spur patient safety efforts

In 2004 two patients undergoing continuous renal replacement therapy in one of the CHR's ICUs died after receiving a lethal potassium chloride (KCl) dialysis solution prepared by the region's central pharmacy. These deaths refocused CHR on the need to ensure safe, high-quality healthcare. Senior leaders and physicians disclosed the facts of these incidents publicly and acknowledged responsibility for the deaths. They then commissioned an external review (referred to internally as the Robson Report) that fully examined the circumstances that led to these deaths and verified the conclusions of their own internal reviews (Robson et al. 2004). CHR's board of directors also asked the review team to look beyond these deaths to examine the strength of the patient safety culture in the various facilities providing healthcare services in the Calgary region.

The Robson Report confirmed that, in many ways, CHR was already a leader in patient safety and QI. Strong evidence of CHR's commitment to improvement appeared in the region's efforts to learn from leaders elsewhere (e.g., IHI, Intermountain Healthcare and Minnesota Children's Hospital) in order to help establish a pan-Canadian collaborative of ICU specialists to evaluate and adopt evidence-based safe practices and in its conducting of more than 25 multidisciplinary patient flow collaboratives (Robson et al. 2004). Moreover, CHR had a number of national and international experts, including Dr. Jan Davies, an anesthesiologist and patient safety expert who had developed methods and tools to understand the causes of adverse events.

Despite these efforts, external reviewers felt that there was a gap in performance across the region. Although there had been funding and support for many innovative improvement initiatives, the majority of the clinical and support staff, as well as patients, families and the public, remained relatively untouched by this work. Closing the loop and spreading knowledge and enthusiasm generated by these projects was seen as necessary to make QI and safety core organizational values and to translate the organization's vision and mission into reality (Robson et al. 2004). The latter objective was particularly challenging given that the region's vision and mission statements did not explicitly emphasize quality and safety. The accidental ICU patient deaths highlighted the need to overhaul CHR's vision, mission and values statements to reflect the importance of quality and safety. These are now central tenets and explicit components of the regional values statement (see Appendix C).

Jack Davis, CHR's chief executive officer (CEO), and the executive team established a new executive role to keep QI and patient safety front and centre at the regional level. In 2004 Dr. Ward Flemons became vice-president of QIHI; his mandate was to oversee a systematic approach to QI and patient safety. Additionally, safety was formally embedded into QIHI and its new name: the Quality, Safety and Health Information (QSHI) portfolio. Clinical safety leaders (similar to QI consultants) and safety committees were established for each portfolio; the safety structure generally mirrors that of the QI stream. QSHI's structure and position and the dual reporting of improvement consultants and clinical safety leaders facilitate learning across portfolios, programs and facilities throughout CHR. The senior operational leaders in each portfolio must approve all recommendations and tested changes before changes and innovations may be spread to other portfolios. QSHI then publishes approved recommendations, which are also regularly evaluated to determine their impact and sustainability.

According to Ward Flemons, the development of key safety policies and procedures has enriched QI work throughout CHR. Core safety policies (Calgary Health Region nd b) include the following:

- A just and trusting culture of safety
- Disclosure of harm to patients
- Reporting of harm, close calls and hazards
- Informing partners and stakeholders about safety hazards, failures and fixes

Rather than assigning blame, a just and trusting culture supports disclosure and transparency. This creates an environment that encourages (and expects) reporting of system vulnerabilities and defects. Greater transparency and sharing of lessons learned across programs helps to address system vulnerabilities and reduce recurrences. In 2007 the safety learning reporting system was developed and implemented as a pilot project. This system allows healthcare providers to easily report hazards, close calls and adverse events, and it helps them to monitor progress on recommended system improvements. Glenn McRae, the director of quality and safety at QSHI, noted that "the most critical piece of the safety learning reporting system is its ability to accelerate a culture of safety and QI by enabling knowledge into action."

CHR's senior executive team works to entrench the organization's vision, mission and values through visible commitment to safety policies at the provider and patient levels, regular use of "fireside chats" with staff members and patients, and Safety WalkRounds™. During the latter, senior operational and medical executives meet with front-line staff members from each unit to discuss new and ongoing safety concerns. Staff members are asked to highlight problem areas relating to system vulnerabilities and propose potential solutions wherever possible.

New directions

In late 2007 CHR reviewed its organizational and leadership structures. Many in the system believed that the portfolio organization and dual administrative and physician leadership model had helped to link physicians into regional strategies and accelerate improvement. Eagle reported, however, that there were concerns that the structure had created overlapping and redundant accountabilities and inhibited change. For example, according to Eagle, despite the emphasis placed on safety practices and policies, much of this work seemed "pasted to the outside of portfolios" rather than residing within. The structures seemed to slow fundamental changes at the front line and needed to be more adaptive in order to meet the evolving needs and requirements of the system and patients. Additionally, the region needed to use data more effectively to track and improve population-based health outcomes.

In January 2008 CHR reorganized its portfolio and leadership structures and refocused its use of data to support improvement in a variety of outcomes. The new portfolios were structured according to the population(s) served and/or services provided, and were aligned around the core clinical businesses. These new portfolios are:

- Health Outcomes (formerly QSHI)
- Public Health
- Wellness and Citizen Engagement
- Continuing Care, Medical Services and Seniors Health
- Community Health Services
- Interventional Services (diagnostic imaging; surgery; cardiac sciences; neuroscience; trauma; human organ procurement and exchange, and tissue; bone and joint)
- Critical Care, Emergency, Laboratory and Clinical Support Services
- Child and Women's Health and Specialized Clinical Services

An executive vice-president was appointed to lead each portfolio; these individuals were responsible for operations across the continuum of care. Most of the previous physician leaders (executive medical directors) were reassigned as associate chiefs of medicine in each portfolio, with a direct reporting relationship to the chief of staff. The goals of the restructuring emphasize increased accountability, enhanced performance and flexibility for core clinical programs. As Eagle noted, CHR is entering an uncertain environment in which the organization must move fast; the region needs the agility and flexibility to drive change more quickly: "we [CHR] believe that this new structure brings this [flexibility]."

Much like Intermountain Healthcare's strategy, CHR's leaders seek to prioritize improvements for the high-cost, high-volume and high-risk clinical programs, creating more robust metrics to help drive substantive improvements. Eagle observed that quality, safety and health information now reside within the Health Outcomes portfolio and are distinct entities that have been recast to support defined clinical priorities, outcomes and metrics.

Strategic value of QI and safety

As CHR has progressed in its approach to QI, it has increased the number and type of staff members who have QI knowledge and skill, built an infrastructure to develop useful data and methods to guide performance and emphasized a culture of quality and safety. New projects are now addressing broader corporate goals: improving the patient experience and creating healthy communities.

Project GRIDLOCC (Getting Rid of Inappropriate Delays that Limit Our Capacity to Care) and Clinical Integration are projects that target areas of strategic priority. Project GRIDLOCC involves a number of QI initiatives designed to decrease wait times, minimize system bottlenecks and alleviate emergency department congestion. Flemons described GRIDLOCC as "a strategic QI initiative which focuses on 'end to end' patient care – from first contact with a family physician or emergency department, through to hospital care and transition to an appropriate level of care in the community." He added that "wait times in emergency departments are a symptom of patient flow problems throughout the system. We must redesign our work and ensure that discrete processes link appropriately to meet patient needs across the continuum of care."

Clinical Integration involves a disciplined approach for improving patient care beyond acute care. It relies on a structured methodology to implement evidence-based practice for cross-functional teams. "Cross-functional teams represent the entire patient journey. These teams are better able to design or redesign services such that patient care needs are met at all points in their care," said Dr. Joe Dort, the medical director of Clinical Integration. Data extracted from PCIS, e-health record, patient feedback and population health databases are used to inform process design and redesign. Clinical integration pilot projects in spine health and retinal surgery began in 2007. These projects will be expanded to focus on high-risk, high-cost (financial and social) or high-volume clinical priorities.

Barriers and facilitators to improving quality and safety

Barriers

Like other Alberta health regions, CHR has benefited from the province's strong economic growth. Funding for healthcare services is generally higher than in other parts of Canada. However, the resources boom has created difficulties in recruiting and retaining staff. Generating an environment that supports QI is difficult when staff members and physicians are overworked. There continues to be tension between some direct care providers and QI staff. Some front-line clinicians feel that available resources should be deployed to patient care rather than QI. They believe front-line staff members have always worked diligently to provide the highest quality of care possible – and would do more if given more resources. Moreover, the range of different initiatives has created, in the words of one staff member, "too many burning platforms," a situation that leads to confusion, fatigue and reduced capacity to change for some individuals.

Physician engagement has proven difficult in the absence of financial incentives. QI projects require dedicated time, something that affects physicians' incomes. It has been difficult to engage residents in QI initiatives because they have limited exposure to quality, performance and patient safety in their academic training and are not given protected time to participate in local QI initiatives.

The QSHI portfolio team made considerable progress in creating data sets that evaluate performance across a variety of dimensions to guide improvement. However, decision-makers require data that will enable them to evaluate team or system-wide performance for specific patient populations or processes. For example, measures that focus on specific processes in the cardiac program may be evaluated by time of arrival in emergency to admission, patient length of stay, rehabilitation time, number of readmissions and time for patients to return to work.

CHR (like other Alberta regional health authorities) is publicly funded by the Alberta Ministry of Health and Wellness, which allocates funds and sets healthcare policies (Alberta Ministry of Health and Wellness nd). Regional health authorities are mandated to collect a variety of administrative measures; however, these metrics often do not align with or support system-wide QI. Provincial health priorities and foci depend on the priorities of the current minister of health. Ongoing initiatives and resources may be interrupted or redirected with changes in the minister's office.

Facilitators

The commitment of CHR's CEO and senior executive team to service excellence and the provision of high-quality patient care is broadly recognized by managers, physicians and other staff members. In addition, development of the QSHI portfolio has provided resources, training and expertise that have accelerated QI and patient safety throughout programs, organizations and the region. The development and use of data for planning, improving and monitoring healthcare services at all levels has been important in identifying QI targets and guiding local efforts.

CHR has been effective in developing a cohort of influential physicians with QI knowledge and training. These people bring visibility and expertise, and they communicate the relevance of QI work to CHR's entire physician workforce.

Next steps

"The CHR is at the end of the beginning of the development stage," noted QSHI's Glenn McRae. He (and others) described the region as "moving into the implementation stage, the hallmark of which is a regional approach that operationalizes improvement, links pockets of excellence and integrates all components of the patient journey." The following are some of the key strategies CHR has implemented:

- An e-health record
- PCIS
- GRIDLOCC (the safety reporting learning tool)
- Clinical Integration
- Alberta Matrix for Health
- An integrated learning strategy

The last strategy aims to increase awareness of the science and principles that underpin regional safety policies and to assist leaders, middle managers, front-line staff and physicians to work collaboratively to build a culture of safety.

CHR has invested considerable financial and human resources in the development of QI knowledge and skills across the organization. Despite this, many front-line staff members have yet to participate in improvement work. Moreover, human resources are scarce and all three acute care hospitals run near 100% capacity; consequently, staff members are often unable to dedicate time to improvement projects. CHR's senior leaders hope that many more direct care providers will participate in projects to improve patient flow in order to help increase capacity and free up time for education and professional development. Creating a critical mass of individuals with improvement knowledge, skills and experience will accelerate improvement work across the region. Restructuring the QI consultant and physician roles so those staff members work more closely with portfolio directors and assist in identifying strategic priorities may also increase the impact of improvement efforts and enable innovations and tested changes to spread more rapidly to operational leaders. According to Flemons "the goal is to further operationalize quality and safety rather than having QSHI staff and consultants lead and develop initiatives."

CHR has developed a strong track record of improvement; however, many of its efforts have focused on pilot projects (albeit with good results). Moving from demonstration and pilot projects to realizing substantial changes in key areas is the next challenge. Eagle summarized the region's strategy determining priority areas, focusing on these areas and achieving desired outcomes: "Good ideas and demonstration projects only get you so far. Without change in philosophy and behaviour, very little [change] can really happen."

Conclusion

Over the last 14 years CHR has evolved from a collection of independent organizations with different structures, policies, procedures and practices into one of Canada's largest integrated healthcare systems. CHR's board of directors and senior leaders have led a shift from an external focus on revenues, resources and finances to an internal transformation that focuses on improving care and creating innovative approaches to care delivery. New regional patient safety policies support a just culture and provide a clear set of principles that underpin improvement.

Physician leadership, engagement and adherence to evidence-directed practice have advanced improvement in all programs. A key strategic decision to establish the QSHI portfolio to develop improvement capability, performance measurement, health system analysis and evaluation, QI and patient safety has also been integral to CHR's progress. The development of integrated, region-wide information systems provides timely data for decision-makers at all levels of the organization, and the ability to link key clinical process, outcome and finance measures enables managers to monitor a balanced set of measures for accountability and clinical process improvement.

Many QI projects have been launched over the past eight years, and they are now resulting in measurable improvements. But they also present pragmatic challenges. For instance, how can the region continue to support staff members and physicians in ongoing QI work while it is under pressure to deal with high service demands? How can CHR better utilize and develop its leaders to advance improvement and spread change? Will recent changes enable CHR to improve patient outcomes in core clinical areas and move the region closer to its goal of becoming fully integrated and capable of system-wide improvement?

References

Alberta Bone and Joint Health Institute. 2007. *Alberta Hip and Knee Replacement Pilot Project. Scientific Evaluation Report.* Retrieved June 23, 2007. <http://www.albertaboneandjoint.com/projects/arthroplasty/Hip%20Knee%20Scientific%20Report.pdf>

Alberta Ministry of Health and Wellness. nd. *About Us.* Edmonton: Government of Alberta. Retrieved May 27, 2007. <http://www.health.gov.ab.ca/about/minister.html>

Calgary Health Region. 2004. *Report to the Community 2004.* Calgary: Author. Retrieved April 26, 2007. <http://www.calgaryhealthregion.ca/communications/pdf/2004_report_to_the_community.pdf>

Calgary Health Region. 2005. *Strategic Service Plan – Overview. Changing the Face of Health Care: Our Five Year Plan.* Calgary: Author. Retrieved October 21, 2007. <http://www.calgaryhealthregion.ca/corporate/about_us/pdf/healthplan.pdf>

Calgary Health Region. 2007. *Annual Report 2005-2006.* Calgary: Author. Retrieved April 20, 2007. <http://www.calgaryhealthregion.ca/communications/pdf/2005-2006_annual_report.pdf>

Calgary Health Region. nd a. *Vision, Mission and Values.* Calgary: Author. Retrieved March 29, 2007. <http://www.calgaryhealthregion.ca/communications/about_us/mission.html>

Calgary Health Region. nd b. *Patient Safety Policies.* Calgary: Author. Retrieved February 29, 2008. <http://www.calgaryhealthregion.ca/qshi/patientsafety/policies.htm>

Calgary Regional Health Authority. 1999. *Annual Report 1997-1998. Working Together for Health.* Calgary: Author.

Calgary Regional Health Authority. 2000a. *CCHSA Accreditation Update Report.* Calgary: Author.

Calgary Regional Health Authority. 2000b. *Physician Partnership Steering Committee Report.* Calgary: Author.

de Villier, J.S., T. Anderson, J.D. McMeekin, R.C.M. Leung and M. Traboulsi. 2007. "Expedited Transfer for Primary Percutaneous Coronary Intervention: A Program Evaluation." *Canadian Medical Association Journal* 176(13): 1833-38.

Health Quality Council of Alberta. 2005. *Alberta Quality Matrix for Health.* Retrieved February 23, 2008. <http://hqca.ca/templates/HQCA5/pdf/Final_Matrix_2005-06-23.pdf>

Prostate Cancer Institute. 2006. *Annual Report.* Retrieved November 2, 2007. Calgary: Prostate Cancer Institute. <http://www.prostatecalgary.com/client/whats_new/85/86/2006_annual_report.pdf>

Quality, Safety and Health Information. 2006. *2006 QSHI Annual Report.* Calgary: Calgary Health Region. Retrieved May 14, 2007. <http://www.calgaryhealthregion.ca/qshi/qshi_annual_report_12oct06.pdf>

Quality, Safety and Health Information. 2007. *2007 QSHI Annual Report.* Calgary: Calgary Health Region. Retrieved October, 2007. <http://www.calgaryhealthregion.ca/qshi/qshi_annual_report2007.pdf>

Quality, Safety and Health Information. nd. *About Us.* Calgary: Calgary Health Region. Retrieved February 23, 2008. <http://www.calgaryhealthregion.ca/qshi/about_us.htm>

Robson, R., B. Salsman and J. McMenemy. 2004. *External Patient Safety Review.* Unpublished.

Scott, C. and N. Gall. 2006. *Knowledge Use in the Calgary Health Region: A Scan of Initiatives that Support Use of Evidence in Practice.* Calgary: Calgary Health Research. Retrieved June 18, 2007. <http://www.calgaryhealthregion.ca/research/images/Knowledge_Utilization_Scan_Full_Report_%20Aug_28_2006.pdf>

Watson Wyatt Worldwide. 1999. *Calgary Regional Health Authority: Organizational Review.* Calgary: Calgary Health Region.

Appendix A. CHR's transformation from 1999 to 2007

1999
- CHR's first full Accreditation Survey:
  - Recommends a More Purposeful Approach to Quality Improvement (QI)

2000
- Quality Improvement & Health Information Department Created (reports to Chief Medical Officer)

2001
- Department Based Q1 Physicians and Consultants Hired
- Department Q1 Projects Started
- Regional Collaborative Project:
  - Waits and Delays

2002
- Regional Collaborative Project:
  - Surgical Patient Flow

2003
- Regional Collaborative Projects:
  - Patient Flow
  - Surgical Site Infection
  - Medication Safety

2004
- KCI Dialysis Tragedy
- External Review – Robson Report
- Quality, Safety & Health Information Portfolio Created (reports to Chief Clinical Officer)
- Regional Clinical Safety Committee Formed

2005
- Clinical Safety Evaluation Department Created
- Regional Patient Safety Policies Created
- Portfolio Clinical Safety Leaders Hired
- Accreditation Moved into QSHI Portfolio
- Hosted National Patient Safety Symposium (Halifax 5) Public Forum Video Presented

2006
- Patient Advocates Hired
- Office of Patient Concerns Created
- Regional Q1 Project:
  - GRIDLOCC Started (Access and Flow)
- Patient/Family Safety Council Created
- Procedures & Guidelines Created to Support Policies
- Leading the Way: Policies & Procedures Rollout

2007
- Safety Learning Reporting System Piloted
- Automated Performance Measurement Software (Static piMD)

Source: Adapted from Quality, Safety and Health Information (nd). Used by permission.

Appendix B. Alberta Hip and Knee Replacement Pilot Project – Six Dimensions of the Alberta Matrix for Health

Dimensions of Quality	Current Approach	New Continuum of Care
Accessibility	Referral to seen – 145 days Seen to surgery – 58 weeks	Referral to seen – 21 days Seen to surgery – 7.5 weeks
Efficiency	Surgery time – 119 minutes Acute LOS – 6 days Cost change – toward new	Surgery time – 109 minutes Acute LOS – 4.7 days Cost change ↓ 15% hospital ↓ 2% overall
Acceptability	Long waits = decreased quality of life and increased cost	Reduced wait = minimal decrease in quality of life and cost More personal and more intense
Effectiveness	Improved physical and social function and reduced pain	Even greater increase in physical and social function and pain reduction
Safety	4.8 joint-related adverse events per 100 patients <30 days after surgery 2.2 joint-related adverse events per 100 patients ≥30 days after surgery	4.1 joint-related adverse events per 100 patients < 30 days after surgery 1.2 joint-related adverse events per 100 patients ≥30 days after surgery
Appropriateness	31% mobilized day of 75% spinals Discharge change – toward new	85% mobilized day of 82% spinals Reduced use of surgical wound drains

No difference in patient age, sex, BMI, health status, socio-economic factors.
Source: Alberta Bone and Joint Health Institute (2007). Used by permission.

Appendix C. CHR vision, mission and values

VISION, MISSION AND VALUES

vision: healthy communities
mission: leaders in health - a partner in care
values:

WE VALUE	AS SHOWN BY
caring respectful relationships	Providing patient and family centred care Showing respect, equality and fairness Being compassionate Maintaining dignity Valuing contribution
quality and safety	Committing to safety Providing accessible services Working in partnerships Providing best practice, evidence-based care
accountability	Being honest Building trust and being trustworthy Displaying integrity and the highest level of ethical behaviour Being accountable for our decisions and actions

Source: Calgary Health Region (nd). Used by permission.

8

Trillium Health Centre

Mississauga, Ontario

Introduction

The product of a merger between the Mississauga Hospital and Queensway General Hospital, Trillium Health Centre is a 751-bed community hospital serving over one million residents in Mississauga, west Toronto and the surrounding area. Its staff includes 4,400 employees, over 700 physicians and 1,100 volunteers (Leddy 2007). Trillium is guided by an ambitious mission called "Transforming the Health Care Experience" that aspires to "set the standard for outstanding health service delivery" and to be "courageous, innovative and evidence-based in efforts to improve the quality of services" (Trillium Health Centre 2007a). This bold aim, established by Ken White, the inaugural president and chief executive officer (CEO), has been matched by important achievements during the organization's 10-year history. Trillium has won local, national and international awards for excellent performance in clinical and administrative areas (see Table 1).

This case study explores key factors contributing to Trillium's success, including leadership, strategic alignment of improvement activities, investments in staff capability and cultural development.

Table 1. Key awards granted to Trillium Health Centre

Year	Name of Award
2007	• National Quality Institute Progressive Excellence Program Level III
2006	• Ontario Laboratory Accreditation (OLA) 5-year Accreditation • Recipient of Ontario's first Innovation Award for Improving Quality and Patient Safety (Trillium Order Sets System) • First multi-site hospital in the world to receive ISO 14001 registration
2003	• 3M Health Care Quality Team Award
2002	• 3M Health Care Quality Team Award (acute care facility category) • First hospital in the history of the Medical Users Software Exchange (MUSE) to be awarded an International Education Exchange Award
2001–2004	• Ranked as one of Canada's Top 100 Employers (Yerema 2004)

Method: Exploring a system capable of improvement

A team from the University of Toronto Department of Health Policy, Management and Evaluation prepared this case study. One member of the team spent three months in a practicum at the health centre and collected information for the case between March and May 2007 (follow-up interviews were conducted in November 2007). She interviewed key corporate and physician leaders, as well as those in clinical and support services, and reviewed selected corporate documents. Two initiatives were researched in detail: The Safer Healthcare Now! (SHN!) initiatives in the Medical Surgical Intensive Care Unit (MSICU) and the Non-Nursing Task Force (NNTF) redesign of nursing and support service roles.

Quality improvement at Trillium

Trillium leaders described their quality improvement journey as occurring in two phases. During phase one (1998–2005), board members committed to risk management and patient safety as strategic priorities. They adopted an innovative enterprise risk management approach to systematically prioritize investments within these areas of strategic focus (see Appendix A). Between four and five improvement initiatives focusing on high-risk, high-volume and high-cost patient groups were completed each year.

Staff development was undertaken in several areas. CEO White promoted the concept of distributed leadership, suggesting that all staff members – with or without formal leadership titles – should develop and exercise their ability to lead. Resources were allocated to develop and implement the "Foundations of Leadership" course (see Appendix B). External experts were also used to mentor staff in improvement methods, and project management consultants introduced a systematic approach to planning, implementing and evaluating projects. These methods included identifying quantitative outcome measures for all proposed projects and identifying the staff resources required to lead and implement proposed projects.

Front-line clinical staff were seconded to improvement projects across the health systems. These secondments were designed to build individuals' improvement capabilities and assist later in project implementation. However, there were no formal ways to ensure the spread of improvement knowledge and skills once the seconded individuals returned to their local health systems. While this strategy was successful in some cases, it failed to ensure organization-wide diffusion of improvement expertise.

In 2000 the Performance Excellence (PE) portfolio (the term used at Trillium to refer to quality improvement) was created. Given equal status with the clinical health systems and strategic business units (SBUs), the creation of the PE portfolio signalled leadership commitment to quality improvement. PE supports health system and SBU improvement work, develops quality improvement expertise and enables the spread of best practices.

By 2005 Trillium's improvement strategy had broadened from building baseline capability to a focus on transforming the healthcare experience "beyond the walls of Trillium to the broader community at large" (White 2007). Use of external consultants was de-emphasized while internal resources were augmented. In 2007 White put forth a new management strategy aimed at "all aspects of service, and in partnerships with others, to lead the industry in recognition for quality, outcomes and leading edge health service innovation."

Investments in staff education accelerated in phase two (2005–2007). Three new courses were developed to educate team members about quality improvement tools and to teach managers and staff members about project management tools and techniques. Internal project management services were also developed to sustain the systematic approach to project planning and implementation.

Trillium also strengthened its commitment to pursue external awards to reward staff members, validate Trillium's achievements and provide an external forum for knowledge exchange. Investments in information technology (IT) were increased in phase two, commencing with the THINK (Transforming Healthcare into Integrated Networks of Knowledge) project. THINK was aimed at providing a standardized platform for clinical and administrative data collection and strengthening decision support capabilities based on electronic health records.

Trillium's board, guided by an innovative risk monitoring matrix (see Appendix A), increased its support of risk management and patient safety initiatives. Board members also established the Quality Monitoring Committee to oversee care quality. This committee identified and monitored indicators for clinical excellence, including hospital standardized mortality ratio (HSMR), the number of adverse events causing harm per 1,000 patient days and other targeted clinical benchmarks.

Criteria for prioritizing quality improvement initiatives shifted in phase two from a focus on improvements for high-volume, high-cost and high-risk patients in targeted areas to improved care across multiple health systems involved in episodes of care. This change was also intended to create a system perspective, shifting staff views of patients from one that identified them as patients of a local unit (e.g., emergency department patients) to one that identified them as "Trillium" patients from admission through discharge.

Five new areas of strategic priority were articulated in 2007 (Figure 1):

1. Create the Ideal Patient Experience (IPE)
2. Create a Healthy Workplace Experience
3. Focus on What Is "Ours to Do"
4. Drive Patient Access and Flow
5. Enable Holistic Health

These priorities were selected in order to advance the delivery of safe, evidence-based care; to establish Trillium as an "organization of choice" (see Figure 1) for staff and volunteers; and to align strategic priorities with Ontario's health system transformation agenda.

The development of structures and processes to support improvement work was accompanied by efforts to shape Trillium's organizational culture. Explicit messages from the CEO on topics such as innovation and leadership combined with capability-building opportunities aimed at creating "the Trillium way" and an optimistic "just do it" culture that embraced change. Staff members described this culture as an enabler of quality improvement and as a source of pride and identity. They expected to be innovators in Canada's healthcare system and to participate in transformative projects.

Staff members viewed the distributed leadership philosophy as having created the perception of a flattened organization. They felt the new philosophy allowed clinical staff to engage in improvement work and to build on long-standing team relationships with considerable success. Staff were encouraged to participate in these activities and the detailing of care processes, and identification of improvement opportunities were provided by the most knowledgeable team members, rather than only the most senior team member. This approach enriches discussion and improves each team's ability to identify changes most likely to result in further improvements at the front lines.

Figure 1. Trillium Health Centre strategy map

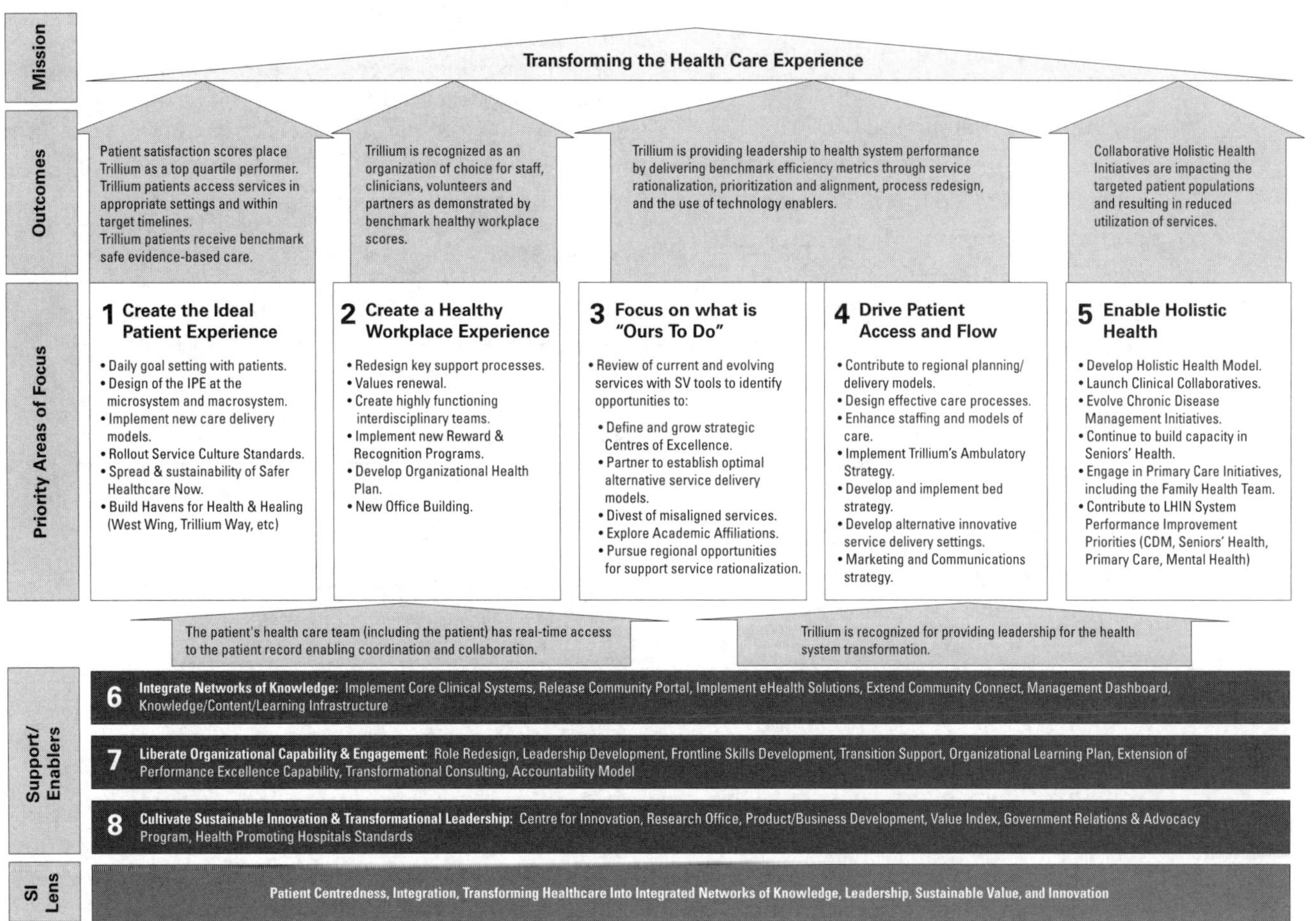

Source: Trillium Health Centre (2007d). Used by permission.

Leadership, strategy, staff capacity-building and organizational culture developed in phases one and two contributed to an environment that enabled Trillium to participate effectively in SHN! and to develop new improvement initiatives, such as the NNTF.

The Safer Healthcare Now! campaign

In 2003 Director of Medicine Patti Cochrane was introduced to the medical emergency teams (METs) concept at an Institute for Healthcare Improvement (IHI) conference. Cochrane brought the concept back to Trillium.

METs (also known as rapid response teams or critical care outreach teams) are interdisciplinary groups of intensive care staff that provide assistance to patients outside of intensive care units (ICUs). In early 2004 members of Trillium's medical surgical ICU (MSICU) attended an IHI Critical Care meeting, where they learned more about the role and organization of METs. Later that year Trillium joined the Canadian ICU Collaborative, which is an effort of ICU staff from across Canada focused on using quality improvement methods to implement evidence-based practices to improve care outcomes (Canadian ICU Collaborative 2007). Through participation in the ICU Collaborative, Trillium members learned the skills needed to implement an MET as well as the interventions required to reduce ventilator-associated pneumonia (VAP). Team leaders were named for both of these efforts and later for other initiatives launched as part of SHN! (see sidebar).

The Safer Healthcare Now! campaign (Safer Healthcare Now! 2007a)

The Safer Healthcare Now! (SHN!) campaign and its partner campaign in Quebec, Together, Let's Improve Healthcare Safety, is a pan-Canadian patient safety campaign. Modelled after the 2004 Institute for Healthcare Improvement (IHI) 100k Lives campaign, SHN! introduced six evidence-based interventions to reduce avoidable deaths in hospital during phase one of the campaign. These were: AMI – Improved Care for Acute Myocardial Infarction, CLI – Prevention of Central Line–Associated Bloodstream Infection, Medication Reconciliation, RRT – Rapid Response Teams, SSI – Prevention of Surgical Site Infection, and VAP – Prevention of Ventilator-Associated Pneumonia.

Six hundred teams from over 180 healthcare organizations are presently enrolled in SHN! Thirty teams from 15 healthcare organizations are presently enrolled in the Quebec campaign.

Trillium Health Centre participated in all six bundles offered in phase one of the campaign.

Early phase one campaign results, presented in Montreal in March 2007, demonstrate improved quality of care and patient outcomes. Phase two of the campaign was launched in Spring 2008.

METs require high levels of team communication and coordination. The organization of registered respiratory therapists (RTs)[1] at Trillium enabled the development of an MET. RTs were already being used at Trillium as the first staff responding to calls when patients outside of MSICU showed symptoms of cardiovascular deterioration. The introduction of an MET team, comprised of nurses and RTs, built on established team relationships and patterns of communication.

[1] RT will be used when referring to a registered respiratory therapist to avoid confusion with rapid response team.

Trillium's experience with quality improvement and patient safety initiatives also helped the MSICU staff in their work on SHN! interventions. Membership in the ICU Collaborative, availability of order sets applicable to the VAP bundle, continuity of team leaders for METs and central line–associated primary bloodstream infection (CLI) teams as well as positive relationships between RTs and floor nurses formed a ready foundation when the SHN! campaign was introduced to the MSICU in May 2005.

Unlike many other organizations that enrolled in SHN!, Trillium developed a project management structure and implementation plan for its SHN! efforts (Trillium Health Centre 2005a). Following project management principles, a project profile was completed that identified critical project elements (see Table 2), including project rationale and scope, objectives and outcome measures, critical success factors, cost/benefit analysis, staging and spread of bundles and communication plans. Trillium's project management structure requires significant resource allocation. Senior management approved the funds required for the campaign's process interventions (see Appendix C). This decision was shaped by the view that Trillium needed to provide the safest care possible if it were truly to transform patients' healthcare experience.

The project support provided to Trillium teams involved in SHN! was an important contributor to their success. Chief Nurse Executive Pam Pogue remarked that, in her view, releasing staff to do improvement work, rather than expecting that it be added to regular responsibilities, has been the single most important success factor in Trillium's quality improvement efforts. The project management framework, which requires identifying the staff and time commitments needed to implement each initiative, provided this structure for the SHN! campaign. In August 2005 an SHN! project board was established to coordinate the campaign, guide team leads, provide decision support and support resourcing requirements. This board, along with physician champions and leadership support, provided stewardship throughout the campaign's first 18 months.

Three SHN! initiatives were introduced into the MSICU in 2005–2006:

- Reduction of CLIs
- Reduction of VAP
- MET

As discussed earlier, MSICU staff members' participation in the ICU Collaborative provided them with eight months of experience prior to the implementation of an MET and the VAP bundle.

The CLI team, led by Tina Leon-Garcia, was launched in February 2006. Its goal was to reduce CLI in MSICU by 50% by December 2006. A two-stage pilot was planned that involved implementing two groups of evidence-based practices recommended for reducing infections: The insertion bundle and the maintenance bundle (see Table 3).

Table 2. Excerpt from Safer Healthcare Now! project profile

<table>
<tr><th colspan="2">Pilot Objectives and Expected Outcomes</th></tr>
<tr><td colspan="2">1. Medical Emergency Team (MET): To decrease the number of cardiac arrests by 60% in the medical health system by the end of a 6-month trial (November 30, 2005)

Outcome Measures:
• Number of cardiac arrests
• Number of patients who died from cardiac arrests
• Hospital mortality
• Number of ICU bed-days occupied by survivors of cardiac arrest
• Number of hospital bed-days occupied by survivors of cardiac arrest
• MET utilization
• Codes per 1,000 discharges
• Codes outside the ICU</td></tr>
<tr><th colspan="2">Critical Success Factors</th></tr>
<tr><td colspan="2">• Project lead required to manage overall SHN! implementation, including provision of regular progress reports to internal stakeholders (e.g., Medical Advisory Committee)
• Initiative leads required seconded time to successfully implement the six bundles over the 18-month campaign
• Health records analyst support required for data collection
• Decision support required to support data collection and analysis
• PE support required to mentor in rapid cycle improvement methodology
• Infection prevention and control participation required
• Project management consultation required</td></tr>
<tr><th colspan="2">Scope of Pilot</th></tr>
<tr><td>In Scope – MET</td><td>Outside Scope – MET</td></tr>
<tr><td>• Pilot in Medicine until November 2005
• November 2005: Stage participation of next pilot health system(s) until December 2006</td><td>• Organization-wide implementation</td></tr>
</table>

Source: Trillium Health Centre (2005a). Used by permission.

The CLI team faced several challenges, including how to collect the measures requested by the SHN! campaign. Information required to calculate the rate of CLI per 1,000 catheter days was not readily available and involved manual chart audits of all MSICU patients with positive blood cultures. Moreover, the total number of catheter days was required to calculate the first measure, and these data were also not routinely collected at Trillium. Several trials were undertaken in order to establish an efficient collection process. These included paper-based manual counts completed each shift by the MSICU charge nurse and data capture by health records coders. In the end, partnership with THINK's IT consultants provided a better solution, and MSICU staff can now enter real-time CLI day counts into a database.

Table 3. Safer Healthcare Now! (SHN!) central line–associated primary bloodstream infection (CLI) bundle components

CLI Insertion Bundle Components	CLI Maintenance Bundle Components
• Hand hygiene • Maximal barrier precautions • Full-body drape for patient • Cap, mask, gloves and gown for physician • 2% chlorhexidine skin antisepsis • Optimal catheter site selection	• Daily review of line necessity, with prompt removal of unnecessary lines • Dedicated lumen for total parenteral nutrition • Ascetic access to lumens • Check entry site for signs of infection with every change of dressing
CLI Measures	
• CLI/1,000 catheter days • Compliance with the insertion bundle • Compliance with the maintenance bundle	

Source: Safer Healthcare Now! (2007b). Used by permission.

The development of standardized order sets by Intensivist Dr. Chris O'Connor facilitated implementation of the VAP bundle. By 2007 over 275 order sets had been developed to improve quality of care. Of those developed, the oral care routine and deep venous thrombosis prophylaxis order sets were implemented as part of the VAP bundle (see Table 4). Access to these order sets, and team familiarity with VAP through membership in the ICU Collaborative, created a ready environment for implementation of the bundle. At inception, the VAP team, led by Rosanne Leddy, sought a 50% reduction in the rate of MSICU-acquired VAP.

Table 4. Safer Healthcare Now! (SHN!) ventilator-associated pneumonia (VAP) bundle components

Components of the VAP Bundle
1. Elevation of the head of bed to between 30 degrees and 45 degrees 2. Daily sedation vacation, and an assessment of readiness to extubate by performing a spontaneous breathing trial (SBT) 3. Use of oral versus nasal tubes for access to the trachea or stomach 4. Use of evacuation (EVAC) tubes for the drainage of subglottic secretions Additional components of care: 1. Oral care routines 2. Deep venous thrombosis prophylaxis

Source: Safer Healthcare Now! (2007c). Used by permission.

Multiple improvement cycles were required to implement several other aspects of the VAP bundle. Variation in the identification of patients with VAP led to greater standardization and use of RTs in identifying patients with VAP in MSICU. RTs also assumed accountability for monitoring head of bed (HOB) elevation, a procedure that previously had low compliance. Random HOB audits and electronic reminders were trialed in 2005, but proved ineffective. After conducting several small change tests, RTs identified two successful strategies: posting signage at the heads of beds and educating families at the bedside. These improvements led to HOB compliance of between 95% and 100% for 18 months. As a result of these and other changes, the VAP rate in MSICU fell 74%, from 20.71/1,000 ventilator days to 5.43/1,000 ventilator days between January and November 2006, thereby exceeding the project's initial goals.

Because the team functioned outside of MSICU 24/7, the MET pilot differed from the CLI and VAP pilots in both scope and visibility. Staffed by critical care nurses and RTs, and supported by intensive care physicians, the MET brought critical care support to patient bedsides throughout the hospital. One challenge team members faced was the historically strained relations between floor and ICU nurses and the perception of some ICU nurses that floor nurses' critical care assessment skills were deficient. To overcome this barrier, a hospital-wide campaign, led by the MET leader Michael Cass, was carried out prior to launch to educate staff on the role of the MET and to foster collaboration. In addition, critical care staff members selected for the MET were chosen for their soft skills: communication, mentorship and team-building abilities. Team practices reinforced these skills and the MET provided prompt feedback on individual patient outcomes to staff members on the pilot unit. Within nine months of launch, the volume of medical health system patients diagnosed with cardiac/respiratory arrest decreased 55%, the ICU readmission rate for this patient group decreased 14% and MSICU mortality fell 28% (Cass 2003). Table 5 presents the results after 22 months of operation on medicine, surgery and neuromusculoskeletal (Neuro/MSK) services.

The data presented in Table 5 were extracted from the discharge abstract database as a proxy outcome measure for the MET. Deceased patients may or may not have been seen by the MET prior to death, and cause of death may or may not have been cardiac/respiratory arrest.

Early success, measured by a reduction in cardiac/respiratory arrests and downward trending in unit-level mortality data, facilitated the spread of the MET throughout the hospital. Subsequently, the MET began to receive requests to provide support for many aspects of nursing practice beyond its initial scope, including calls to assist with dispensing medication and dealing with challenging family situations. These issues led to new workshops developed by clinical nursing educators.

Several other quality improvements emerged in the MET pilot. Among them, medical directives were developed to enable MET nurses to order lab work, chest X-rays and electrocardiograms. Other directives allowed nurses and RTs to order blood gases before contacting the most responsible physician (MRP). Together, these directives created significant team efficiencies. Weekly patient safety rounds were also established in MSICU to disseminate lessons learned from actual cases and to solicit ideas for improvement. Finally, monthly patient safety rounds were provided organization-wide to generate interest across multiple health systems.

Table 5. Cardiac/respiratory arrests and deaths increase/decrease since medical emergency teams (METs) started

	Cardiac/Respiratory Arrest ↑ or ↓ : MET Start Date until September 2007		Cardiac/Respiratory Arrests and Hospital Disposition Died ↑ or ↓ : MET Start Date until September 2007		
Unit	**#**	**% Change**	**Unit**	**#**	**% Change**
Medicine (Data: June 2005–September 2007)	-57	-34%	Medicine (Data: June 2005–September 2007)	-51	-34%
Surgery (Data: April 2006–September 2007)	-5	-45%	Surgery (Data: April 2006–September 2007)	-1	-14%
Neuro/MSK (Data: August 2006–September 2007)	-6	-75%	Neuro/MSK (Data: August 2006–September 2007)	-1	-14%
Total	-68	-36%	Total	-53	-33%

Source: Cass (2007). Used by permission.

The Non-Nursing Task Force (NNTF) quality improvement journey

In addition to the SHN! initiatives at Trillium, there are a number of other projects that have generated important improvements. The NNTF is one such example.

Frustration expressed by nurses in a hospital forum and survey results on the involvement of nurses in tasks that took them away from bedside care led to the creation of the Non-Nursing Task Force in 2005. Data from a survey administered to 133 medical/surgical nurses revealed the five most frequently completed non-nursing tasks:

- Searching for equipment or wheelchairs
- Searching for missing medications

- Searching for supplies
- Preparing patients for transport
- Performing housekeeping activities

These tasks occurred on all shifts (although more frequently at night) and required each nurse to spend, on average, 24 minutes looking for linen and 44 minutes performing housekeeping duties on each shift. Completing these tasks reduced nurses' time available to complete bedside care, delayed the admission of new patients to the units and decreased nurses' job satisfaction. Moreover, these findings did not align with the vision of future nursing practice espoused by senior nursing leadership or with Trillium's strategic goal of providing an "ideal patient experience." Interruptions in nursing care were also thought to increase the likelihood of error (Chisholm et al. 2000), which introduced a patient safety component to the project.

The NNTF was co-led by a front-line nurse, Karen Kallie, and a porter, Lakis Faragitakis. A steering committee guided the planning and delivery of NNTF work. The NNTF's aims were to improve patient care by designing a service model that would enable nurses to work within their optimal scope of practice and enlarge the support staffs' contributions to patient care. Internal and external environmental scans were completed to inform small- and large-scale tests of the changes required to redesign the service model. Performance metrics – including patient satisfaction, nursing satisfaction and unit cleanliness – were compared pre- and post-pilot to determine whether changes to the service model resulted in improvement.

Once the pilot was operational, the NNTF worked diligently to develop baseline process maps to describe in-patient admissions, missing medications, dinner tray delivery, night cupboard stocking, portering/paging and portering for diagnostic imaging processes. A number of improvement ideas were developed based on this analysis. Those that were achievable within existing budgets were tested and, if proven successful, were implemented. For example, volunteer service teams assumed accountability for several non-nursing tasks, such as greeting and directing family members on units and distributing water to patients. These teams were assigned to dedicated units on an ongoing basis, rather than receiving daily assignments throughout the hospital. Pharmacy services installed a uniform bin system on all in-patient units to expedite medication drop-off and pick-up, thereby reducing the frequency of missed medications.

Other changes included redistributing the work done by nursing, portering and environmental/hospitality associates. The availability of environmental/hospitality associates was matched to service demand at peak in-patient unit admission times (see Appendix D). The new service model that emerged required environmental associates to clean all non-patient areas. It also required hospitality associates to help nurses transfer patients to stretchers and to clean patients' rooms. Evaluation of the new model suggested it resulted in less time spent by nurses on non-nursing tasks (see Table 6) and cleaner patient units (see Table 7).

Table 6. Non-Nursing Task Force (NNTF) pilot results

Description of non-nursing task (NNT)	Pilot Medical Surgical Units: Mean Number of NNTs Completed by Nurses/Shift n=56 Nurse Respondents	Comparison Medical Surgical Units: Mean Number of NNTs Completed by Nurses/Shift n=15 Nurse Respondents	% Difference in Mean Number of NNTs Completed by Nurses/Shift
Performing housekeeping	7	9	23%
Searching for equipment and wheelchairs	8	13	39%
Searching for missing medications	3	4	25%
Meal tray set-up	3	5	40%

Source: Trillium Health Centre (2007e) and NNTF co-team lead. Used by permission.

Table 7. Non-Nursing Task Force (NNTF) pilot CareSmart continuous quality improvement (CQI) patient survey results

Name of Pilot Unit	Pre-pilot CQI Score (Unit Cleanliness)	Post-pilot CQI Score (Unit Cleanliness)	% Improvement (Unit Cleanliness)
2B Neurosurgery	77%	94%	17%
2B Surgery	80%	90%	10%
4D Medicine	74%	92%	18%
4B Medicine	79%	92%	13%

Source: Trillium Health Centre (2007e). Used by permission.

Benefits to patient safety were not directly measured during the pilot; however, nurses reported that they perceived the new service model resulted in enhanced point-of-care safety.

The NNTF pilot's positive results led to the spread of the new service model to other units across the hospital and to additional quality improvement initiatives. One project focused on missing medications, a critical source of frustration identified by nursing staff on in-patient units. Results of the Trillium survey indicated that searching for missing medications consumed 24 minutes of each nurse's shift and contributed negatively to nurse–patient and nurse–pharmacist relationships. An improvement team with membership from nursing, pharmacy, medicine, portering and hospital administration, and guided by 3M Canada consultants, used Failure Mode and Effects Analysis (FMEA) and Six Sigma methodology to analyze and improve the processes required to communicate with and dispense and deliver medication to in-patient units (Mills 2007; Trillium Health Centre 2007e). Among the process changes made to reduce missing medications were the following:

- Improving the timeliness of the pharmacy's receipt of physicians' orders
- Adjusting the medication cart exchange time to coincide with the largest order entry time
- Modifying the morning dosing time from 9:00 am to 10:00 am in order to provide additional time for the pharmacy to process medications

Collectively, these process improvements decreased the mean number of missing medication from 1,231 per week (June 2005) to 370 per week (November 2007). This change represents a 70% decrease from the peak and a 32% reduction from the rate observed in November 2006. These improvements reduced the length of time nurses spend searching for missing medication by 50% per shift and, reportedly, improved team dynamics.

In an effort to measure the outcome of this type of work at a system level, senior leadership developed a new indicator: "capacity liberated for staff and physicians." This indicator measures the percentage of full-time equivalent positions created annually through waste reduction and process improvements.

New leadership: New phase of improvement

Ken White stepped down as CEO of Trillium Health Centre in early 2007 and Janet M. Davidson began her tenure as president and CEO of Trillium in March 2007. Coupled with continued financial pressures on hospital budgets in Ontario, this leadership transition led to changes in Trillium's corporate strategy. One key change was the disbanding of the PE portfolio and the redistribution of its quality improvement functions to the patient services and quality portfolio, and to the chief financial officer's portfolio. A new portfolio, Strategic Planning and Business Transformation, was created and additional accountability mechanisms were introduced to promote effective resource management. Senior leadership also committed resources to project management consultation and the use of Lean improvement methodology.

The board's Quality Monitoring Committee has also evolved under Trillium's new leadership. A quality reporting framework was developed in 2007 (see Appendix E) that organizes key quality indicators (and performance targets, where applicable) around six quality dimensions:

- Patient centred
- Accessible
- Safe/effective
- Appropriately resourced
- Integrated
- Efficient

A new quarterly report was created for the Quality Monitoring Committee that draws in mandatory indicators from various sources (e.g., SHN!, Canadian Council on Health Services Accreditation). In addition, the vice-presidents of patient care and medicine have been nominated to support the committee by providing clear communication links between the committee and Trillium's senior team.

The growing regional focus on service delivery in Ontario has increased the pressure on Trillium to collaborate with many agencies. As a regional cardiac care centre, for example, Trillium serves patients from across the region and the province, and depends on the smooth operation of the larger system to provide quality care to these patients. System issues, such as the availability of emergency transport and variations in standards of care from facility to facility, can affect patient outcomes. Trillium is participating on a regional cardiovascular steering committee with other hospital representatives, paramedics, primary care representatives, the Ontario Ministry of Health and Long-Term Care and community care access centres to address system-wide issues.

Summary

Four key factors have contributed to the success of quality improvement efforts at Trillium:

- Leadership
- Strategy
- Staff development
- Culture

Leadership has provided clear, consistent messaging in areas of strategic priority. Notably, this has included commitment to the provision of safe, evidence-based care and the creation of the ideal patient experience. This strategy has supported structures, such as the PE portfolio, and processes, such as the routine use of the project management model to guide cycles of improvement work.

The timing of investments has also contributed to Trillium's success. In phase one, the CEO introduced an innovative system-wide framework of distributed leadership to engage staff at all levels of the organization. Staff development focused on leadership, quality improvement and project management skills capable of moving the Trillium strategy forward. The evolution of unit-level improvement work to system-level efforts such as the MET and NNTF has benefited from both the new support structures and staff members' skills. Collectively, these investments have shaped an organizational culture now known as "the Trillium way."

With growing experience, the application of improvement methods has spread from the patient care portfolio to the business and financial portfolios. Leadership support for the Quality Monitoring Committee and a framework to monitor key quality indicators provides a strategic perspective on quality performance. The PE portfolio has been redistributed on the premise that this structural change will "embed" quality improvement expertise across the organization.

Trillium's continuing success rests on its ability to address several challenges. These include the need to continue developing staff members' leadership and improvement skills in order to sustain investments in improving care, despite financial pressures; to fully realize IT efforts; and to ensure that emerging regional service delivery and governance arrangements support local initiatives as well as system improvements.

Emerging shortages in nursing, medicine and other health human resources make secondment of front-line staff to improvement roles difficult. For nearly a decade, Trillium has selected and trained front-line clinical staff for improvement projects as a means of building skills and improving care. The NNTF, for example, was co-led by a front-line nurse and a porter. Health human resource shortages may limit Trillium's future ability to second staff members, to backfill resulting vacancies and to redesign clinical positions for staff returning from secondment terms to facilitate their ongoing participation in improvement work.

The sustainability of improvement work presents a second challenge. While Trillium's "just do it" culture has stimulated much activity, it often results in staff participating in many concurrent improvement activities. The sheer volume of these competing priorities may limit the sustainability of individual projects. This challenge emphasizes the continuing need to prioritize project commitments systematically, to divest those projects that produce marginal outcomes and to complete priority projects before engaging in new ones.

The IT infrastructure available to support Trillium's improvement work presents a third challenge. One objective of the THINK project is to create a standardized platform for clinical and administrative data collection; however, this goal has not yet been realized. In the interim, a gap exists between desired and actual IT functionality, requiring some manual data collection. The capability to produce the routinely collected data SHN! teams and other projects require is still not available, a lack that further adds to the burden of data collection and analysis.

A fourth challenge arises from the immediate fiscal pressures experienced by all Ontario hospitals and reliance on a funding model for long-term, large-scale improvement projects. Buoyed by an emerging improvement culture, the immediate challenge for Trillium leadership is to support continued investments in improvement capability while responding to fiscal pressures. Members of the Strategic Planning and Business Transformation portfolio will face tough decisions on these issues. SHN! was funded from fiscal year 2005–2006 to fiscal year 2006–2007 by using "project dollars" from outside of health system budgets. Project dollars are available on a time-limited basis; ultimately, improvement projects' operating costs become the responsibility of their respective health system(s). The impact of this funding model on the sustainability of initiatives such as SHN! is unknown.

Finally, Trillium's position as a high-performing organization within an evolving regional care delivery system has created challenges. Discrepancies between organization-level and regional capabilities have constrained the organization's ability to deliver consistent high-quality patient care in the past. New structures such as Local Health Integration Networks amplify Trillium's need to provide regional leadership for health service transformation.

References

Canadian ICU Collaborative. 2007. *What Is a Collaborative?* Retrieved November 4, 2007. <http://www.improvementassociates.com.ns74.alentus.com/dnn/CanadianICUCollaborative/tabid/190/Default.aspx>

Cass, M. 2003. *Trillium Medical Emergency Team.* PowerPoint presentation. Unpublished.

Cass, M. 2007. *Trillium's Medical Emergency Team.* PowerPoint presentation. Unpublished.

Chisholm, C., E. Collison, D. Nelson and W. Cordell. 2000. "Emergency Department Workplace Interruptions: Are Emergency Physicians Interrupt-Driven and Multitasking?" *Academic Emergency Medicine* 7(11): 1239–1243.

Leddy, R. 2007. *Ventilator Associated Pneumonia: Our Journey and Preliminary Results.* PowerPoint presentation. Unpublished.

Mills, A. 2007. *"It Just Isn't Here!": Using a Six Sigma Approach to Reduce Missing Medications.* PowerPoint presentation. Unpublished.

Safer Healthcare Now! 2007a. *The Six Interventions.* Retrieved May 21, 2007. <http://www.saferhealthcarenow.ca/Default.aspx?folderId=82>

Safer Healthcare Now! 2007b. *Safer Healthcare Now! Getting Started Kit: Prevent Central Line Infections How-To Guide.* Retrieved May 21, 2007. <http://www.saferhealthcarenow.ca/Default.aspx?folderId=82&contentId=184>

Safer Healthcare Now! 2007c. *Safer Healthcare Now! Getting Started Kit: Prevention of Ventilator-Associated Pneumonia in Adults How-To Guide.* Retrieved May 21, 2007. <http://www.saferhealthcarenow.ca/Default.aspx?folderId=82&contentId=180>

Trillium Health Centre. 2005a. *Safer Healthcare Now! Project Profile.* Mississauga, ON: Author. Unpublished internal document.

Trillium Health Centre. 2005b. *Safer Healthcare Now! Project Budget Final.* Mississauga, ON: Author. Unpublished internal document.

Trillium Health Centre 2005c. *Baseline Number of Hospitality Associates Available/Hour and Number of Patient Transfers/Hour.* Mississauga, ON: Author. Unpublished internal document.

Trillium Health Centre. 2007a. *About Us: The Trillium Way.* Mississauga, ON: Author. Retrieved May 14, 2007. <http://www.trilliumhealthcentre.org/about/theTrilliumWay.html>

Trillium Health Centre. 2007b. *Enterprise Risk Management Risk Monitoring Report.* Mississauga, ON: Author. Unpublished internal document.

Trillium Health Centre. 2007c. *THC Foundations of Leadership Course.* Mississauga, ON: Author. Retrieved May 14, 2007. <Trillium Health Centre Intranet>

Trillium Health Centre. 2007d. *2007-2009 Strategy Map.* Mississauga, ON: Author. Unpublished internal document.

Trillium Health Centre. 2007e. *Trillium Health Centre 3M Health Care/Canadian College of Health Service Executives Health Care Quality Team Award Submission.* Mississauga, ON: Author. Unpublished internal document.

Trillium Health Centre. 2007f. *Trillium Corporate Key Quality Indicator Report.* Mississauga, ON: Author. Unpublished internal document.

White, K. 2007. *Turning Trillium Inside Out: A Leaders Perspective.* PowerPoint presentation. Unpublished.

Yerema, R. 2004. *Canada's Top 100 Employers.* Toronto: Mediacorp Canada Inc.

Appendix A. Sample enterprise risk-management, risk-monitoring matrix

Sample Outcome Dimension	Risk Identification	Definitions	Measurement	Monitored by	Status 2006	Status 2007	Action Plan
Clinical Excellence	Confidentiality	Maintaining the security and integrity of Trillium information and operations	Number of incidents regarding breaches of confidentiality or improper release of Trillium information	Director, Health Records	G	G	
	Consents (equipment, treatment, privacy)	Informed consents obtained by the correct person at the correct time	Ratio of claims involving consent incidents	Medical Advisory Committee legal services privacy officer	Y	G	
	Infection prevention and control	Issues related to the identification, prevention and management of hospital and community-acquired infections	TB: number of patients C. DIF: Nosocomial/1,000 admissions BACTEREMIAS: Nosocomial/1,000 admissions BACTEREMIAS: Primary/1,000 admissions MRSA: Number of new MRSA patients (POA)	Infection Prevention and Control Committee	Not included	Y	

Definitions of risk:

G(reen)	Risk management plan is in place. Risks have been identified and mitigation strategies have been put in place.
Y(ellow)	Risks or mitigation strategies have not been fully developed.
R(ed)	Risks may not have been fully identified. Mitigation strategies are not fully in place.

Source: Trillium Health Centre (2007b). Used by permission.

Appendix B. Foundations of Leadership course

Foundations of Leadership – Cohort #7: April 25–May 30, 2007

Who Should Attend: All Formal, Informal and Emergent Leaders

Prerequisites: General Orientation; PACE Recommended

Duration: Six half-day modules plus team-based project work

The Approach: The modules include:

Understanding the Context
To be effective, leaders must understand the "DNA" of Trillium and our future plans, and see them in the context of a changing world.

Developing Authentic Self-Awareness
Develop an understanding of the true nature of who you are and what you bring to the role of leadership.

Mastering Change
Learn to use transformational change as a catalyst for enhanced performance and how to work with change resisters and those who feel like the victims of change.

Becoming Other-Centred
Learn to engage others and to create support for strategies and solutions with such skills as other-centred communication and listening.

Influencing Others
Learn to guide problem-solving when working with individuals or teams by clearly identifying root causes, finding creative solutions and developing a commitment to move forward.

Organizations as Systems
Participants will begin to make sense of the constant ebb and flow of change and explore how they can apply new learning about complex, adaptive systems to their work.

Special Considerations: Each participant is expected to identify a learning partner who will meet with his/her each week to help them understand and apply their learning.

Source: Trillium Health Centre 2007c

Appendix C. Trillium Health Centre's Safer Healthcare Now! project budget

Description	2005–2006 Projected Costs ($)	2006–2007 Projected Costs ($)	2005–2006 Incremental Costs ($)	2006–2007 Incremental Costs ($)
Phase one program development (e.g., backfill project lead, staff training, administrative support)	54,987	40,927	36,847	47,216
Annual program-specific costs (e.g., total annual costs for six bundles)	161,361	175,756	-	-
One-time costs	82,183	75,372	-	-
Ongoing operating costs	79,179	100,385	-	-

Source: Trillium Health Centre (2005b). Used by permission.

Appendix D. Baseline number of hospitality associates available/hour and number of patient transfers/hour

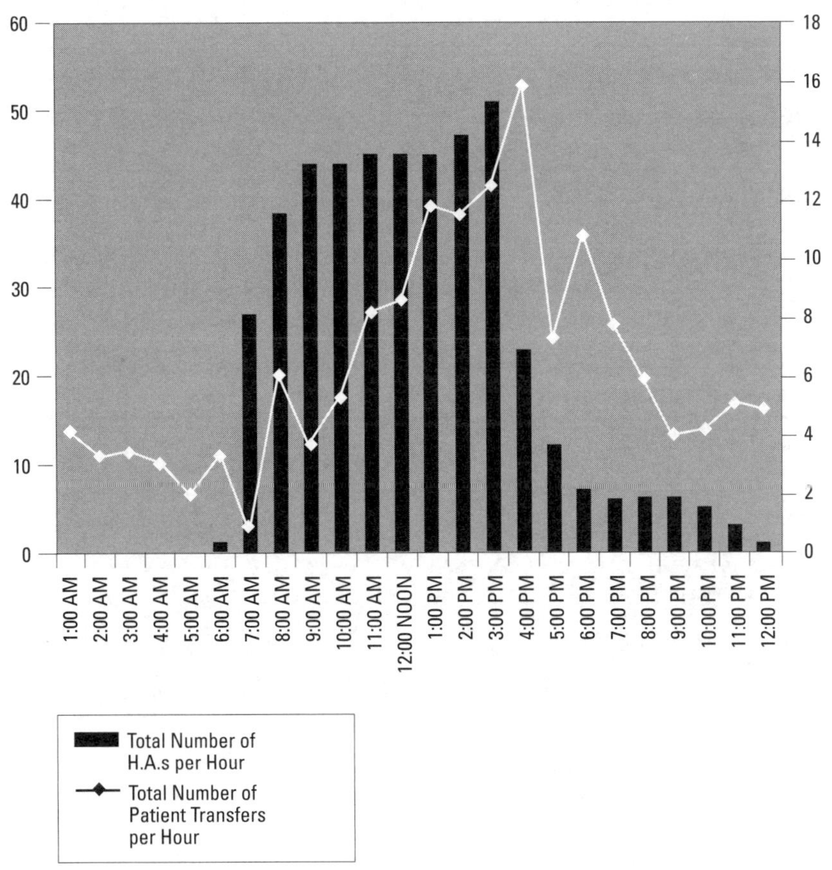

Source: Trillium Health Centre (2005c). Used by permission.

Appendix E. Excerpt from the 2007–2008 *Trillium Corporate Key Quality Indicator Report*

Dimension	Indicator	2005–2006	Target	Previous Year 2006–2007	Q1	Q2	Q3	Q4
Safe/Effective								
	HSMR							
	Actual number of deaths							
	Unplanned rate of readmissions within 7 days of discharge							
	Unplanned returns to OR (cases)							
	Number of high-risk incidents							
	Number of high-risk incidents leading to death							
	Number of medical/legal claims (quarterly)							
	Infection rates							
	Rate of nosocomial MRSA/1,000 admissions							
	Rate of nosocomial C. diff/1,000 admissions							
	Central line infection/1,000 line days							
	Surgical site infections							
	Ventilator-associated pneumonia							
	Rate of patient falls/1,000 patient days							
	Reported medication incidents/1,000 patient days							
	Safer Healthcare Now!							
	% of admitted patients receiving med reconciliation							
	% of AMI patients who received all six appropriate AMI evidence-based elements							
	Medical emergency team: reduction of respiratory/cardiac arrests							

Source: Trillium Health Centre (2007f). Used by permission.

Afterword

Reading these stories about high-performing health systems should make Canadians uncomfortable. From a small county in Sweden to a large, Canadian-style dispersed system in the United States; from a focus on primary healthcare to the pursuit of excellence in acute care; from implementing tools and techniques to the development of system-wide cultures – these narratives describe achievements to which Canada aspires but rarely achieves.

Our inability to make things right despite huge investments in healthcare is no longer a private failure. Chris Ham from the University of Birmingham, an astute international healthcare system observer, tells a revealing story. As the architects of the UK's National Health System (NHS) transformation charted their course at the beginning of this century, they looked, Ham recounts, elsewhere for inspiration and cautionary tales. The worst possible outcome, they concluded, would be to increase spending from 6% to 10% of GDP and end up looking like Canada. By this they meant it would be a travesty to spend so much and achieve so little.

Damn them for their prescience. In 1997 total Canadian healthcare spending was $79 billion. Ten years later the tab had reached $160 billion. Yet that decade of spending increases far above the rate of inflation did not fundamentally improve performance. In addition, public confidence has not been fully restored, and international rankings on measures such as public satisfaction and value for money, however controversial, do not flatter Canada. We support dozens of demonstration projects but rarely generalize proven success. We learn a lot *about* others' successes – everyone seems to know about the prerequisites for high performance and regiments of Canadian front-line workers, managers, board members and government officials have visited the UK, Intermountain Healthcare, Virginia Mason and their cousins. They all sing lustily from the Institute for Healthcare Improvement (IHI) hymnal. Whether we learn from them is another matter.

Why this apparent contradiction: on the one hand we are willing and able to learn, seem to want to change, sign up in droves to improve safety, succeed on a small scale, but on the other, we can't seem to close the deal system-wide? As careful comparative health systems analysts remind us, context is everything. What works in Sweden might not work here. So what is it about our context that holds us back? Are we in the end a learning-disabled nation, frozen by tradition, paralyzed by the power of vested interests, as complacent as Canadian hockey prior to the wake-up call of the 1972 summit series with the Soviets?

Peculiarly Canadian challenges

Our expensive mediocrity is not entirely an accident. Canada faces challenges that are less daunting elsewhere. They are not insurmountable, but we ignore them at our peril. Among the most prominent:

Mon pays, ce n'est pas un pays …

Yes, the state of federalism holds us back. It is no secret that federal–provincial relations are at a low ebb. Canadians reliably support the involvement of both levels of government in policy-making and direction, yet their governments do not share this view. Ottawa's role is to be a cash cow (see the accords of 2000, 2003 and 2004). With a guarantee of billions of new dollars coming down the pipeline for years to come, the predictable result is increased expectations for higher pay and plans to add capacity. The unintended (but inevitable) consequence is that our new money mainly buys the status quo while other countries' buys change. (We should have gone to the UK for counselling.)

Clinical autonomy rules

It is quite possible that clinical autonomy is more firmly entrenched in Canada than anywhere else. We know about and accept huge variations in practice with equanimity. Most physicians feel little attachment to health regions or larger systems, and medicine remains primarily a cottage industry. Autonomous judgment is a hallmark of professionalism and, properly applied, it is a fundamental building block of excellence. But autonomy without accountability is a recipe for huge variations in practice and an invitation to plunder public resources. It also makes managing wait times and achieving real equity of access extraordinarily difficult.

Perverse incentives breed cynicism

Everyone familiar with Canadian healthcare knows the following:

- It is more lucrative to practise bad medicine than good medicine, particularly in family practice. See 80 basically healthy patients a day for five minutes and you'll prosper. See 20 complex frail elderly patients and apply all of your learning and wisdom and you'll make a modest income at best. Medical associations by and large determine which specialities will make how much money and which practice patterns will be most lucrative – yet another example of a healthcare system designed to get the results we observe. Governments need to find ways to eliminate these perverse incentives.
- Governments send mixed signals about whether they wish to fund volumes or excellence and prudent use of resources. Their rhetoric supports needing and using less healthcare, but their behaviour rewards volumes. It is hard to take seriously their population health and prevention messages when they hold the system accountable for activity but not outcomes. Governments must commit to a population- and needs-based approach, and find ways to reward ingenuity that improves access and quality with less volume.
- Many professionals are woefully underused. Nurse practitioners are probably the best-studied occupational group in human history. Three dozen randomized controlled trials have confirmed that they can deliver a wide swath of effective primary care services. Lured by every imaginable form of incentive, family doctors still largely will not go to or stay in rural and remote Canada. Yet the juxtaposition of these two firmly established realities has not led to the obvious transformation. The guilds are powerful and it is instructive to observe how medicine has managed to change the focus to physicians' assistants (i.e., a hierarchical, doctor-controlled approach) from an expanded nurse practitioner model (i.e., collaborative and egalitarian approach). All health human resources stakeholders need to rethink the whole approach to education, credentialing and the division of labour.

Success notwithstanding

The barriers to improvement are real, but there are solutions – even in Canada. Most do not require wholesale rebuilding. They often rest merely on the removal of a few important barriers to improvement and on policies that encourage the behaviours to which we aspire.

Beyond pretend-management

Eight provinces have health regions, and Ontario has Local Health Integration Networks (LHINs). In theory, these structures have been established to decentralize authority, encourage experimentation and innovation, and set creativity free. Yet health ministries cannot resist looking over (even sitting on) the shoulders of health regions and LHINs, wading into mini-crises and generally letting the public know that they, and not the local authorities, are in charge when the going gets tough (and even when it doesn't). If ministries were brilliant micro-managers, with policies and incentives aligned, one might forgive them for their meddlesome and demoralizing hubris. Moreover, there is a lot of pretend-governance and pseudo-management. Costs are still heavily driven by independent and largely autonomous physician contractors. There is sufficient confusion about who really makes decisions to allow clever players several options for getting what they want. These are the elephants in the room, leaving scant room to pursue a truly needs-based, efficient and effective public interest mandate. The solution is to let organizations manage within sensible accountability frameworks and expand the concept of management into the domain in which it is needed most: clinical service.

Embrace the information revolution

When it comes to comprehensive, real-time health information, Canada exhibits all of the characteristics of a country that doesn't want to know and doesn't want to tell. Those responsible for the health information and information technology (IT) agenda have said over and over that it may take 10 times as much money as we have thus far been prepared to invest to produce real-time performance information accessible to providers, the public, managers and policy-makers. Every high-performing health system story has electronic, standardized, widely used information at its centre. The next frontier is the office-based electronic medical record, which has to be standardized, interoperable, linkable and useful at multiple levels. Otherwise, we will end up with less analytical power than we had a decade ago.

Learn from the best – including ourselves

The key object lessons from the inspiring stories in this collection of case studies are:

1. Policy and leadership matter. Success cannot be optional. Accountability must be clear. Performance improvement is a serious business that requires steely commitment and a refusal to tolerate persistent failure.
2. Policy without tools is ineffective; tools without policy are highly limited.
3. It may take a village but it doesn't have to take a generation. Transformation is never complete, and in some areas progress can take a long time. But some transformations have been rapid – notably, at Veterans Affairs (VA) and in some aspects of the UK's healthcare system. Always aim for fast, even if sometimes slow is all you can get.

4. Integrating key providers fully into the system and engaging them in goal-setting and performance improvement are essential to success. Fostering a culture of cooperation and participation requires a dedicated strategy, resources and policy framework. In Canada, there are several competing cultures at play: hierarchical vs. egalitarian; primary care focused vs. intensive specialized care; a population focus vs. a patient focus. Creating a unified approach to system improvement will not come about by osmosis. Great organizations invest a lot in building common cultures; healthcare must as well.
5. Let people experiment, fail, regroup and improve. Let them organize their own work. Once they have embraced the culture of performance, the need to instruct, cajole, persuade and intervene vanishes.
6. Be wary of narrow targets and paying for isolated successes. Incentives are important, but they must be carefully calibrated, and there is always the risk of unintended consequences. Healthcare is a public service with powerful ethical underpinnings. The greatest international successes seem to have abandoned flirtation with market concepts and pseudo-competition; instead, they have focused on cultural change supported by tools, relationships and a powerful sense of common purpose.
7. Successful transformers are fundamentally dissatisfied with the status quo. Canadians are slow to see the flames on the platform even when we feel the heat. Let's get constructively agitated and apply the resulting energy and sense of urgency to getting better. Every delay means that people will suffer needlessly.
8. Learn from Canadian success stories. There is hardly a species of excellence that cannot be found in Canada. From the Ontario provincial Cardiac Care Network to the Group Health Centre in Sault Ste. Marie to the Alberta Bone and Joint Institute, there have been triumphs of access and quality. Making excellence mandatory is the next step. That's what high-performing healthcare systems do, and that's what Canada ought to do.

Steven Lewis
President, Access Consulting Ltd., Saskatoon
Adjunct Professor of Health Policy,
University of Calgary and Simon Fraser University

Selected Additional Resources

Jönköping County Council and Sweden

Garpenby P. 1997. "Implementing Quality Programmes in Three Swedish County Councils: The Views of Politicians, Managers and Doctors." *Health Policy* 39(3): 195–206.

Andersson-Gare, B. and D. Neuhauser. 2007. "The Health Care Quality Journey of Jönköping County Council, Sweden." *Quality Management in Health Care* 16(1): 2–9.

Bodenheimer, T., M. Bojestig and H. Goran. 2007. "Making Systemwide Improvements in Health Care: Lessons from Jönköping County, Sweden." *Quality Management in Health Care* 16(1): 10–15.

Elg, M., B. Kollberg, J. Lindmark and J. Olsson. 2007. "Goal Orientation and Conflicts: Motors of Change in Development Projects in Health Care Service." *Quality Management in Health Care* 16(1): 84–97.

Malmvall, B.-E., I. Franzen, P.-E. Abom and M.-B. Hugosson. 2007. "The Rate of Influenza Immunization to People Aged 65 Years and Older Was Increased from 45% to 70% by a Primary Health Care-based Multiprofessional Approach." *Quality Management in Health Care* 16(1): 51–59.

Malmvall, B.-E., S. Molstad, J. Darelid, A. Hiselius, L. Larsson, J. Swanberg and P.-E. Abom. 2007. "Reduction of Antibiotics Sales and Sustained Low Incidence of Bacterial Resistance: Report on a Broad Approach during 10 Years to Implement Evidence-Based Indications for Antibiotic Prescribing in Jönköping County, Sweden." *Quality Management in Health Care* 16(1): 60–67.

Øvretveit, J. and A. Staines. 2007. "Sustained Improvement? Findings from an Independent Case Study of the Jönköping Quality Program." *Quality Management in Health Care* 16(1): 68–83.

Quality Management in Health Care 2007 16(1) issue focused on Jönköping and Sweden:

Peterson, A., R. Carlhed, B. Lindahl, G. Lindstrom, C. Aberg, B. Andersson-Gare and M. Bojestig. 2007. "Improving Guideline Adherence through Intensive Quality Improvement and the Use of a National Quality Register in Sweden for Acute Myocardial Infarction." *Quality Management in Health Care* 16(1): 25–37.

Rejler, M., A. Spangeus, J. Tholstrup and B. Andersson-Gare. 2007. "Improved Population-based Care: Implementing Patient- and Demand-Directed Care for Inflammatory Bowel Disease and Evaluating the Redesign with a Population-Based Registry." *Quality Management in Health Care* 16(1): 38–50.

Strindhall, M. and G. Henriks. 2007. "How Improved Access to Healthcare Was Successfully Spread across Sweden." *Quality Management in Health Care* 16(1): 16–24.

Intermountain Healthcare

Clayton, P.D., S.P. Narus, S.M. Huff, T.A. Pryor, P.J. Haug, T. Larkin, S. Matney, R.S. Evans, B. H. Rocha, W.A. Bowes, F.T. Holston and M.L. Gundersen. 2003. "Building a Comprehensive Clinical Information System from Components: The Approach at Intermountain Health Care. *Methods of Information in Medicine* 42(1): 1–7.

Jimmerson, C., D. Weber and D.K. Sobek. 2005. "Reducing Waste and Errors: Piloting Lean Principles at Intermountain Health Care." *Joint Commission Journal on Quality and Patient Safety* 31(5): 249–257.

Nelson, E.C., P.B. Batalden, K. Homa, M.M. Godfrey, C. Campbell, L.A. Headrick, T.P. Huber, J.J. Mohr and J.H. Wasson. 2003. "Microsystems in Health Care: Part 2. Creating a Rich Information Environment." *The Joint Commission Journal on Quality and Patient Safety* 29(1): 5–15.

Thompson, D.I., C. Sirio and P. Holt. 2000. "The Strategic Use of Outcome Information." *The Joint Commission Journal on Quality and Patient Safety* 26(10): 576–586. National Health Service, UK.

National Health Service, UK

Ham, C., R. Kipping and H. McLeod. 2003. "Redesigning Work Processes in Health Care: Lessons from the National Health Service." *Milbank Quarterly* 81(3): 415–439.

Ham, C. 2005. "Lost in Translation? Health Systems in the US and the UK." *Social Policy & Administration* 39(2): 192–209.

Ham, C. 2006. "Reforms to NHS Commissioning in England." *British Medical Journal* 333: 211–212.

Hawkes, N. 2006. "English NHS Reforms Made Easy." *British Medical Journal* 333: 645–648.

Higgins, J. 2007. "A New Look at NHS Commissioning." *British Medical Journal* 334: 22–24.

Veterans Health Administration

Armstrong, B., O. Levesque, J.B. Perlin, C. Rick, G. Schectman and P.M. Zalucki. 2005. "Reinventing Veterans Health Administration: Focus on Primary Care." *Journal of Healthcare Management* 50(6): 399–408.

Asch, S.M., E.A. McGlynn, M.M. Hogan, R.A. Hayward, P. Shekelle, L. Rubenstein, J. Keesey, J. Adams and E.A. Kerr. 2004. "Comparison of Quality of Care for Patients in the Veterans Health Administration and Patients in a National Sample." *Annals of Internal Medicine* 141(12): 938–945.

Healthcare Papers 2005 5(4). Issue focused on Veterans Health Administration.

Hynes, D.M., R.A. Perrin, S. Rappaport, J.M. Stevens and J.G. Demakis. 2004. "Informatics Resources to Support Health Care Quality Improvement in the Veterans Health Administration." *Journal of the American Medical Informatics Association* 11: 344–350.

Kerr, E.A. and B. Fleming. 2007. "Making Performance Indicators Work: Experiences of the US Veterans Health Administration." *British Medical Journal* 335: 971–973.

Longman, P. 2007. *Best Care Anywhere. Why VA Health Care is Better than Yours.* Sausalito, CA: PoliPointPress.

Ohldin, A., R. Taylor, A. Stein and T. Garthwaite. 2002. "Enhancing VHA's Mission to Improve Veteran Health: Synopsis of VHA's Malcolm Baldrige Award Application. *Quality Management in Health Care* 10(4): 29–37.

Oliver, A. 2007. "The Veterans Health Administration: An American Success Story?" *The Milbank Quarterly* 85(1): 5–35.

Weeks, W.B., L. Hamby, A. Stein and P.B. Batalden. 2000. "Using the Baldrige Management System Framework in Health Care: The Veterans Health Administration Experience." *The Joint Commission Journal on Quality Improvement* 26(7): 379–387.

Weeks W.B., J. Waldron, P.D. Mills, S.H. Brown, L.R. Coulson and T. Speroff. 2003. "A Model for Improving the Quality and Timeliness of Compensation and Pension Examinations in VA Facilities." *Journal of Healthcare Management* 48(4): 252–261.

Acknowledgements

This book reflects contributions from a large number of people, and we wish to thank them for their important efforts and sage advice. We especially thank Paula Blackstien-Hirsch, whose energy, sound judgment and continuing guidance has been critical to the Quality by Design project. Paula played an important role in the project's design, the coordination of team activities and, most importantly, the analysis and review of the case studies. Her commitment to Quality by Design and her wisdom about many issues have been invaluable elements for more than two years. Michael Murray also offered important advice on the design of the project, especially in its early stages, and provided insights into how to translate the lessons learned for different audiences. Sonya Pak did a brilliant job in capturing the essence of each case and developing short versions that could be used to support presentations and overviews of the project. Adalsteinn Brown, assistant deputy minister in the Ontario Ministry of Health and Long-Term Care, supported the project as our "decision-making partner" and provided a strategic perspective and critical commentary that helped ensure that the project both met high academic standards and maintained relevance to healthcare policy issues.

Leaders and staff members at each of the seven sites we visited gave important assistance, and we deeply appreciate their gracious receptions and generous contributions of time and effort. In particular, staff members at the sites were extraordinarily helpful in providing information, assisting our efforts to meet with many individuals and engaging in extended discussions about their work. Many people at the sites read and reread our case studies, thereby helping to ensure the accuracy and relevance of our observations. We also recruited external readers who were familiar with our cases to provide additional review and commentary. We thank Patricia Stolz, William B. Weeks, Chris Ham, Cliff Norman, Howard Waldner and June Duesbury-Porter for their careful considerations and valuable comments.

To help ensure that Quality by Design's information and outcomes will be useful in informing policy decisions, we assembled an advisory group of healthcare leaders who offered advice on the project's goals, methods and products: Tony Woolgar, John McKinley, Arlene Bierman, Bob Baynham, Cynthia Majewski, Jonathan Lomas, Ben Chan, Barry Monaghan, Ken White, Paul Darby, Marilyn Emery, Dave Murray, Hy Eliasoph and Sandra Hanmer. We benefited from discussions with these people, and we sincerely thank them for their time and insights.

To help identify how these cases might contribute to improvements in Canadian healthcare we asked several leaders across the country to comment on the international case studies. We thank Maura Davies, Jack Kitts, David Levine, Murray Martin and Rick Roger for sharing their thoughtful reflections on the possible lessons for the Canadian system. Finally, we asked Steven Lewis to review how these cases might inform policy and we were rewarded with a discerning assessment of the challenges.

In thanking the many people who have contributed to this work we must add that while the final product is much better as a result, any remaining deficiencies result from our shortcomings, not theirs.

G. Ross Baker, PhD
Anu MacIntosh-Murray, PhD
Christina Porcellato, MHSc
Lynn Dionne, MHSc
Kim Stelmacovich, MHSc
Karen Born, MSc

Toronto, Ontario
March 13, 2008

Index